Never Follow
The Wolf

Helao Shityuwete

Never Follow
The Wolf

The autobiography of a Namibian
freedom fighter

KLIPTOWN
BOOKS
LONDON

Published in 1990 by Kliptown Books Ltd.
Canon Collins House, 64 Essex Road, London N1 8LR.

British Library Cataloguing in Publication Data
Shityuwete, Helao
   Never Follow The Wolf: the autobiography of a Namibian
      freedom fighter.
   1. Namibia. Political events, history
   I. Title
   968.8
   ISBN No. 1 871863 06 6

Phototypeset in 10pt Melior and
printed in England by A. G. Bishop & Sons Ltd,
Orpington, Kent.

Dedicated to my wife Jane
and daughter Tuli

Contents

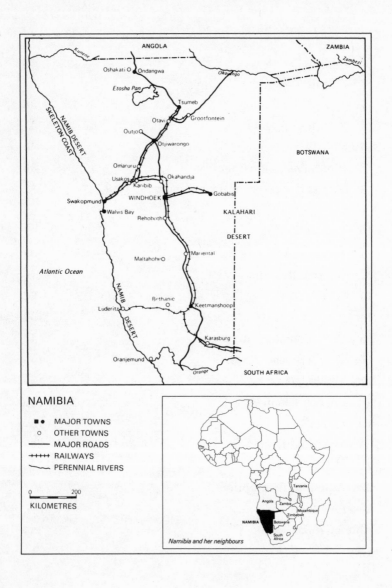

NAMIBIA

■ ● MAJOR TOWNS
○ OTHER TOWNS
— MAJOR ROADS
+++++ RAILWAYS
〜 PERENNIAL RIVERS

0   200
KILOMETRES

Namibia and her neighbours

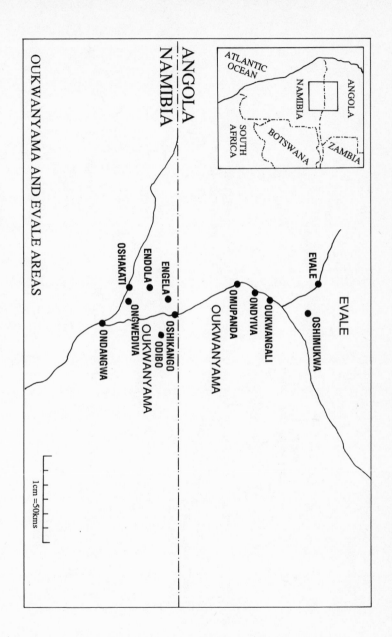

OUKWANYAMA AND EVALE AREAS

ANGOLA
NAMIBIA

ATLANTIC OCEAN

NAMIBIA

ANGOLA

SOUTH AFRICA

BOTSWANA

ZAMBIA

OSHAKATI

ENDOLA

ENGELA

EVALE

OMUPANDA

ONDYIVA

OUKWANGALI

OSHIMUKWA

ONGWEDIVA

OSHIKANGO

ODIBO

OUKWANYAMA

OUKWANYAMA

EVALE

ONDANGWA

1cm =50kms

ix

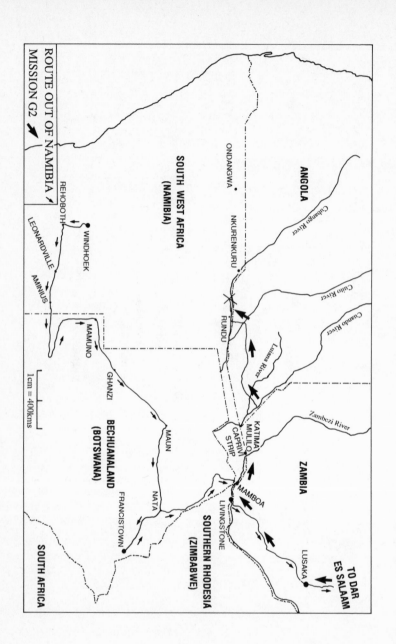

ROUTE OUT OF NAMIBIA

MISSION G2

1

Childhood

I arrived on 25 August 1934, the year of the Great Flood and the date of the death of a great king. The date might not have been recorded, except for the fact that King Samuel Maharero died in exile in Bechuanaland on that day, where he and some of the Namibian people had been driven by the Germans. For a child to be born on the date on which a great leader died is seen as a good omen. The spirit of the leader is believed to enter those born on that day and to pass on leadership qualities.

My father, Nelindi Shityuwete, was a descendant of the Evale Royal Family, from the Evale area of southern Angola. My mother came from the Ovakwanyama people who lived south of Evale, in an area straddling the Angola/Namibia border. My father's title as the head and ruler of Ovavale people included that of Rain King. He was believed to hold divine and rain-making powers, but he himself was sceptical of magic powers. My father had four or five wives and my mother was the youngest. I was the nineteenth child of my father's 22 children but the only child of my mother.

My earliest memories are of looking after my father's calves with one of my little brothers, from a different mother, who was almost the same age as me. Sometimes our big brothers took us with them to look after the cattle. We were inseparable little brothers, so close to each other that we were able to share our mothers when it came to breast feeding. We used to take on the first mother we came across – his or mine. Though we sometimes had fights over who should take which breast, they were minor and we were able to sort them out - with the help of our mothers of course.

I don't remember much of my father because he spent much of his day hunting leopards with his 'subjects'. As a child, my neck was decorated with all sorts of claws from animals and birds that my father had killed – it was difficult for my mother to carry me on her back because she would be scratched by the claw necklace.

For reasons unknown to me my mother left my father when I was about four years old. I stayed behind with my father, his other wives and my brothers and sisters. I do not remember

1

missing my mother and was content to be looked after by my father's other wives. But one hot summer's day in 1939 or so, when I was taking the calves to water, I saw a strange woman coming out of the bush towards me and I was frightened. I was five years old and it was almost a year since I had last seen my mother, and I did not recognise her after such a long period. I do not know how long she had been lying in wait for me or how she knew when I would visit the water-hole. She approached me cautiously, looking to and fro to make sure I was unaccompanied.

When she was satisfied that I was alone, she called me to her. Not knowing who she was, I refused. But when she told me that she was my mother and that she was taking me to my granny, of whom I was very fond, I agreed. She picked me up and threw me onto her back and we disappeared into the bushes. When we reached the road leading to my father's house she hid me under a thick bush, telling me to wait and be silent. She then ran off in the direction of my father's homestead.

After a while I heard horse hooves approaching from the homestead and my mother appeared running in front of a chestnut stallion ridden by my (maternal) uncle. They stopped next to the bush and my mother called to me to come out. They picked me up and put me on the horse's back behind my uncle and, with my mother in the lead, we set off towards the Evale/Oukwanyama borders.

We travelled for about four hours non-stop in case my absence was discovered and for fear that my father might send someone after us. My mother never reduced her speed nor did she appear to show any signs of tiredness. I admired her endurance and stamina and I longed to have the same qualities when I grew up. We stopped at a homestead along the route to have some lunch. I expected to find my grandmother there and when I did not I became suspicious that my mother and uncle were not really taking me to her after all. I became impatient and demanded that they should take me back to my father. But when we set out again in the late afternoon they promised that they were taking me to my grandmother. We eventually got to my granny's home at Oshimukwa, in the Oukwanyama area of southern Angola, near midnight. I was very tired but happy to see my granny after such a long and tiring journey and she too was pleased to see me. My mother, who had by now remarried, left me there and disappeared with my uncle.

My grandmother was the chief wife of my grandpa's six wives. Besides my mother she had two other daughters, aunts Beata and Maria Ishinda, both of whom were grown up and had left home, and were living at Endola, a village in the north of Namibia. The former was to play an important role in my life.

Granny, being the chief wife, had great responsibilities. She looked after the whole household, making sure that everybody had enough to eat and to wear. If there was something needed she would report to my grandfather to make the necessary arrangements. Besides her official duties she had some children from distant relatives under her care. Among them was my distant cousin Vatuva ya Kainzi who was eleven years my senior. She treated me badly by beating me for no reason at all when my grandma was not looking.

1938–1940 was a period of great famine in the region and food was scarce. Though we had enough to eat, unlike many other people, Vatuva, under cover of darkness, used to hold my hand down when we had our meals in the evenings. She would prevent me from eating until she had had her fill and only let me eat what she had left. Despite the fact that she mistreated me I never bore any grudge against her – nor did I report her to my grandmother who would have punished her for her behaviour.

My grandfather, like my father, had many children. I had some difficulties in relating to my younger uncles and aunts, especially as I was forced to call them tatekulu (uncle) and meme (aunt), terms usually applicable to older people.

My grandpa was a nice old man in his 60s and he spent much of his time teaching me all that a boy of my age ought to know: he treated me as his equal and made me feel very grown up. He made me a bow and arrows and also taught me how to make them. I was happy and pleased to have such a wonderful grandfather. One evening, however, when I was about six years old, we had an argument.

It happened when everybody else went to bed and he and I were left alone in the sitting place. He was yawning and ready for bed but I was not. He expected me to volunteer to go to bed and when he found that I was not going to, he ordered me to go to bed. I said no, I was not ready yet. He stood up and told me that he was going to get his horse-whip to punish me – he did not want to use it but he would if I forced him to. I said

3

in that case I was going for my bow and arrows and we would meet and settle the matter like men. I ran off and when I came back I found him waiting for me. He gave me one lash before I could do anything with my bow and arrows and I went yelping to bed like a puppy. We never had any more disagreements after that.

My relationships with his other wives were very good except with one who used to tease me by calling me Mwaandyai (His Royal Highness), which I hated. This was a reference to my status in relation to my father, the Rain King. She also used to shout at me: Ovambwela must go back to their Ombwela! – a reference to my father's principality. She had a keen sense of humour and although she was only teasing me I was very hurt.

In mid-1940 my father suddenly took ill and, being his favourite child, he sent for me because he wanted to see me before he died. Traditionally the first-born son was the heir-apparent to his father's title but my father was determined to waive this and make me his heir instead. But due to religious factors – my mother was a practising Catholic and she had had me baptised in my infancy and granny had recently been baptised – my mother's family were opposed to the idea and did not take me to see him before his death. He died a non-believer.

My family did, however, take me to the funeral and that is where I saw tradition at work. Though I was only six years old I can vividly remember seeing all my father's children standing in a row in the cattle kraal where we were taken for the traditional rites. Standing in the order we were born, we were all made to drink from one cup and were cleansed in beer-scented water. We were then anointed with oil and blessed by everyone we passed on our way out to the place reserved for us. We spent the whole night eating and drinking home-made brew. A big log fire kept us warm for the night.

Though I was very sad at the loss of my father, I was pleased to be reunited with the rest of my brothers and sisters, some of whom I had not met before, and did not meet thereafter. After the ceremonies the following morning, my escort took me back to my grandparents at Oshimukwa, my grandpa's district.

The following year, when I was seven years old, my settled life was again disturbed by the arrival of my father's younger brother, Fumah. He arrived in the late afternoon with a

4

contingent of about 20 men all on horseback. I did not know he was coming – my teasing 'grandmother' was the first to tell me. 'Your father is here and would like to take you back with him to your Ombwela,' she said.

I stared at her in disbelief and told her that my father was dead.

'No, I am talking about your father's brother, Fumah,' she said proudly.

But I did not recognise the name Fumah and had not heard of that uncle before. Fumah! I started laughing at the name because Fumah means Frog. What a funny thing for a person to be called Frog. I was curious to meet Mr Frog and find out what kind of a man he was.

I did not meet him until suppertime when he sent for me to come and have dinner with him. My curiosity turned into terror. Fumah was not an ordinary man. My father was not small, but Fumah was really huge. He had the eyes of an owl and his long brittle hair stood up on his head like spikes on a fence. He was dressed in animal skins with a necklace of all sorts of wild animal teeth and claws from birds of prey. I stopped in my tracks and wanted to turn and run. But he called me to him softly, that we could perform the customary greeting, which is to rub our faces and noses together (no longer practised). My legs were as heavy as lead and I could not move them forward or backward.

When he realised that I was frightened, he stood up slowly and came towards me. He was the tallest man I had ever seen. He came over to me, bent down and reached out for me, calling my name at the same time. I braced myself for the worst but his touch was very gentle and it drove away all my fears. 'Helao, my son,' he said softly. His voice was as kind as one could want and this reassured me that he was a man like any other.

He picked me up, then carried me in his arms to his chair. Putting me in his chair he knelt in front of me to have a better look at me. He bent forward in greeting and gently rubbed his face against mine. I accepted him but did not trust him. We then sat down for dinner and I watched him through the corner of my eye throughout the meal. After dinner he told me the purpose of his visit.

'Helao, I have come to take you with me to Evale,' he said, watching me. 'Since your father's death I have been meaning to come and fetch you but I did not have time until today. I did not want to send someone on my behalf because I also wanted to talk to your grandparents and to your mother. What do you think?'

'I want to come with you, uncle,' I said. Though I was not keen to go with him, I did not want to show it in case he felt offended.

He was pleased with the outcome and told me to go to bed early and have a good night's sleep. 'See you in the morning, my son,' he said.

I bade him good night with a troubled mind. Should I go with someone I had just met and who claimed to be my uncle?

The following day I was still undecided. At midday my uncle sent for me to have lunch with him and for us to make final preparations. Seeing him for the second time decided me, and I planned to escape if I could. After lunch I was asked to take the plates back to the kitchen. The kitchen was at the far end of the house and this provided me with an excellent opportunity to make my escape unnoticed. The kitchen was deserted. I left the plates there, slipped out of the house, climbed the perimeter fence then went to hide in the bushes nearby. After an hour or so I thought I should find out whether my uncle and his party had left and went to wait near the road they would be taking.

They did not come for three hours or so. I was about to give up and step out into the road when I suddenly heard many horses approaching from the homestead. I dived into the nearest bush to avoid being seen or run over by the horses. With my heart pounding with fear I managed to count them as they passed within a hair's breadth of my hiding place. Even though I was satisfied through my counting that they had all gone, I did not step outside my hiding place until I was sure. Slowly, I crept out of the bush, surveyed both directions, stepped into the road, then breathed a deep sigh of relief. I waved goodbye as their dust disappeared in the distance and then went home to face the accusations of cowardice. My grandmother, however, was pleased with me and that made me feel proud of myself. Most unfortunately, I did not see my uncle again until his death in the 1950s.

My grandmother was getting old and wanted to leave my grandpa under a mutual agreement. So granny and I went to set up house in 1941.

Our new household was not far from my grandfather's and I spent most of the afternoons with grandpa when granny did not need my services. However, I had a lot of work to do around the house. Because I was still very young I was unable to perform difficult duties and left all of them to my grandmother. She was a hardworking woman and did all the men's work around the house. My cousin who treated me badly had married before we left my grandpa's, so I was the only child living with my granny. Thus I grew up doing both girls' and boys' work in the house. I was able to cook meals at the age of seven, pound corn when I was eight and prepare home brew when I was nine. I was therefore able to relate to both male and female roles and was happy that I could do things that other boys and girls of my age could not.

However, I was opposed to some traditional rituals. As youngsters, our society expected us to undergo certain traditional rites, for example, the piercing of ears, the removal of two lower front teeth, and chipping off bits from between the two upper front teeth. All these were done for beautification purposes only and had nothing to do with sacrosanct traditional norms.

Having failed to see the logic of mutilating my body I refused to be part of any of it. I found myself isolated by my friends because I did not conform. Looking back, I am pleased that I did not give in to their ridicule because many of them have had to spend much time worrying about the damage they have done to their bodies. I did participate in other traditional events like dancing and attending festivals. Our two societies, that is Ovakwanyama and Ovavale, do not practise circumcision on either male or female as many African (and some non-African) peoples.

As kids, we did not receive any kind of formal education. Home or parental education was the only thing known to us and no other educational institutions were open to us. I thus grew up illiterate, but my aunt, Beata Ishinda from Endola, opened a new chapter in my life.

She arrived one evening in 1941, the year my granny left grandpa's. She was with her sister, Aunt Maria, and another lady. They all looked special and different from us. They practised a different form of religion, Protestantism, and I thought that could possibly have been the reason why they looked so different. Like many people who grew up as Catholics in our region we were taught how to chant prayers three times a day – in the mornings, middays and in the evenings. My aunts were able to read and write. Furthermore, while our prayers were the same, day in and day out, my aunts were free to pray from memory, and they closed their eyes when they prayed whereas we did not.

My aunt's arrival in 1941 was the beginning of important events leading to my education. It was not until her second visit in 1943 that plans for my education were discussed. It was then decided that I would accompany her to Endola on her next visit. They came again in the summer of 1945, when I was 11, and preparations were made. Although I was pleased at the prospect of going to school I was sad to leave granny alone. I did not even know what the word school meant, but I was overcome by curiosity to find out all about it.

When the time of departure came, I clung to my granny and would not let her go. It was really difficult for both of us. It was the first time I had seen granny crying, which made me feel guilty at leaving her. She did not want me to leave although she had agreed to the plan. But we had to part, and we left early that day, arriving at our first stop, Oukwangali, towards late evening.

Oukwangali was about 25 miles from Oshimukwa, my grandpa's district, and had a few shops belonging to Portuguese businessmen. It also housed administrative offices, a police station, a prison and a church. We spent the night with one of my aunt's Portuguese friends. This was a revelation to me because it was the first time I had come into close contact with people of different skin colour from mine.

The man, a white Portuguese who owned a shop, was married to a black woman and they had three children, the oldest of whom was the same age as myself. They were a very nice couple and they invited us to have supper with them. The meal consisted of rice, pork and vegetable soup. It was unfamiliar to me but I found it tasty and wondered why granny did not grow rice or rear pigs for pork so that we could have nice food like the Portuguese. The grown ups washed down their meal with vinho tinto (red wine), while we kids drank carsosa (cold drinks).

Throughout the meal, I watched the man with the white skin. Although I had seen an albino before, this man was not an albino. I had heard about the Portuguese but had never seen one before and thought they were also black like myself. After the meal I asked my aunt about it. She told me that all the Portuguese people were white and that they were not albinos.

The couple's children had beautiful brown skin and dark

curly hair. We made great friends and they taught me a few Portuguese words like bon dia (good morning), bo a noit (good night) and atte a manha (until tomorrow). I could not teach them any Oshikwanyama words (my Oshivale had long since disappeared) because they were fluent in both Portuguese and Oshikwanyama. I was impressed with the easy way they could switch from one to the other. I slept in the children's room and we chatted throughout the night. In the morning, after breakfast, we bade everybody goodbye and headed south. I was sorry to leave my new friends behind but school was my target now. We intended that day to reach Ondyiva, the capital of Cunene Province about 50 miles or so away. I had never walked a long distance before and having walked for the whole of the previous day I was beginning to tire.

We could not reach Ondyiva that day and spent the night half way there. I had never left my granny before and although the journey was beginning to tell on me I found it very fascinating and I enjoyed every bit of it. We arrived at Ondyiva the following evening.

Though it was a small town, it looked unusually big to someone like me who had never seen a town before: I was fascinated by the big houses standing together in rows. We spent the night at the home of one of my aunt's friends and in the morning went into town to do some shopping. I had never seen so many people gathered together in one place in my life. We visited several shops and went to see the barter market where people exchanged cattle for other goods such as tobacco and beads.

'Do they all live here?' I wanted to know.

Not all of them, my aunt told me. Some of them had travelled long distances to come to town and some had come to look for work.

'Work? What kind of work do you do in town?' I asked, because I regarded ploughing and hoeing as the only work.

'Selling in shops and working as domestic servants and messengers,' I was told.

I was about to ask another question when around a corner, along a dusty road, came a car hurtling at full speed towards us, or so it seemed to me. What a noise! Clinging to my aunt's skirt, I cried out for help. It swept past us, leaving behind a cloud of dust and a strong smell of petrol in the air.

'What was that?' I asked.

'Etuwa (a car),' my aunt said, pulling me away from her skirt.

I had been looking forward to living in a town but how could I with such noisy fearful cars? I was assured that cars did not do people any harm and that they were good for transport, but I was not impressed and swore that if our group was to go by car, I would rather go on foot. After shopping, we went to pack our things and prepare for the next day's journey.

We left Ondyiva early in the morning for Omupanda, which is 25 miles from the Namibian border. We walked for the whole day and arrived there in the middle of the night. After a short rest we set off for the border and Engela, the Finnish Mission just inside Namibia. We crossed the border at midnight and arrived in Engela in the early hours of the morning. We visited the Engela hospital, where one of my distant aunts had been getting some medical treatment. I was to spend a week with her because I had some spots on my scalp and because I was feeling really tired. So it was decided that my aunt and her group would proceed to Endola and I would join them a week later.

I had been in the hospital for two days when one night, while I was playing with my friends rolling eendunga (palm tree stones), I found myself in the vice-grip of a Fraulein connected to the hospital staff. No noise was permitted in the hospital, especially at night. She was shouting and I was screaming and struggling to get away from her grip. She asked me where I came from - she meant the hospital room number. But instead of telling her the room number I told her that I came from Oshimukwa, my grandfather's place. Everybody around broke down with laughter at the misunderstanding.

*   *   *

It is never too late to learn – a maxim I have used all my life. However, when my aunts Beata and Maria Ishinda put me in school I was 13 years old and I did not appreciate what they were trying to do for me. At the beginning I suspect they wondered if it was indeed too late for me to learn.

In January 1947 I started at Endola Finnish Mission School where both my aunts were teachers. Aunt Maria was teaching 'Enongopalo', primary class, and Aunt Beata taught the pre-primary classes. My other teachers were Natalia Kakonda, David Shiponeni, Sara Moses and Eunike Nguloshi.

I was placed in Aunt Maria's pre-primary class where the majority of students were seven to nine years old. I stood out like a sore thumb because I was the tallest in the class but hardly knew what the word education meant. This state of affairs had an adverse effect on my progress: I was ill at ease competing with very young children and felt that I was wasting my time. I told my aunts that I was not feeling confident in my studies, which consisted mainly of the alphabet, some basic arithmetic and Bible chanting in Afrikaans, which all seemed rather boring.

However, my aunts were not impressed with my complaints and after two months they took it upon themselves to improve matters and I was made to read to them every evening before I went to bed. Because of the scarcity of reading material at the time, I was made to read verses from the Bible, which was the only book available. This only added to my discomfort.

The breakthrough, however, came in the third month when one evening my aunts organised a reading competition between some children in the house, including myself. I came second and this encouraged me to improve my reading. Another competition was held before the end of term in March: this time our whole class competed and I managed to come top!

When school commenced again I was moved up one class and in January 1948 I went up again, leaving my original classmates far behind. By 1949 I was already in Enongopalo, Aunt Beata's class, the highest I could go in the school.

Normally children from Endola went on to Finnish Mission schools at Engela or Ongwediva, but my aunts did not send me there. Instead they sent me to St. Mary's Mission, an Anglican-run religious institution at Odibo, 20 to 25 miles north-east of Endola. I arrived at St. Mary's Mission in January 1950 and because its boarding facilities were full to capacity I went to stay with my uncle Peter Kalangula at Olunghono, about three miles from Odibo, which meant walking six miles each day to and from school.

There was a good range of subjects to choose from at St. Mary's. My aunts sent me there because it was the only place in the north where English was spoken and taught. Pupils came from several northern areas for this reason and English was the most popular subject. Amongst those I met at the school were Andimba (Hermann) Toivo Ya Toivo, now the Secretary General of SWAPO; Jakob Kuhangwa, also at one time Secretary General of SWAPO; James Hamupanda

Kauluma, now the Anglican Bishop of Namibia and his brother Joseph, who later became one of my teachers.

Due to the popularity of English the classes were overcrowded and to me, who had been used to Bible chanting in Afrikaans, this new language seemed strange and wonderful. The most difficult letters to pronounce were F, H, Q, W and Y. It took me a month to conquer their pronunciation, particularly at the beginning of words, where I was inclined to pronounce the letter separately, before adding the rest of the word! However, after this everything was plain sailing and I started to enjoy my studies. Before the year was out I had already been moved up one class. My favourite subjects were English, Arithmetic, Geography, History and Nature Study.

I had the most wonderful time at St. Mary's but I did experience some difficulties. In the five year period of my study there, 1950–1954, I had to move three times due to accommodation and food shortages. Though I used to bring food from home whenever I went to visit for a weekend, I sometimes had only one meal a day and often had to go without altogether, relying on fruit I could find growing locally, such as eembe and eenyandi. Another problem was that I had to walk long distances to and from school, especially when I changed from Peter Kalangula's place to Aunt Aile Mwatotele's place at Omafo, about 10 to 15 miles west of Odibo.

2

Contract work

I spent 1955 at home after I failed to gain entry to Standard VI, the first year of secondary school, which was now closed to most black Namibian scholars. Apartheid 'Bantu Education' had been imposed in Missionary-run schools and they were prohibited from teaching beyond Standard V, the last year of primary school. While at home and looking after the family's livestock, I paid close attention to the situation at St. Mary's, hoping that I would be able to resume my studies. But things never improved. Sakkie Kapulwa, my cousin, decided at the end of 1955 to go in search of employment and I joined him. My aunts, who had supported us through thick and thin during our school years could no longer do so.

As black Namibians resident in the north we were only allowed to work on contract, a modified form of slavery. The whole system was run by the South West Africa Native Labour Association (SWANLA), which provided labour for the towns, farms and mines to the south. We were given no choice of employment and could not negotiate over the pitiful wages. Breaking the contract – which was usually for 18 months – was a criminal offence, and once the contract was up, we would be forced to return home. Sakkie was fortunate to be sent to Windhoek, but I and 11 others were despatched to the small town of Outjo.

Outjo is notorious in Namibian history. The majority of the farming community are descendants of the 'Angola Boers', Afrikaners who had trekked into Angola but were brought back by the South African government to colonise Namibia. They are known for their cruelty towards their black employees, especially the contract labourers from the north, many of whom allegedly disappear without trace, reportedly killed and their bodies fed to the pigs.

Our group of 12 arrived at the Outjo railway station in the afternoon. The contract workers' hostel was close to the station and we walked there without waiting to be fetched. On our arrival we were greeted by a group of workers from the north who were about to leave and they briefed us on the situation there. It was not encouraging and I found myself wanting to run away. Before the briefing was over a

13

big-bellied lady came round the corner of the kitchen. She was the school superintendent's wife and we had been told that she was a very hard and unpleasant woman. She was so huge that the labourers in the hostel nicknamed her 'Nangutula', a reference to her way of walking.

Nangutula was looking for a house-boy and she came to where we were standing in a line. My heart sank when she picked me out. Everybody started telling me I was in big trouble as she did not tolerate any opposition or failure to carry out instructions.

The woman put me to work in a small hostel she ran for white girls, mostly the daughters of the Afrikaner farming community around Outjo. The situation in the hostel as a whole was terrible. People who worked in the kitchen had to get up at 3 am to prepare breakfast for the children. Failure to arrive on time meant that the woman summoned the police who took the offender away for six lashes, without any attempt to establish any wrongdoing. Six people were given this treatment while I was there. My work was made difficult because all the instructions were issued in Afrikaans, but as time went by I began to master the relevant Afrikaans words and Nangutula turned out to be not quite as bad as she was painted.

Many employers beat their workers. There were disturbing incidents of workers with swollen faces and other injuries being taken by their bosses to catch trains back to the north. Some workers were not allowed to wash or bath for the whole 18 months of their contract.

One of the worst cases was that of Paulus Jona Musheko from the same area as myself, who worked for a farmer in the Outjo district. He became ill but was never offered any treatment. When he was close to death his boss ordered him to go back to Ovamboland. However, Paulus found his way to the Outjo hospital where he stayed for two weeks before he was able to move at all.

One day I was told by my colleagues that Paulus was at our compound asking for me. The Paulus I found was not the one I knew: he was just skin and bones and could hardly speak or walk. He had not had a haircut, a wash or a change of clothes for nine months. I shaved his head clean and took him to the shower where I washed him. I fed him and gave him some food to take back with him to the hospital. For the first time in nine months he felt alive again, he told me.

After a month he was discharged from hospital but he had nowhere to stay in Outjo. Because he was not fully recovered I took him and hid him in our compound for another month, but the hostel's white staff spotted him one day and I was forced to tell him to go home. To my surprise he told me that he had not been paid for the services he had rendered to the farmer for the nine months. I took him to the police in order to contact his boss and ask for the money, but the farmer was indignant and did not want to acknowledge that he owed Paulus any pay.

It was appalling to witness the arrogance of the Outjo Boers. Having heard about their attitudes towards blacks I was now experiencing apartheid at first hand. This created in me, as in many black people of this country, a hatred towards people of Afrikaner origin. It was only in later years that I came to realise that not all Afrikaners are alike.

* * *

When I came home from my first contract at Outjo in 1957 I learned that a cousin of mine, Daniel Shifulah, was studying in Angola. I contacted him and he told me that education there was of a higher quality than in Namibia and was open to anyone who wanted to study. Shifulah and his friends spoke Portuguese, English and French and that really impressed me – so much so that I decided to go and join them in Angola to improve my education. But because I had not earned much on my first contract I could not finance my schooling and my aunts who had helped me before were unable to do so. So I made up my mind that I would take up one more contract to earn a little more money and would join Shifulah later. I explained the matter to my Aunt Beata, who had by now become my inspiration on matters educational, and she understood and agreed with my project.

With her encouragement I therefore set out one rainy February morning in 1958 with my friend and neighbour, Publius Jona Haufiku, for Ondangwa. The months of January to March were the periods of heavy rain in those days in northern Namibia (they are no longer because of changes in the weather pattern). Because we could not get any transportation of any sort due to floods in the region, we walked all the way to Ondangwa, which is about forty-five miles from Endola, our village. It never stopped raining and we thought we were never going to make it. However we eventually arrived in the middle of the night at Ondyondyo, near Ondangwa, where SWANLA had its Ovamboland regional headquarters and a compound for workers who had finished their contracts and those taking up new ones. We were wet, tired, cold and hungry but happy to have arrived at all. It was a pitch black night and we wanted to find ourselves a spot to lie down and rest but we were frustrated. The compound was overcrowded, wet and smelly. We could hardly find room for our things let alone a dry space where we could rest our tired limbs. We decided to move to a nearby tree and wait for the dawn.

In the morning we joined the long columns of job seekers at the recruiting offices at Ondangwa. Several foremen addressed us, explaining the basic rules and conditions. It was brought to our attention that jobs were scarce and were only available to those wanting to work on the farms and those who had certificates from previous jobs. Furthermore, things were made worse by the fact that for some reason the few jobs available were not open to Namibians but only to Angolans – many people from Angola and Botswana used to come and work in Namibia. These restrictions resulted in bribery of the foremen by job seekers.

My friend and I were not successful because we were both opposed to bribery and did not want to stoop that low; in any case we did not know anyone to bribe or how to go about it. On the second day we left the office early to find a place to stay for the night. We found a room to rent not far from the recruiting depot and sat down to plan our strategy. The situation was getting desperate and after the fourth day with no success we decided to consider the bribery option. That evening we approached the owner of the house where we were staying and asked him whether he knew any of the recruiting personnel who could help. He gave us the name of a Mr. Eliaser Ndakukamo as a likely candidate.

That evening we went to see Mr. Ndakukamo and asked him about job prospects. He told us that jobs were available for clever and intelligent people. It would not be difficult for people like us to get good jobs, he said. He was prepared to help if we could give him a 'tip'. When we asked what sort of tip he meant he said that he would leave that to our discretion. We bought a bottle of home-made brandy and took it to him the following morning before he left for work and then went with him to the recruiting depot. On the way there he told us that when we arrived we should join the queue of applicants and he would come and pick us out. He further advised us to pretend to be Angolans and to give false Angolan names and addresses. We were well coached and when we got to the depot we did as we were told. We took off our shirts, stood in the line, pushed our chests forward and our chins up and, like obedient sentinels, waited for the eleventh hour.

No one who had ever been on a forced contract of employment liked to repeat the experience, but poverty and large-scale unemployment forced people to do it again and again. The whole process was utterly dehumanising. We had only been in the line a few minutes when Mr Ndakukamo arrived. He picked out one man here, another there, and when he had reached his quota he disappeared inside the office and another man appeared to go through the same process. I was picked but my friend was not – why, I do not know.

Our group of about twenty men was joined by another of forty. We were sent to stand outside a doctor's surgery for medical inspection, and one of the foremen came to tell us that a shipping company in Walvis Bay wanted able-bodied men and those of us interested should proceed inside. While we were entering the surgery a group of about twenty men who were standing on the sidelines rushed in and joined us. Because nobody knew who had been selected and who had not, they were allowed to stay and we all went inside. In all, eighty men were cramped into a room 16 feet square. In the surgery, everyone stripped naked and we stood in eight lines of ten men each, waiting for the doctor.

When the doctor arrived, he ordered us all to bend forward with our hands on the floor. He then went behind us, checking our bottoms, heaven knows what for. When he finished, he told us to stand straight again. He started fiddling with our penises, not bothering to wash his hands after each man. I guessed he was checking for VD. I do not remember how many were found to be positive, but there were a few. It was embarrassing for them when they were led out to be sent to the hospital later. While it is clearly important to stamp out diseases I thought it disgusting to ignore individual privacy.

Because big industries such as shipping and mining needed able-bodied men, the doctor went on to classify us into three categories – A, B, C. He called in three assistants, each one armed with tags from one of the classification categories.

Standing to attention we all pushed out our chests again for the doctor's satisfaction. He checked not only our chests but also our fingers and eyes before telling his assistants which category we were given. They then attached the appropriate tags on our wrists. We proceeded into another room to be vaccinated and issued with another tag round our necks – like parcels. No matter how degrading the whole exercise was, people still left the doctor's surgery smiling, happy because they felt luckier than those who did not manage to be recruited. We then went to the Native Commissioner's Offices for recruitment passes to Grootfontein. They took down all our particulars, including our fingerprints. We proceeded to the SWANLA stores to be issued with a blanket, a shirt and some shorts and some rations. We were told that trucks to Grootfontein would be leaving early next morning.

After a hectic day I went to find my friend. I felt sorry he had not been picked. He told me that after I had been selected and left for the Native Commissioner's Offices he had gone to see Mr Ndakukamo who denied all knowledge of having met him before. There was nothing I could do for him and I was sad when I bade him goodbye next morning. The trucks were already waiting when I got there.

Up to one hundred men were loaded into a 15-ton open truck. We were packed so close to one another that there was only room to stand. Grootfontein was a day's drive from Ondangwa in those days, due mainly to the sandy and circuitous roads. We left Ondyondyo at sunrise and arrived in Grootfontein at sunset. I was hungry by the time we arrived as I had not brought any food or water with me and nobody had offered me anything to eat or drink in the truck. I was so tired I could hardly stand when I alighted from the truck. Someone, however, assisted me to get to the compound where we were made to stand in lines for our rations of maize meal and salt. The compound was even dirtier than the one at Ondyondyo and was very smelly and overcrowded. But because it was still raining and the compound was surrounded by a high fence, we had no alternative but to remain within its confines. I was the only Namibian in a group of fifty men who were going to work for the shipping company in Walvis Bay – the rest were all Angolans. They looked at me with great suspicion, and thought I was planted amongst them as a police agent. I thus found myself ostracised. I did not carry cooking utensils with me, and when I wanted to prepare myself a meal no one was willing to lend me any.

Fortunately I happened to know somebody, Steven, from our area who was working in the SWANLA offices and his quarters were in the compound. I found him and he took me in. I was happy to be comfortable again after the many discomforts since leaving home and the long and tedious truck ride from Ondangwa.

'Hey, Helao, how come you are the only one amongst the Angolans?' Steven asked me. I explained what I had done and he told me that I must be lucky because many people had tried that trick before but were found out and turned away at the Native Commissioner's Offices at Ondangwa.

When we left Ondangwa we were not told the name of the company we were going to work for. So I asked Steven if he knew anything about a certain shipping company in Walvis Bay recruiting Angolans only. He told me that there was an order for 90 men from Sturrock & Woker Shipping Company. I was pleased to hear this because I had heard that their working conditions were good and they paid well (I was soon to be disappointed).

The following morning we went to the SWANLA office to undergo the same process we had been through at Ondangwa. We were all found to be healthy and we were sent to wait in front of the recruiting offices. Someone came out of the office to confirm that we were going to work for Sturrock & Woker, loading and off-loading ships, and that our contracts would be ready for signing that afternoon. We thought we were lucky to have our contracts dealt with so soon. Many people whose contract agreements were not assured had to wait for weeks or even months.

It took the whole day to process our contracts, and towards afternoon we were called in for signing. The contract agreements were never read to us – all we had to do was to put our fingerprints on the paper to confirm the agreement. Each of us was then issued with two blankets, a khaki shirt and a pair of shorts. Our train would be leaving early in the morning, we were told. The loudspeaker would wake us up at five and someone would lead us to the station.

Grootfontein is a small town perched on a hill, with sprawling valleys to the south and a carpet of thorn bushes in the north. The station was situated near the town and we had to walk for half a mile from the compound to get there. It was still dark when we started out: we trudged through muddy puddles and by the time we got to the station we were wet and cold. The train arrived a few minutes later and, to my dismay, I saw that we were to travel in cattle trucks which had been off-loaded not long ago. The cattle dung was still fresh and no attempt had been made to cover it or clean the trucks. Twenty-five men were put into each of the trucks. To make matters worse the trucks were not open at the top: the air was so stale and heavy with dung that we could not breathe properly. I could not believe that human beings could be treated this way by fellow human beings. Each of us was given two loaves of bread by SWANLA but we were given no water containers and there was no way of obtaining water on the train. We travelled for thirty-six hours in such conditions before we changed trains at Kranzberg. I was pleased to get onto a clean and spacious train and to breathe clean and fresh air. I quenched my thirst and dozed off: we arrived in Walvis Bay that evening.

A truck took us to the company offices the following morning where we were welcomed by the manager. He read out the terms and conditions of our employment but did not give us a chance to ask any questions. Our working day was from 8 am until 5 pm, with a one hour lunch break. We would be expected to do overtime as necessary. The pay would be as specified in our contracts but overtime would be paid at 3 pennies per hour. Each of us was given a work number and a time ticket.

We then went straight to the docks. There were three large ships berthed along the quay. We boarded one of them, a German merchant ship, the Hamburg. It was a new experience for me to set foot on a ship. How was it possible to build such a thing and for it to float on the water? It seemed incredible. As my thoughts wandered, others opened the hatches and we all went down below to another incredible scene. I had never seen anything bigger than a lorry or a train before. But here were lines of cars and huge boxes all in a single hold. How were we expected to carry these heavy boxes out of the ship, I wondered to myself. My answer came before I could ask someone. A huge hook hanging from the end of a cable was lowered slowly into the hold. We tied some cables round one box in the centre then secured it to the hook on the end of the cable. Slowly the contraption lifted the box and it disappeared with it, to reappear again and again. I had not looked around when we entered the dock area in the morning and had not noticed the cranes standing in a row along the wharf. While we had our lunch break I stood there amazed, watching them turning and carrying things to and from the ships.

This was early March 1958 and I was to do this job for two years. It was hard work for very little money – 17 shillings a month. Working conditions were very bad and dangerous, especially when unloading cement, bone-meal and charcoal with no protective measures at all. But the most dangerous job of all was off-loading rails for the railways. It was difficult for workers to find a safe place away from the swinging rails when a winch or crane was heaving them out of the hold. If the cable round the rails broke we all held our breath waiting to be struck. Other dangers lay in loading copper, manganese or other minerals. The work was hard and sometimes we had to shovel these minerals while the hold covers were in place: the dust would circulate round the hold and breathing would become difficult. Again no protective measures were provided: workers were forced to provide their own protective gear. This was very hard on such low wages. We often put our complaints to the foreman or 'Boss Boy' but he never cared to take them to the management. He was thus unpopular with the workers who thought that he was part of the exploitative system.

Our living quarters consisted of one long building. It had two entrances, one at each end. A passage ran through the middle with several cubicles on either side, each with six cement bunks. The place was overcrowded and lacked storage space. Toilets were buckets and always spilled over before disposal, resulting in a stale stench. No hot water was provided: we had to shower in cold water after a hard day's work. Brack water was supplied for drinking. We had maize meal porridge with meat at lunch and in the evenings, and bread and coffee in the mornings; no vegetables or fruit. We were given our meals outside because there was no dining room but strong east winds blow over Walvis Bay and this made eating outside almost impossible. We were thus forced to eat our food inside the compound, but this was inconvenient due to overcrowding.

In July 1958 myself and a colleague, Ivor Haufiku, were given responsibility for two working spans consisting of 24 men each. Haufiku and I wasted no time in calling our two spans together. After the formal speeches of introduction, we told workers that we would like to have their co-operation and that we would always be prepared to listen to their problems, and to draw the management's attention to their complaints. We emphasised that their interests would be our first priority. By the end of the meeting, we had compiled a list of complaints and requests to be presented to the management. These included better working conditions, provision of protective facilities, and the right to renegotiate wages. Workers also demanded that they should be transported to and from the compound to the docks (they walked a mile in each direction). It was then decided that we should discuss the matter with the rest of the workforce before putting our demands to the compound manager, who would refer them to the work manager. This was done and the list of complaints was endorsed by the whole workforce. Haufiku and I were then appointed to go and see the compound manager on behalf of the workers.

The compound manager was shocked when we told him that we wanted to see him and discuss workers' problems.

'Problems? what sort of problems?' he demanded.

We handed him the list of complaints and by the time he had finished reading it he was shaking with rage. He demanded to know who the author was.

'Workers,' we told him, adding that we were only delegated on their behalf.

He rushed off to the office and came back accompanied by the work manager. The work manager asked whose handwriting it was. I told him that it was mine. He asked whether I was trying to provoke the workers to strike.

'Strike? What strike?' I demanded.

The letter was agitatory, he said, and if I was not careful it could lead to a strike, and I would end up in jail.

I told him that there was not a single passage in the letter amounting to incitement to strike and although it was my handwriting, the contents were the workers', adding that the complaints and requests were legitimate and made in a sincere spirit. I hoped that the management would understand and respond accordingly. He promised to take up the matter with the management and to let us know as soon as was possible.

When the work manager came back to us, he told us that some workers' overtime pay would be raised to 6 pennies an hour. But Haufiku's and mine would remain the same as punishment for 'provoking' the protest action. This led to many workers calling for a strike if the management did not raise our overtime bonuses too. They called for another meeting and decided to ask the manager to come and talk to them directly. He told them on his arrival that the overtime bonuses were calculated according to workers' performances and that there was nothing he could do to change the situation. This led to workers going slow, loading or unloading fewer goods per hour than they normally did. The management was shocked, and to avoid further disruption they agreed to increase overtime bonuses to nine pennies per hour for every worker and a shilling per hour for foremen.

We had scored a great success but there were still more serious problems to contend with. There was discrimination in work. Black workers, though qualified, were not allowed to operate the ships' winches or to drive bulldozers loading copper. White dock workers were earning a hundred times more than their black counterparts. This led to resentment because all the dirty jobs were assigned to blacks with less pay. Medical care was dismally poor and workers who contracted tuberculosis and other respiratory complaints had to be sent to Swakopmund, outside Walvis Bay, for treatment.

One evening, in 1959, when we returned from work to the compound, we found talk about a workers' movement. It did not immediately register with me or any other workers because we had never heard of such a thing at that time. A personal message had been left for me to go and see a Mr Vinnia Helao Ndadi at Ocean Fishing Company, two miles away. I had not met Ndadi before and I did not know who he was.

I found Ndadi buried in a huge pile of newspapers reading something about the United Nations. He told me that he had met a Mr Sam Nujoma from Windhoek who wanted us to discuss workers' problems, especially the situation of the migrant contract labourers. He said they, in their compound, had had a meeting with Nujoma. He had told him that they had formed an organisation to represent the workers, especially those suffering under the contract labour system. Their organisation was called OPO (Ovamboland People's Organisation) and he wanted us in Walvis Bay, with our large population of contract workers, to join them and establish a branch of OPO there. OPO wanted better pay for the workers, better working conditions, the abolition of the 'forced' contract labour system, better treatment for all workers and, above all, the withdrawal of the South African administration from Namibia and independence for Namibia as a whole. South

Africa had been granted a mandate over Namibia by the League of Nations after it had captured it from Germany during the First World War; but South Africa had continued many of the German colonial policies and imposed the racist apartheid system. OPO wanted the United Nations to revoke South Africa's mandate and allow Namibia to become independent, Ndadi explained.

'What's the line of action?' I asked Ndadi.

'First we have to set up a branch here in Walvis Bay and co-ordinate with Windhoek,' he responded. 'We will then make representations to the UN in New York. We will need to organise very hard and we need a lot of money.'

Though I was literate by this time, I did not understand much of what Ndadi was saying. I knew little about world affairs. Why did he specifically want to see me anyway? I asked. Because when he came to our compound, he was told that I was the right person to talk to, Ndadi said.

'What do you want me to do in the meantime?' I asked.

'Well, you can be the organiser in your compound and the surrounding compounds,' Ndadi replied.

We parted with an agreement that we would convene a meeting, but I needed to be given ample time to speak to as many people as I possibly could.

We met again after two weeks. I took my friend Haufiku with me this time and we told Ndadi that there was a lot of enthusiasm everywhere we went. We then decided to arrange for a meeting to be held at Ndadi's compound.

Walvis Bay was the only town in Namibia not affected by a night curfew. This enabled us to organise a huge meeting on the night of 29 June 1959. It was mostly the contract labourers who attended because we were not yet able to communicate with the people in the townships. Ndadi spoke of his meeting with Sam Nujoma, President of OPO. He told them what he had told me, that they were committed to fighting for better working conditions, higher wages and the abolition of the contract labour system, but above all, to demand the removal of the South African administration from Namibia. He told the crowd that many African countries were fighting for their freedom and moving towards national independence. We should do the same thing and fight for our liberation – after independence we would no longer be forced to work under the contract system. We would be able to choose what type of work we wanted to do and to negotiate terms with the people we wanted to work for, Ndadi concluded.

His speech was enthusiastically received but there were also many reservations as to how we were going to achieve all these objectives. Ndadi told us that we had to work very hard. We had to organise and raise money. But where were we going to get the money from, knowing well that we did not earn enough to support ourselves and our families? How were we going to strengthen the organisation without money? We must begin by making little contributions and selling membership cards, Ndadi said. The joining fee was fixed at two and six pence and from then on each one should contribute according to his ability. This was seen as reasonable enough. It was decided towards the end of the meeting that all compounds would be given freedom to choose their own office-bearers and representatives. These representatives in turn would form the executive committee of our Walvis Bay Branch.

Someone in the crowd wanted to know about the fight Ndadi had referred to. How and when was it to take place? To the obvious disappointment of some people Ndadi explained that joining the movement was the fight he was talking about. Many people were ready to take up arms and fight the South African administration like their forefathers who had battled the Germans and the Portuguese. Ndadi said we would only be required to do this if South Africa refused to give back our country. This restored the enthusiasm with which the word 'fight' was first received by the meeting.

The meeting ended in the middle of the night. Thousands of people had attended, and they gave an impression of an army of locusts let loose. Though people in Walvis Bay were familiar with workers going through the town at night, they were shocked to hear and see so many blacks in such a big throng. Many whites came out of their homes to see what was going on – they were frightened and thought there was a revolt in the offing. We learned later that many went to check on their domestic servants. They were surprised and alarmed to find them either out or just returning from the meeting.

Ivor Haufiku, Epaphros Joshua and myself were appointed to represent our compound. I was elected secretary, Haufiku chair and Joshua treasurer. We organised vigorously in and around our compound and managed to raise a substantial amount of money within a short time. By September we had collected over £300 which we took to Ndadi and Nanyemba, his assistant. Then the executive committee was convened to decide what to do with the money collected from our branch as a whole. Ndadi and Joshua Nghilukilwa were assigned to take the money to Windhoek.

Organising the workers was not always plain sailing. We met a lot of opposition from conservative elements. Agents were sent by the Chiefs and Headmen from the north to find out what we were up to. They did this in collaboration with the government, which was also trying to find out what was happening.

Some workers became disillusioned with the pace of our progress. When were contracts going to end? Where was the freedom and independence they were promised? They must be given their contributions back, they demanded. We were faced with a difficult situation. People thought the abolition of the forced contract labour system and Namibian independence could happen overnight. We had to remind them what Ndadi had told them the first day – that they might be called upon to take up arms if South Africa refused to grant us our independence. That was said with the understanding that the struggle we had undertaken could not be expected to last one day but could take years of fierce fighting. Many understood but there were many doubting Thomases.

There were a lot of weaknesses in our organisations, though few will admit it. OPO, which was formed to be the voice of the workers, never took their problems to the managements of firms and companies. No meetings were arranged between workers' representatives and employers. The emphasis was placed on the country's status as a mandate rather than on the inhuman conditions.

In October 1959 I was approached by someone who said that he wanted to go and present our case to the UN in New York. Because no black Namibians were allowed to travel abroad at that time he had to travel clandestinely. Could I help him to stow away? He was Jack Ya Malimba (a nickname), a resident of the black township in Walvis Bay. We did not know each other before but he had been told that I worked at the docks and I could possibly help him. I was doubtful and did not trust him but I inquired about him and was assured that he was one of us. There was an American merchant ship in the harbour and I agreed to let him know as soon as I had found out when it was leaving.

Malimba arrived one evening after he had received my

message that the ship was about to leave harbour, dressed in overalls and looking just like one of us. I escorted him aboard and showed him his hiding place.

He stowed away for seven days and nearly died but he made it to New York where he was looked after by the ship's owners. The authorities were informed and this created a flurry of activity at the United Nations. Eric Louw, then South African ambassador at the UN, was furious and wanted Jack to be expelled immediately to Namibia. Our UN representatives Mburumba Kerina, Rev Michael Scott and Ismael Fortune, together with the Liberian Government, objected to the expulsion request. Jack was then secretly flown out of New York to Liberia where he was immediately given political asylum. This further angered the South Africans. They accused the Americans of treachery and deception, but the Americans denied all knowledge of Jack leaving New York.

By now I had become a fervent newspaper reader and followed events in both Namibia and the world very closely. Jack's flight to Liberia occupied my thoughts most of the time and I myself wanted to stow away. But I was in a conspicuous position and my absence would have been discovered even before the ship left the harbour.

We were also watching the situation which was unfolding in Windhoek, Namibia's capital. In August 1959 the government built a new township now known as Katutura. Immediately part of it was completed, the Windhoek local authorities tried to force people to move there. The people refused and started boycotting the bus services and the municipality's beer hall. The boycott was total.

The authorities responded by sending in armed police and soldiers in armoured cars, on the pretext of defending the location superintendent whose life was allegedly in danger and protecting the people who wanted to use the buses and the beer hall. In reality the economic interests of the authorities were being threatened by the boycotts. The 10th December 1959 is known today as Namibian Women's Day. It was on that day that the women of our divided black society came together for a common purpose: to oppose the authorities' divisive apartheid scheme to remove them from the place they had lived for centuries and dump them five miles away from town. When the women staged a demonstration the police and soldiers started shooting. Many people turned and ran but there were some who braved the rifle fire. Among them was Meekulu Mungunda, who, despite her wounds, set fire to one of the police vehicles before she died. Thirteen people were massacred on that day.

The authorities, to some extent, were caught unawares. They did not expect things to develop as they did. They expected the 'Kaffirs' to move meekly to Katutura without any resistance. In the aftermath of the Windhoek massacre, public meetings were organised by OPO, and two other organisations, the South West Africa National Union (SWANU) and the Herero Chiefs Council, where it was explained to the people that Namibia was a Mandated Territory and that South Africa had been given the task by the United Nations of leading it to independence and self-determination. It was pointed out that, by killing people, South Africa had violated its mandate over Namibia. To many it was the first opportunity to hear and understand this and to question the legality of South Africa's actions.

Our people at the UN were lobbying the international community to take tougher action against South Africa for violating its obligation to the territory and its people and many fine speeches were made in our support. All this boosted our morale and raised high hopes that Namibia was soon to achieve its independence.

The newly established organisations, SWANU, OPO and the Herero Chiefs Council, added their voices to these expectations. Although they lacked proper organisational structures, they did manage to get lawyers from South Africa to come and represent them in their case against the administrator, location superintendent, chief of police and the South African Government for the Windhoek massacre. Advocates Bram Fischer and Oliver Tambo flew into Windhoek airport. But Tambo, because he was black, was refused entry to the territory and the case was never pursued.

Despite its fine sentiments, the UN failed to take the necessary steps to find out for itself what was going on in the territory. No UN mission was sent to investigate the Windhoek massacre. We decided that someone needed to go to the UN to further lobby the world body to take a tougher stand against South Africa. Towards the last week of December 1959 the OPO executive committee met to discuss the situation and Vinnia Ndadi was chosen to go.

It was suggested that he should stow away on a ship bound for New York or somewhere else in the United States – we were firmly convinced that the US was sympathetic to the liberation of all mankind! Nathanael Gottlieb Maxwilili was assigned the task of co-ordinating the whole operation. I was given the task of organising the hiding place on board ship. We went through the rehearsals with Ndadi and gave him full instructions. He had to carry nothing when he boarded and to wear an overall on top of his other clothes, pretending to be one of the Sturrock & Woker workers. Food and a flash light were to be provided. He was supposed to be in hiding for a minimum of 48 hours and a maximum of 72 hours after the ship left the harbour. But the ship was barely out of the harbour when he started knocking at the cover of the hold he was hiding in, because conditions were unbearable.

Six hours after we sent the ship away, our compound manager arrived asking which of our men was unaccounted for. I told the manager that we had all reported back to the compound, although some had since left. He told me that the police had picked up someone claiming to be one of our workers who had stowed away aboard the ship we had sent out to sea that afternoon. My heart sank. How on earth could they have discovered Ndadi so quickly? Something must have gone wrong. The SAP (South African Police) together with the SARP (South African Railways Police) soon arrived in a number of vehicles demanding to see everybody working for the Sturrock & Woker Co. We told them that it was not possible because it was our free time and many people had gone out to visit friends and others were still at work. I told them I was sure that the man found on the ship was not one of us. Next morning the news appeared in the *Namib Times*, a local paper, that a certain OPO man was arrested going to the United Nations to report on the Windhoek massacre.

Though we were not well organised we had enlisted the support of some members of the police force. When Ndadi was arrested we sought their assistance to smuggle one of our members into the prison in order to contact Ndadi. Maxwilili was found 'drunk' in the street and was 'arrested' and locked up for the night. He was released early the following morning having met Ndadi and heard his story. Because Ndadi had not yet been charged, no line of action was decided upon, but arrangements were made for his defence should the case be taken to court. He was eventually charged with trying to leave the country illegally, and sentenced to three months' imprisonment.

The Ndadi case was not the only major issue facing the Walvis Bay OPO branch. The construction of a new township and a new compound by the Walvis Bay town council was approaching completion. The people had already indicated their opposition to moving to both places. They were now to be informed what action was to be taken in the event of forced removals and, in the light of the Windhoek massacre, advised to take precautions not to do anything which could endanger lives unnecessarily. The authorities in Walvis Bay were also aware of the fact that OPO, though an unregistered organisation, was a force to be reckoned with. They had penetrated our ranks and knew something of what was going on. OPO was the only known and well-established organisation in Walvis Bay: many people in the locations were joining up.

* * *

My contract was coming to an end, and at the end of January 1960, I left Walvis Bay for Endola, my home town. Though I was happy to be heading for home I was sorry to leave behind my friends in the movement facing so many difficulties.

My train left Walvis Bay in the evening and arrived in Grootfontein 36 hours later. After Walvis Bay, which does not receive rain at all, Grootfontein was wet and muddy just as it was when I passed through on my way south. Here I met a close friend of mine, Immanuel Shifidi, on his way to Walvis Bay. We exchanged views, he telling me all about my family and me informing him about OPO and its activities in Walvis Bay. He said they had heard about OPO but did not know much about it because it was not yet well known in the north. Shifidi was to become one of the OPO, and later SWAPO, stalwarts. We said goodbye to each other and I left Grootfontein for Ondangwa the following morning and arrived home a day later. I was happy to be home and my family was pleased to see me back.

As soon as my Aunt Beata came home from the school where she taught, I told her about my intentions of going to further my studies in Angola. I also told her about my involvement with OPO and that in addition to my academic ambitions I had to develop my political education. She expressed her support for my venture and told me that she had heard that Hermann Ya Toivo and Jacob Kuhangwa, who were both under restriction orders for their involvement with OPO, were planning to flee abroad and they might welcome me in their scheme.

I knew both Ya Toivo and Kuhangwa when we were all studying at St. Mary's at Odibo in the 1950s. I consulted them and asked if they could include me in their scheme. That was fine with them but they didn't want to follow the same route taken by many who had fled the country before them, from Rundu to Bechuanaland. Their photographs had been given to all the police stations in the land and had also been sent to the Portuguese in Angola, they told me. A new route had to be found. I said I was going back home and would be in touch with them if I heard of something and they should do the same. Back home, I told my aunt all about the plan. She said I should see Julius Nakale Nuyoma, a friend of hers who had been to Angola – he might be of some help. He was indeed. He was ready to guide us through Angola to the town of Lobito, on the west coast, and from there we could travel further afield – to the USA, where there would be greater educational opportunities. Furthermore, it would give us an opportunity to present our case to the UN. I then set up a meeting between Ya Toivo, Kuhangwa and Nuyoma.

3

Angola

It was early April 1960 when we decided to meet and make final arrangements for the journey. Nakale Nuyoma arrived early in the afternoon but we had to wait until dark before Ya Toivo and Kuhangwa arrived: due to restrictions placed on their movements they had to travel under cover of darkness. They eventually arrived towards midnight and after long discussions and reviews of alternative routes, we agreed that Nuyoma should guide us through to Lobito. Nuyoma told us that it was easy to get aboard a ship in Lobito from where we could make our way to the USA. My neighbour, Eliaser Tuhadeleni 'Kaxumba Ka Ndola', would see us as far as Ondyiva, inside Angola. We were to meet at my place and I was to collect Ya Toivo and Kuhangwa's luggage in advance so that they could travel light to meet us. We needed some sort of travel documents and Nuyoma and myself were to go to the Native Commissioner's offices to obtain such documents. Because of restrictions placed on Ya Toivo and Kuhangwa, we had to give assumed names to the official issuing the papers and we would thus travel incognito.

Nuyoma and I obtained the necessary papers without any difficulties. However, to my great disappointment, when I arrived at Ya Toivo's I found that he had changed his mind and was no longer prepared to carry on with the journey. So with a heavy heart I took Kuhangwa's luggage and went to wait for him at my home. When he arrived, he restored my morale because he was as determined as I was to proceed with our journey. To avoid detection we set out after dark, crossing the Namibian/Angolan border at midnight. We walked the whole 36 miles to Ondyiva on foot. We arrived in the early hours of the morning, tired and hungry, but there was work to be done. We had to find transport, submit our papers to the administrative offices and buy some food.

Ondyiva was then a nice little town and in April its tree-lined streets were beautiful. Nuyoma and I set out for the administrative offices while Kuhangwa and Tuhadeleni went to the shops for rations. Nuyoma and I had hardly reached the offices when Kuhangwa was involved in an incident in the street with the Ondyiva Administrator. People in authority always like to throw their weight around and the colonial Portuguese were no exceptions. The Administrator had just left his house and was walking to his office when Kuhangwa and Tuhadeleni passed him on their way to the shops. As is often the case, foreigners are bound to make mistakes. Kuhangwa and Tuhadeleni did just that – they were both wearing hats and they failed to take them off when he passed. To the Administrator this was disrespectful and an insult to his office. He called them to him and, babbling in Portuguese, he started raining blows at Kuhangwa's head. Tuhadeleni immediately realised who the man was – he took off his hat and, speaking in Oshikwanyama, went down on his knees pleading for mercy. He was terrified because Kuhangwa, who knew little about the reputation of the Portuguese, was about to match the Administrator blow-for-blow. The Administrator, realising that neither of his victims knew anything about colonial Portuguese manners let alone understood the language, let them off the hook.

Watching this incident from the Administrator's office, Nuyoma and I were very concerned that the bubble was about to burst. If the Portuguese had insisted on bringing Kuhangwa and Tuhadeleni to the offices, their photographs could have possibly revealed their true identities and it would have had dangerous consequences for all of us. We were relieved when our papers were finally dealt with and we left hastily and went to meet the others to find out what exactly had happened. Nothing much, they said, except that Kuhangwa had experienced his first Portuguese baptism. This became a big joke throughout our journey to Lobito. In a matter of time, we were also to learn something about Kuhangwa which we didn't know before – he was unpredictable and short-tempered. After the incident we went in search of transport, any transport, to Lobito.

We found an open truck bound for Huambo, in the central highlands of Angola, which was on the route to Lobito. Beside ourselves, there were five other men, all black Angolans, travelling on the truck. One of them was the driver and the rest were returning from business trips. We left Ondyiva at four o'clock the next morning and took 48 hours to reach Huambo.

We arrived in Huambo without any further incident. From there we caught an evening train to Lobito, travelling the whole night and arriving late the following afternoon. Lobito is a small coastal town up the coast from Benguela, with one of the best beaches in Angola. The town was well kept and clean, but its townships were dirty, muddy and overcrowded. Passenger liners and merchant ships berthed in the quiet waters of the bay and the town was frequented by sailors of all nationalities and mariners of the Portuguese navy. Our aim was to get on board any ship which would accept us or, if none would take us, to stow away. Nuyoma had a friend living there and I had an aunt, Maria Ishinda II (she had the same name as my aunt in Endola), who had worked and lived there for a number of years. We hoped they would put us up.

We caught a taxi from the railway station to the township in search of Maria. Neighbours showed us into her house – she was still at work. Word had got round Lobito that Sam Nujoma, OPO's president, was expected in the town – his escape from Namibia just before we had set out had been widely reported in the media all over the world. On hearing our names, the neighbours thought that Nuyoma was Sam Nujoma.

My aunt arrived back from work in the evening to find her house besieged by a crowd of people wanting to have a glimpse of 'Nujoma'. She did not recognise me as her nephew – I was nine years old when we had last met and now I was a man of 26. She was not happy with the situation because she was terrified of being accused by the Portuguese authorities of bringing 'Nujoma' to Angola to cause trouble for them. She did not hesitate to spell this out to us. However, she recognised Nakale from previous meetings and he explained who we all were. Only then did she accept us as her guests of honour, and told the crowds that this was not the Nujoma who they were curious to see. When we settled in, Nuyoma went to see his friend Miguel Neves in town, where he spent the night.

Kuhangwa and I came down with malaria the following morning. In the evening, Miguel and Nuyoma came to see us, only to be told that we had taken ill. They took us in Miguel's car to his house where we had nice hot baths. Miguel called in a private nurse to take our temperatures and give us treatment – she gave us camoqin tablets and recommended a good night's sleep. We had dinner with Miguel and he offered us the hospitality of his house. We would be welcome to stay there as long as we wanted to, he said. We did not tell him our intentions but only that we were visiting: he was shocked when he later discovered our true identities and wanted to know why we had not told him before. We explained that it was better for no one to know. We had not realised that he was interested in politics, but from then on he started political discussions with us. He told us that he knew a Namibian by the name of Daniel Michael Shifulah who was studying at the College of Alvaros, in Benguela. Shifulah was the distant cousin who had so influenced my study ambitions – I did not know that he was in Benguela. We made an appointment to meet him.

Basking in the African sun and breathing the salty but fresh air of the Atlantic, Benguela is one of the most beautiful cities in Angola. Her broad streets were lined with trees, beaches teemed with bathers of all ages and colours and the smell of fish filled the air. I did not tell Miguel of my relationship to Shifulah and he was surprised to see that we knew each other. We sat down, had some tea and then started discussing politics and Shifulah's studies, which were funded by an American charity organisation. He then invited us to meet some of his friends and took us to a nearby college where the students sang us lovely songs in Uumbundu, the language spoken in central Angola. He introduced us to four distinguished looking men who turned out to be high officials of UPA (Uniao Popular de Angola). UPA was one of the first political organisations in Angola which later became FNLA (Frente Nacional de Liberetacao de Angola), after it split. Their activities were strictly underground operations. They asked us whether they could trust Miguel, who was a Portuguese national. We told them that he seemed sympathetic to the plight of blacks.

It was suggested that we move to another place for further discussions and Shifulah and his friends took us to his in-laws. He introduced us to his fiancée Maria and her parents. We were given a private room and immediately got down to the business of political discussions. They told us about their organisation and its activities and membership. They had heard about OPO and were pleased to meet its president (Nuyoma again mistaken for Nujoma!). They asked why we were in Angola. To assess the socio-political situation of the Angolan people, we told them. Though we trusted Miguel to a certain extent, we could not reveal our plans as yet, for fear that they might be leaked to the police. From then onward, we had regular contact with Shifulah to whom we did reveal our plans. He assured us that we could confide in his friends and they could find a safe passage for us through which we could leave Angola for independent African states or the USA. But after our return to Lobito it became clear that he and his UPA contacts would not be able to help us to escape. Leaving on a ship proved impossible because of tight security at the docks.

We continued to stay with Miguel, who had a business of his own, Miguel Neves Imports and Exports Shipping Company. He popped in for a word with us whenever he found the time after a day at the office. Our discussions with him now centred mainly on politics. The Belgian Congo was about to be granted its independence on 30 June 1960. He, like us, was interested in Congolese independence. Kuhangwa and I wanted to attend the independence ceremonies in order to get out of Angola – having done his part, Nuyoma was to return home. We faced one big problem. Our finances and time were running out. Kuhangwa sent a telegram to OPO members in Cape Town for help but when the money arrived, it was inadequate for both of us to travel. Faced with a desperate situation, we had to make a decision as soon as possible. We had to make some sacrifices or end up going nowhere, I argued, although Kuhangwa was determined that both of us should proceed to the Congo. Fearing being stranded in a foreign country, I told him that I was ready to go back home, collect some more money and resume my journey again. We agreed on this and on 18 May 1960, we said our goodbyes and Kuhangwa caught a train to the Angolan-Congolese border.

I stayed a few more days in Lobito after Kuhangwa's departure, thinking about and planning my next moves. By now I felt lost and dejected and I made up my mind not to waste more time. I had tried several times to get through to the docks, but I looked conspicuous. I did succeed once in penetrating the security and boarded a Liberian-registered ship, but I found no one to help me.

At the end of May, I left by train bound for Huambo, from where I caught a goods delivery truck heading south. I met one of my distant uncles on the truck. He was travelling back from Chamutete Copper Mine, near Kassinga in southern Angola, and told me that he was living with Vavali, my sister, and she would be cross with me if I did not go and visit her. They were living at Oshimukwa, the area of southern Angola where I had grown up. Because I had not seen Vavali for over twenty years, I longed to see her.

The truck dropped us two miles away from my sister's

house and we walked the rest of the way. I was overcome with joy and excitement to meet my favourite sister and her big family. Though I was only six when I last saw Vavali she did not seem to have changed at all, she was as beautiful as ever. I loved her because she was always kind to me. She too, was pleased to see me after so many years. She told me that another sister was her next-door neighbour and was holding a 'naming' party for a daughter of my brother, Shapetama, the following morning.

It was one of the most memorable occasions of my life when I met not only my two sisters but also my eldest brother whom I had not seen for more than two decades. He, like our father, had married many wives and had many children. He wanted me to visit him at his home which was miles away but, having promised myself to spend only a week in the area, I felt I could not fit it into my programme. I had to leave that same day for my mother's home. I was sorry to leave but happy to have seen so many of my relatives.

I spent a few days with my mother and then with my grandmother before I headed for Endola. They were both as pleased to see me as I was them. I felt sorry for my grandmother because she was now very old and was sharing the house with her cousin who was even older than herself. They had nobody to look after them and she had no grandchildren staying with her. I could not help but feel guilty and helpless being so far away and unable to assist in her time of need. My uncle Haihambo, her cousin, had accumulated a debt of three years' rent. He was too old to do any work in order to earn a living let alone pay rent, so I gave the little money I had to him to pay part of his debt. I left with a heavy heart and a troubled mind, wondering what would happen to them in the event of their few subsistence resources running out.

4

The Prodigal Son

My journey back home, though uneventful, was not a pleasant one. My mind was preoccupied with my granny's and uncle's plight. I had nothing to offer them and I could not stay with them. I had too much to do, both politically and academically, I had no time to spare.

When I suggested that they come and join us at Endola, they had not even agreed to consider it. This added to my general confusion and lack of direction. I had nothing to take back home but myself. Not even the news that granny and uncle were coming to stay with us, which was what everybody wanted. I was uncertain of everything now. When I arrived home I was visibly disturbed and depressed.

My Aunt Beata, however, welcomed me with open arms and thought my depression was due to my failure to find my passage overseas. When I explained that it was due to my concern for grandma and Uncle Haihambo she said it would pass with time. She slaughtered an ox and prepared a big party to celebrate my return home. All my friends were invited to the party and I was well received by everyone who came. I was reminded of the Biblical story of the prodigal son, who asked his father for part of his inheritance, went to a distant country and squandered all his wealth. Destitute and hungry, he returned home to his father, who welcomed him with open arms. I was that prodigal son. Everybody was pleased to see me back, they all had questions to ask and wanted to know all about my journey into Angola. How did the Portuguese treat me? Didn't they beat me up? Are blacks treated better in Lobito? What about education? Is it segregated like in Namibia? Because I was not able to answer all the questions at the same time, I suggested to everybody present that I would give them a briefing before the big meal. They gave me a standing ovation after the briefing. We then had our party and everybody went away satisfied.

After I had rested for about two days, I looked up my political acquaintances. I was told that OPO's activities were going well, but communications with Windhoek and the outside world were minimal. Many OPO members in the north - Eliaser Tuhadeleni, Vinnia Ndadi, Lot Homateni, Ya

Toivo and others – were banned from going to any other parts of the country and from taking any employment. The authorities had accused the OPO leadership of inciting the workers through the organisation of trade unions and political meetings – maintaining that workers were happy with the contract labour system and those seeking to abolish it were work-shy communist agitators. Many leaders were blacklisted by employers and their movements curtailed by the authorities. Their families were harassed and many were threatened with deportation to Angola.

Some church leaders too, especially the then Finnish Mission Society's leaders in the north, such as Pastor Erickson at Engela, had taken a hostile attitude towards OPO members. Erickson allegedly had a heavy machine-gun hidden under a tarpaulin in his sitting room. He was said to have acquired it from Strydom, the Native Commissioner of the Oukwanyama District at Oshikango, to protect himself from OPO's 'Anti-Christ' elements. This made him unpopular with many people including some of his own colleagues in the church, and as a result he was banished to the wilderness of Kongo, about a hundred miles east of Oshikango. He served among the Eastern San (Bushmen) for about two years before he returned to Finland. Many ovafita (reverends) belonging to the Lutheran churches, such as Nhinda of Engela, and Shindongo of Oniimwandi, were outspokenly against OPO members. They branded them as Anti-Christ, refused to conduct baptism, confirmation or marriage services for them and banned them from holding OPO meetings on or near church premises. As a result, many people left the Lutheran churches because of what they saw as persecution and joined the Anglican and the Roman Catholic churches which were not hostile towards OPO and later SWAPO members. Thus the Lutheran churches lost the monopoly they had enjoyed in the north.

People like Reverend Theophilus Hamutumbangela of St. Cuthberts (Anglican) at Onekwaya, in Oukwanyama, played an important role in defence of workers' rights. He was the first church leader to be detained for speaking against apartheid laws and the injustices perpetrated against black Namibians by the authorities. He exposed the robbing of contract workers by the Namutoni Police who confiscated goods from returning workers. (Namutoni was the inland border post between what is known as Ovamboland and the so-called Police Zone to the south). He was then nicknamed 'Nghuwoyepongo o Pamba he i lotoka', literally meaning, 'the wailing of the poor is only heard by God'. His name, together with that of Reverend Michael Scott (though not a Namibian by birth) would go down in Namibian church history for the great contribution they rendered to the Namibian struggle.

With the ordination of Pastor L Awala of Oniipa as Bishop of the then Evangelical Lutheran Ovambo-Kavango Church in the early 1960s, the hostile attitude of the Lutheran Churches changed. Bishop Awala began to revolutionise the church. Old guards were removed from positions of influence: young and energetic new blood was infused within the church hierarchy. This in turn helped to facilitate OPO and later SWAPO activities. The churches began supporting our aims and objectives; they became part of the struggle.

I myself had become involved in church youth activities by this time as this was a major social outlet for young people. My aunt's house was just a stone's throw from Endola parish church and I had joined its Youth Group. We organised youth choirs and community activities, such as helping the aged and the needy.

Apart from the political and trade union issues, OPO activities in the north centred round the abolition of the forced contract labour system, the rejection of foot-and-mouth disease vaccinations for cattle (people feared the authorities were intent upon killing the cattle), the rejection of plans for the erection of a barbed-wire fence along the Angola/Namibia border, and protesting against the confiscation of goods from returning migrant workers by the police at Namutoni.

Meanwhile the OPO leadership in the north had heard unconfirmed reports that a new organisation had been launched in Windhoek. In August 1960, with all prominent OPO members in the north banned from entering the Police Zone, I was asked to go through Tsumeb to Windhoek to deliver verbal as well as written messages to the comrades there. Early one morning I went to the Oshikango Native Commissioner's Offices to get a travel pass to Windhoek. Peter Kalangula, my distant uncle, was then working in the offices as a secretary. He issued me a pass without question. He only inquired about his cousins, my aunts Beata and Maria Ishinda (as I have mentioned I have two aunts called Maria Ishinda, one living in Lobito).

I called at Tuhadeleni's house on my way back from

Oshikango. Tuhadeleni was the chairman of OPO in the north and he dictated a letter which I was to deliver to John Ya-Otto in Windhoek. The letter was to be published in 'The Contact', the Liberal Party of South Africa's news magazine, to highlight the repression, deportations to Angola and torture of our members by the Native Commissioner and Tribal Chiefs and Headmen. For example, Godfrey Nangonya and Mateus Nghikupulwa were deported to Angola for being OPO members and for organising against the vaccination of cattle. Tuhadeleni had been internally exiled for a year to Kongo, for refusing to stop OPO activities. Immanuel Shifidi had been beaten up by Headman Nehemiah Shoovaleka's tribal policemen when he was arrested at an OPO meeting held at Omafo.

I left home and spent the night at Ya Toivo's. He gave me messages to take to headquarters before he bade me goodbye in the morning. I caught the bus bound for Tsumeb, arriving there in the early evening.

My friends and I had all been wrong to think that I was less likely to be suspected. Although none of us knew it, and the authorities had not shown their hand, I too was one of the blacklisted persons. When the Native Commissioner at Oshikango realised that a mistake had been committed in granting me a travel pass to Windhoek, he alerted the Namutoni and Tsumeb police. But by then I had already reached Tsumeb. My colleagues picked me up from the bus station and, taking no chances, they took me to comrade Levi Mwashekele's home where I kept a low profile. Mwashekele was chairman of the Tsumeb branch. An extraordinary meeting of the executive committee of the Tsumeb Branch was convened and I gave them the messages from the comrades in the north. They gave me some information relating to the formation of the new party, the South West African People's Organisation (SWAPO). Since I was going to headquarters, I was told I would get further information in Windhoek.

OPO members reported to us that the police had been at the bus station, checking the papers of all travellers from the north. OPO scouts were posted to watch strategic roads to the railway station and they found that the police were watching all roads. It was now obvious to me that the police knew I was in Tsumeb and were hoping to catch me when I went to buy my train ticket to Windhoek. It was decided that someone should go and buy a ticket for me and I would be smuggled to the station. They gave me messages to take to Windhoek.

After the meeting, a car drew up in the back yard. I got in and was driven at full speed through the back roads of Tsumeb while the police were watching normal routes to the station. I got out, slipped into the station unnoticed and boarded the train to Windhoek. I sat down and took out the newspaper my friends had given me to read. Newspapers were impossible to get hold of in the far north and I was hungry for world news. I knew the risk of being caught reading such a paper but I could not suppress the yearning to read before the ticket collector arrived.

We roared out of the Tsumeb railway station towards the south. The ticket inspector came in. 'Ticket!' he demanded. I gave it to him and went back to my paper – he returned the ticket without looking at me. I sat back with relief and could not stifle the pleasure of being a wanted person, yet able to travel openly in comfort. I resumed my reading. No police came on board to check and there was no need to change trains at Kranzburg as had been the case in the past (a main line had replaced the narrow gauge from Tsumeb to Windhoek). The journey was as peaceful as I could have wished and I arrived in Windhoek with no problems.

I took a taxi from the station to the home of my cousins, Wendy Hipangelwa and Sackie Kapulwa in the Old Location. They had not yet moved to Katutura, but further forced removals were on the cards and everybody was bracing themselves for the fight ahead. Wendy and her children were home when I arrived but Kapulwa had gone to work. When he came back in the evening I told him that I wanted to meet other comrades.

He took me to John Ya-Otto's. Ya-Otto was Secretary-General of OPO and later of SWAPO. We had never met before but it was as if we had known each other for years. I told him my mission and handed him the letters from the comrades. He told me that the situation in Windhoek was tense and could explode at any time. Looking around the township, I could only see rubble and devastation. Houses were destroyed everywhere. He briefed me on other issues and the creation of the new party. It was difficult for people to meet in Windhoek but they always managed, he said, and he would arrange a meeting of the Executive Committee.

We gathered at the house of Gabriel Mbidi, not far from Wendy and Kapulwa's. Present were David Meroro (Chair), Jason Mutumbulwa (Information and Publicity Secretary),

Ya-Otto and two more people whose names and positions I don't remember. After the opening speech by Meroro, the chairman, I was given the floor. I told them about the difficulties we were having with the authorities in the north and the difficulties in communicating with our comrades in the south. I stressed the need to establish an information network and pointed to the fact that we did not know about the change and creation of the new organisation. I told them that they would find more information in the letters addressed to the secretary. They too pointed to the problems facing them in disseminating and distributing information. They were presently preoccupied with the pending forced removals and were short-handed.

Ya-Otto and myself left together after the meeting. He told me that he wanted me to go to his place to edit Tuhadeleni's letter for publication. It was the middle of the night when I returned to my cousins.

I left with Kapulwa in the morning for the city, to meet some friends. When I returned at lunchtime, Wendy told me that the police Special Branch were looking for me.

'What did they want?'

They had not said, but would come back that afternoon.

I waited for them the whole afternoon. They never showed up and I thought they had given up. I was wrong. They came again the following morning when I was out again. They did not leave any message. To make matters more complicated Wendy's boyfriend, Gabriel David, was a policeman. He arrived that evening but he was off duty and did not want to discuss anything. All he would say was that the police were investigating suspected forged documents and wanted to check the travelling papers of some visitors from the north. He would not be drawn into any further discussion.

I decided that as there was no chance of avoiding arrest, I would rather report to the police myself. In the morning I set out for the police station to present myself. On my way there, I passed some police looking for me at the edge of the location. They did not see me and I did not draw attention to myself. I met them again near where my cousin Kapulwa worked. This time I stopped them, introduced myself and asked why they were looking for me. They said it was not they but the Special Branch who wanted to see me – they were only messengers. I proceeded to the Special Branch office and was directed to the white policeman who wanted to see me.

He was outside the office washing his car and asked me to help him.

'Is that what you wanted to see me for?' I demanded.

He replied by asking if it was not normal to offer to help when one found someone working.

I became extremely irritated and after increasingly hostile exchanges I was about to leave when he stopped me and finally got to the point. He wanted to know what the purpose of my visit to Windhoek was.

'None of your business,' I replied.

He asked to see my pass. I threw it at him. He picked it up, smiled, and asked who had issued it. I suggested he looked at the signature. He now wanted to know whether I had collected it myself, and how I had travelled to Windhoek. Next he wanted to see my train ticket and to know where I had got it from. When I said it had come from Tsumeb railway station he jeered, 'You think that I am a stupid Boer, Mr. Shityuwete?'

As the questioning continued it became clear that the police had indeed been trying to follow me on my journey to Windhoek, but had lost me in Tsumeb. He even admitted as much, saying that I had been clever to slip through the net without them noticing.

He again asked what I was doing in Windhoek. I told him I was visiting my cousins in the Old Location, at which he said that the people living in there were communists who did not want to co-operate with the government. Our conversation concluded, he handed back my papers and warned that he would be keeping an eye on me. I told him he was welcome.

I met my colleagues for more discussions. They gave me more details of the new organisation, SWAPO. The change of name was suggested because OPO represented only a certain group of people and was concerned mainly with workers' problems. A broader, more political and more representative movement was needed to cater for all Namibians, irrespective of race or creed. Membership would be open to all Namibians and the aim was to unite Namibians in the call for the withdrawal of the South African colonial administration and the granting of independence. Full details were still to be worked out but a draft programme of action had been sent to our representatives at the United Nations. They gave me more messages to take to Tsumeb and to my friends in the north. I went to buy newspapers to take with me before I left and was pleased to see Tuhadeleni's letter and photograph in 'The

Contact' September 1960 issue – I bought a few copies to give to friends and one for Tuhadeleni. I said goodbye to my cousins and friends then left Windhoek for Tsumeb. Whether the police kept an eye on me, I had no idea.

Back home, I went to see Tuhadeleni, who was my neighbour. I briefed him on my journey and experiences with the police. He suggested that we should meet others in the Executive Committee and possibly arrange for a public meeting, so we sent out messages to the committee members to meet at Tuhadeleni's.

All members, except Ya Toivo who was under house arrest, arrived at Tuhadeleni's a week after I returned from Windhoek. I gave them the picture of events in the south as well as in the rest of the world. The information was well received but there was disappointment when they heard of my experiences with the police and that I was also a listed person. They were, however, pleased with what I had achieved and hoped that something could be worked out to enable us to keep in touch with our colleagues in the south. It was agreed that a public meeting be held at Tuhadeleni's in two weeks' time, to inform people about SWAPO.

A week before the public meeting I was struck down with an attack of malaria which was so severe that it prevented me from attending. Tuhadeleni, who was the chair, gave the report I brought from Windhoek on my behalf. He and Vinnia Ndadi, as well as John Kemanye from Okalongo, addressed the meeting. Letters from Windhoek were read and in addition to the change of the name, political issues were discussed at length. I was told that the meeting was well attended and people responded fairly positively, but very few understood the meaning of 'politics'. The abolition of the contract labour system was their main priority and they were not really sure about broadening the scope. No police came to disrupt the meeting, as many had expected.

My malaria was getting worse mainly because I was not receiving any medical treatment for it. Eventually I went to the local Endola clinic where I was given penicillin injections, to no avail. I visited Okatana Mission Hospital for further treatment, where I was given quinine injections, but this too had no effect.

It was now October and there were no signs of recovery. Instead, my condition was deteriorating - I was becoming increasingly weak and began to experience hallucinations and fits. I was alarmed and thought I was suffering from epilepsy. I desperately needed treatment. The question was where?

There were no state-run or well equipped hospitals in the north. The only two were Onandyokwe and Oshikuku, both of which were mission-run institutions. The former was run by the Finnish Mission Society and the latter by the Catholic Mission. I decided to go to Oshikuku Hospital which was 25 miles away and the nearest to me. The examination confirmed that I had a severe dose of malaria but there were no traces of epilepsy, as I had feared. What a relief! Though malaria had claimed many lives in our region, I thought it was at least better to suffer from something with a cure. Dr Elisabeth Freundlich, a German woman, gave me the best treatment available. I was almost dead by this time but she saved my life.

My three weeks in hospital badly affected my political activities. My colleagues were being intimidated and hunted down by the authorities and many had gone into hiding. It was difficult for me to contact any of them and I was unaware whether SWAPO was off the ground because no one could brief me.

5

Return to Angola

After I was discharged from the hospital I spent a week at home recuperating. This was now November 1960, and before the week was out, I had made preparations for my second trip to Angola. My plan was to find a passage through Angola to go abroad. I collected some money, said goodbye to my aunt then left for the Oshikango Administration Offices for travelling papers. I crossed the border into Angola without bothering to present my documents at the Angolan border post - a mistake I was soon to regret.

I walked to Onamacunde, a village 10 miles inside Angola, because there were no transport connections between Namibia and Angola. There a commercial and timber truck from Huambo, in central Angola, had just finished delivering its cargo and I was offered a lift for 200 Escudos (£2.10s.). We arrived in Huambo after two days. The security man on the truck and I became good friends and he invited me to spend the night at his home.

Early the next morning I went to the post office to post a letter to my friend Miguel Neves in Lobito. After I had posted it, I thought it would be better to send a telegram as well. I went to the telegram window and, speaking in English, I asked the woman clerk for a telegram form. She asked me to speak in Portuguese and when I explained that I could not, she went away, returning some time later with the form. I filled it in and she asked me to wait.

When she eventually returned, and using a good deal of sign language, she wanted to know why I had sent such an expensive telegram. I replied that I did not know it would cost so much, and collected my papers to leave, but found a policeman blocking my way. He beckoned me to accompany him. Was this the reason they had taken so long to process my telegram? I wondered. I mentally reviewed the contents of the telegram to check if I had said anything incriminating. There was nothing, I thought.

The policeman led me outside, picked up his bicycle and signalled that I should go with him to the police station. It took us half an hour to get there. He ordered me into one of the offices and closed the door behind me. Pacing about the office was a police captain – I could see that he was already agitated and cautioned myself to tread carefully. He stopped and turned towards the window with his back to me. When he started firing questions at me in Portuguese I was, of course, unable to understand or respond, which infuriated him still further. He clearly thought I was bluffing but after a while, when we had got no further and he had calmed down a little, he decided to seek help at the Administrative Governor's office. There a carpenter was found, who claimed to speak English. His English turned out to be worse than Pidgin but he did at least make it possible for the captain and myself to understand each other.

The captain wanted to know how, when and where I had entered Angola and he accused me of entering illegally. He further wanted to know why I went to Huambo and what I was doing there. Why did I not go directly to Lobito, which I had told him was my destination? (I told the captain I was going to study there.) He was particularly interested to know where I had spent the previous night and when I told him he immediately asked me to take him there in his Land Rover. As we approached I was surprised to notice that the people in the house had got wind of our coming. They had left the house, locked it, and gone to stand on a nearby hillside.

I had no key and there was nobody to let me in. The captain was of hefty build. When he tried the door and it did not open, he retreated a few yards and came rushing at it with the intention of breaking it down but I placed myself between him and the door. He became angry but I explained I had responsibilities to the gentleman of the house and would not allow him to break down the door. Clearly no black man had ever spoken to him like that before and he trembled with rage. I offered to ask the people on the hill for the keys. Though they were terrified of the consequences of putting me up, they were enjoying the situation. It was the first time they had seen a black man standing up to a Portuguese, and the fact that he was a captain made things even more entertaining for them. They gave me the key to the house.

I opened the door and we entered. I suspected that the captain thought I was a smuggler of some sort. He searched my luggage thoroughly, checking each item. Satisfied that I did not carry anything contraband, he put everything back, gave me a lift back to the city and told me I was free to go.

I set out to see my cousin Daniel Shifulah, who had now

joined the Portuguese army in Huambo. When he heard it was me asking for him at the barracks he asked for an afternoon off. I was extremely pleased to see him and hoped that he would be able to assist me in my problem with the captain. We went to a hotel nearby for lunch where he told me that he had met Hilia France, another cousin, who was also working in Huambo. We went to see her and because there were no trains to Lobito for a couple of days, I decided to spend the nights at her home.

The following morning Shifulah brought me a telegram, a reply from Neves in Lobito. It said: 'Welcome back to Lobito. Do not forget to include "six girls" in your suitcase.' I was mystified by this reference to 'girls'. I later found that when the post office had received the telegram they had sent a copy (translated into Portuguese) to the police. After reading it, the captain went to the house where I had spent my first night in Huambo to question me about the contents. When he did not find me there, he had confiscated my luggage.

When I went to collect my things the people were surprised and happy to see me. When the captain had taken my luggage he had told them I was in prison. Angry and upset, because I was going to miss my train that evening, I dashed off to the police station to demand an explanation.

I was immediately ushered into the captain's office. Using a mixture of Portuguese and sign language we somehow managed to communicate. He wanted to know where I had been for the last two days and I wanted to know why he had confiscated my belongings.

He explained that he had taken them to ensure that I did not leave town without seeing him. After asking me whether I had heard from Neves, he revealed his translated copy of the telegram and demanded to know its meaning. He was particularly interested in the reference to the six girls. Feeling that I was getting into deeper water I told him about my cousin at the Huambo military academy and asked whether I could bring him as an interpreter. At first he would not hear of it but in the end he agreed and I went to fetch Shifulah.

Immediately I introduced them to each other, the captain went on the offensive. Though I could not follow what was being said, I already knew that they were not arguing my case, otherwise Shifulah would have interpreted for me. He later told me that the captain suspected him of evil intentions in joining the Portuguese army because he was a Namibian.

49

Shifulah, however, had convinced him by explaining that when the border was drawn between Angola and Namibia, it had cut our nation in the middle and we had found ourselves on either side of the border.

'Now tell your cousin to explain to me about this six girls business,' he ordered Shifulah. Because I did not actually know the meaning, I said it was just a joke. Whether he believed that or not, I do not know, but at least he let me go without further ado. Now that I had missed my train, I had to wait for another two days for the next train to Lobito. To avoid further complications, I left my things with the captain.

I spent the two days at Hilia's. Shifulah and I met at a hotel nearby for our meals. One day we met a group of people outside the hotel after lunch, one of whom asked after me. He said he believed that he was one of my younger brothers. He had come all the way to Huambo to find me - his name was Kondyeni Shityuwete. He did not know me because we had not met before and after our father's death the family had scattered on either side of the border. Immediately he said that he was a Shityuwete, I recognised my father's looks in him.

It was good to meet him after so many years. How did he hear of me, I asked. The word was all over the town and its surroundings that the police had arrested a 'Sud Africano'. He was working in a small town nearby and had heard people who had read the papers talking about the arrest. When he heard the name Shityuwete, he thought I must be his brother and had set out for the city: he had a copy of the newspaper report with him. In Huambo he had gone to the police to find me, only to be told I had been released – that was when he started asking around for me. We went to celebrate our meeting in the hotel.

I was having a siesta at noon the following day when Hilia came in to tell me that a friend of mine was outside.

'A friend of mine from where?' I asked.

Before she could answer, Miguel Neves walked in.

'What are you doing here?' we both asked simultaneously.

'I'm getting ready for my train,' I said.

'And I have come to fetch you,' he said.

We both laughed then hugged. I was really pleased to see him. He explained that he had had to bribe his way to me. We took a taxi to the police station to collect my things before we set off for the train.

The captain was in his office when Neves and I arrived. He asked what Neves was doing in Huambo. He had come to meet me, he said, because he had no faith in Portuguese justice towards blacks, especially foreigners. Inevitably, a heated argument ensued. The captain began to ask Neves many questions, about his import-export business and whether he was a smuggler of some sort. In the end, we were both allowed to go. We collected my belongings and left for the station.

On the way Neves told me that the captain suspected me of illicit diamond dealings – he had understood the 'six girls' to mean diamonds. I asked what exactly he had meant. To my surprise, Neves admitted that he had indeed been referring to diamonds, on the off-chance that I could have brought him some – there was much smuggling of diamonds from Namibia at that time. I was angry that he had done such a stupid thing and caused so much trouble. I was further horrified when he told me that the captain was going to have me placed under police surveillance in Lobito, but he had been persuaded not to. I was not convinced and began to feel uneasy with him.

I stayed on in Lobito for six months, from November 1960 to April 1961. I started taking Portuguese lessons with Neves in the evenings and watched the harbour during the day. In mid-March 1961, my opportunity to stow away nearly came when I managed to evade the security checks at the entrance to the docks. I intended to get on board one of two Liberian-registered merchant ships lying at berth that day. I went straight for the one nearest the entrance but a guard at the foot of the gangway demanded to see my papers. I pretended to reach into my pockets for them and said I seemed to have lost them, but he would not let me go aboard. I then headed for the other ship. I got on the gangway alright and was about to set foot on the ship when again a guard stopped me.

I descended the gangway a dejected person and found my way out of the docks. The situation was getting desperate. Patrice Lumumba ·had just recently been murdered in the Congo. The Angolan revolutionaries had started an armed struggle. Just a week ago they had attacked several Portuguese settler plantations near Benguela. Lobito's streets were being patrolled by soldiers in combat fatigues and armed with automatic weapons. What chance did I have to find my way abroad? I asked myself. I was becoming increasingly nervous. In the end I could stand it no more and decided to head home.

By this time I had acquired Angolan citizenship because I

had lost my travelling documents and had been unable to get replacements. The first week in April 1961, I told Neves that I wanted to leave before things got any worse and questions were asked about me. On 21 April 1961 he drove me to Benguela to catch a bus to Lubango, in Huila Province. The bus was divided into two sections, one for first class, the other for second class passengers.

I bought a seat in the first class section and found myself the only black among the whites and this made me conspicuous once again. We were stopped at a police station half way to Lubango and they demanded to look at my papers. I was ordered off the bus and told I was to be detained. What was the reason for my detention? I asked. Their only reply was that they had received orders to do so. Then a Portuguese woman intervened. When she was told that there was nothing wrong with my papers, she ordered them to give them back to me. We proceeded on our way to Lubango. I could not believe what she had done and her action not only moved my heart but also changed the general attitude I had that all the Portuguese were the same. I thanked her for her intervention.

We were about fifteen miles from Lubango when we ran into a roadblock manned by armed soldiers. They stopped our bus and came on board. A man in civilian clothing came straight for me and demanded my papers – nobody else's papers were checked. Satisfied with the documents, they demanded to search my suitcases which were on the top of the bus. The soldiers on the ground scrambled into position, cocked their guns and aimed at me, ready to shoot. I climbed up and pointed out my suitcases. When they had finished searching, the man in civilian clothing, whom I now learned was from the Governor's office in Lubango, told me to report there in the morning.

We were lined up at the bus depot when we arrived in Lubango. A mixed group of police and soldiers began checking our papers and searched our luggage. Everybody's papers were checked this time but, when they came to me, they ordered me to stand aside. I waited there until everybody had gone before they started searching me and double-checking my papers. They took almost two hours and by the time I left the depot, it was midnight. I spent the night at the Hotel Popular, nearby. On the morning of 23 April, I went to report to the Governor's office and returned to the hotel at lunch. I went to collect my hotel keys from the reception and there I overheard the hotel manager telling everybody in the dining room that I was not Omukwanyama as I claimed to be. He believed that I was either a Congolese or a Ghanaian – countries considered hostile to colonialism. I did not pay much attention to his chatter and left for my room.

I opened the door, sat down with my back to the door and started composing a letter to Neves to tell him that I had arrived safely in Lubango. I did not know that I had left the door open until I noticed a slight movement within the room. I looked over my right shoulder and found myself looking at a pistol barrel directed at my temple. Another appeared to the left. Three soldiers had entered the room. I stopped writing and waited for them to do whatever they intended doing.

'Come with us,' they said. They grabbed my briefcase, collected my suitcases and marched me out of the room.

Outside in the hotel yard, I found two columns of heavily armed soldiers. Although I was at first alarmed, I could not help enjoying the situation in a way and started examining the soldiers as if they were my guards of honour. The hotel gate leading to the main street was closed and when it opened the street was teeming with people – priests praying and nuns weeping – all wanting to see a Congolese/Ghanaian. They put me in a Land Rover with three armed soldiers with their guns trained on me and drove me to the police station where I found another guard of honour waiting.

In the police station, the station commander himself conducted the interrogation – the usual questions of where my papers were, who I was, where I was coming from and going to. He searched my luggage and confiscated several books and some money. I was then driven to the prison. I was only there for a few hours before they took me to the Governor's office to face similar questions again. I spent a week in the Governor's detention and while there a number of people were brought in, some arrested for no apparent reason except that they were found in groups of more than two people and suspected of politicising. I was guarded by up to five policemen day and night. One of the policemen was Omukwanyama and we were able to communicate without others understanding what we were saying. He told me that many of the people arrested and brought to the Governor's detention were killed without ever appearing in court.

On the afternoon of my seventh day in detention, I heard them calling my name and thought that my time to die had come. They led me through a chain of offices before I was ushered into the Governor's office. Seated around the table were the Governor himself and four other people. I did not see them clearly because my eyes focussed on the revolver on the table, assuming it held my fate.

The Governor rose and said, 'Meet your friend Neves!'

It was only then I saw him. Standing up and speaking in English, Neves said everything was alright. Though I was very pleased to see him I was put in an awkward position since I had denied knowing any English. I responded in Portuguese and laughter erupted all round me. Why did I insist on speaking Portuguese even when I was told that everything was alright? I was told I could go. We collected my things and went to find a hotel.

At the hotel, Neves told me that he had had to come because the 'case' against me was so severe that they could have executed me.

'For what?' I asked him.

He told me that the police were told by the hotel manager, where I was arrested, that I had suitcases full of arms. The police requested the army to arrest me because they could not handle it themselves. When they did not find any weapons, and thinking that I had hidden them somewhere, they then began investigating my friends. Neves came to hear of it through his friend, the Administrator of Lobito, who had been contacted by the Governor of Lubango requesting information on Neves. When Neves was shown the telegram from the Governor to the Administrator, he recognised the Governor as someone he had grown up with. He then flew to Lubango to tell the Governor that I was innocent and to demand that the charges levelled against me be dropped.

I was shocked when I heard all these things. Because all roads to Ondyiva were impassable due to heavy rains and flooding of the Cunene River, I decided to catch a plane to Ondyiva from where I could easily cross into Namibia, before the Portuguese changed their minds about releasing me. Neves came to see me off at the airport. Before I boarded the plane, a car pulled up and out jumped some policemen: they had come to make sure that I got onto the plane.

Police and customs officials met me at the Ondyiva airstrip. They took me to the customs offices to search my luggage and wanted to know who I knew in Ondyiva. I knew only my aunt Eunice Hamutenya, who was married somewhere in Ondyiva,

I told them. They sent for her and she came promptly, terrified that something was wrong and that I might be in big trouble. Satisfied that she was not someone with political leanings and that I carried no weapons, the police put me on their Jeep and drove me to the Angolan-Namibian border. They handed me to the border guards who told me never to cross the border into Angola again.

6

SWAPO

The border posts between Angola and Namibia at Oshikango are about one mile apart and, in the 1960s, there was little traffic between the two countries. Even if there had been transport, I could not have got any because of heavy floods. I therefore crossed the border on foot and walked to Oshikango on the Namibian side. I wondered how I was going to make it home - Endola was about 20 miles away and there were numerous rivers to cross during the rainy season. I walked to Engela, six miles away, to see Nghidimundyila Shoombe, a school teacher at Engela Boys' High School and an old friend of mine. Because I was tired, I spent the night there. He told me that OPO was now officially converted into SWAPO. He emphasised that SWAPO was more political than OPO which was mainly a trade union oriented organisation. He and another school teacher were organisers in the area and the response from locals was encouraging. I left my luggage with him when I left for home in the morning.

My progress home was made difficult by the need to cross so many rivers. There was water everywhere. Some rivers were chest high and that made crossing them very tiring. Exhausted and hungry I managed to reach home in the late evening. My aunt and everybody in the household gave me a warm welcome.

I enquired after all my political and personal acquaintances from my aunt. She told me that a lot of things had changed. Repression and persecution had increased. Political meetings in the north were broken up by the authorities. A number of people had been flogged with omapokolo (dried branches of the makalani palm tree). Others were fined and had to pay in cattle or an equivalent amount of money – all for holding political meetings and for 'incitement'. All Headmen in the Oukwanyama District were armed by the Native Commissioner, Strydom. They were given instructions to shoot to kill any defiant SWAPO member. Simon Kaukungua was wanted dead or alive for his defiant stance against both the Headmen and the authorities. Many leaders had gone into hiding but some had managed to flee the country. Tuhadeleni, my neighbour, had been in detention several times. Ya Toivo was still under house arrest. Phillip Namholo, another prominent member of the movement, had been expelled to the north from Tsumeb where he was working as a contract labourer. They were all accused of stirring up trouble in the country.

I called on Tuhadeleni on my second day at home who briefed me on all aspects relating to the political situation. They still had communication problems with the south, but they could get more information through than before. The number of people joining had almost doubled after the changeover from OPO to SWAPO, he told me. He was sorry that I could not find my way overseas but happy to have me back to continue the struggle together. I told him that I had not given up the idea of going abroad as yet and would keep on trying whenever I got the chance. In the meantime I would render to the struggle everything I could, I told him.

Tuhadeleni was visited by Special Branch police from Ondangwa every week – there were no police stationed anywhere in the north beside those at Ondangwa under Captain Ackermann. Before long I experienced the same thing. Every time they called at Tuhadeleni's house, they would check on me first. They would not say what they wanted except that they were paying me a 'friendly' visit. Despite such observation, we managed to hold meetings on a weekly basis, especially on Sundays when the police would not be around. Beside my political activities, I resumed my church youth activities as well. Everything went well until July 1961, when I became ill again.

I was in bed for the whole of August and only got better towards the middle of September. Miguel Neves kept writing to me. The post office at Oshikango, instead of sending my letters to me, kept sending me yellow postal invoices to go and collect my mail. Because I could not go myself, I sent my cousin, Katemo. Every time he went there, he was turned back and told that I must go and collect my mail myself. I did not understand why they wanted me to collect my own mail and would not give it to someone I authorised. I soon found out when I was well enough again to ride a bicycle.

It normally took me an hour to Oshikango by bicycle from Endola, but because I had not fully recovered from my ailment, it took me two hours to get there. The postmaster and I were good friends but he was in the process of handing over to a new postmaster. My friend was busy when I arrived and he delegated his replacement, a white Afrikaner, to serve me.

He looked at the invoice and asked, 'So you are Shityuwete?' He handed me some forms to fill in. I refused to fill them in until I had received my mail. At that, he brought all my letters and parcels and placed them on the counter. 'There! Now fill in and sign those forms!'

I did, but when I asked for my mail he said he was not going to hand it over as yet - he wanted to take me to Strydom, the Native Commissioner.

'What for?' my friend demanded in surprise.

'Because Strydom asked us to, have you forgotten?'

It was now clear why they did not want to give my mail to my cousin, Katemo! They wanted to arrest me and possibly deport me to Angola as they did with Nangonya and Nghikupulwa and tried once with Jacob Kuhangwa. The Portuguese accepted the first two but refused to have Kuhangwa because he was not born in Angola. With my Angolan connection, they would have had a 'legitimate' case.

The new postmaster was already collecting the items and preparing to usher me outside. My friend at first thought his colleague was joking, but when he realised he was serious, he told him not to make a fool of himself. If Strydom wanted me, he knew where to find me. He was not going to let Strydom use the post office as a police station as long as he was in charge, he said. This put the new man in his place and he handed over my mail. But Strydom had not finished with me as yet.

A meeting for some tribal leaders to meet Strydom was convened. It was to take place in October 1961, at Omungwelume, south-west of Oshikango. The authorities were bent on combating soil erosion and to do this, they wanted to limit livestock to seven cattle per family. Furthermore, the cattle were to be put into fenced-off kraals so that children could go to school, instead of looking after cattle. Many people in the north owned more cattle than the authorities were prepared to allow them to possess. So everybody was opposed to the plan. The meeting was called to discuss this, and other issues like access to water and inoculation of cattle. We SWAPO members in the Oukwanyama District decided to attend and, where possible, to challenge the Commissioner over the wisdom of his proposals.

Before the meeting started, I went to say hello to my uncle, Eliaser Kalangula, younger brother to Peter Kalangula, who was a clerk in the Omungwelume Tribal Offices. He told me that he was once asked by Strydom about my political leanings and my Angolan connection. Strydom told him that he suspected me of being one of the 'agitators' and that he would have me watched. Kalangula warned me to be careful. I thanked him for the information and went to the meeting.

Strydom opened the meeting, which was held under a tree, by asking the Headmen present whether they had any complaints or requests to make to the authorities. Silence fell round the tree. None of the Headmen seemed to have anything to complain about or request. When I realised nobody had anything to say, I asked him to tell us his purpose in calling the meeting. Before he answered, he asked who I was (we had never met face to face before). I told him my name and he seemed surprised to see me there.

Omungwelume, where the meeting was held, fell under Headman Vilho Weyulu and immediately after I had spoken, he turned to me and ordered me not to speak as I did not pay taxes to his Tribal Authority. I replied that I paid taxes at the Omungwelume offices and was therefore eligible to speak. The order was then shifted to SWAPO members. No SWAPO member was allowed to speak or ask any questions at that meeting as it was not a SWAPO assembly, we were cautioned. Then turmoil broke out. The Commissioner should tell people what he had called the meeting for. He must not hide behind the Headmen who appeared to have no complaints. If the Headmen did not have complaints, many people there had, and wanted the Commissioner to listen to them. Whether those complaints were asked by SWAPO members was immaterial, the people shouted here and there. What mattered was that people had legitimate complaints and he had to listen to them. Strydom and his staff panicked and, thinking there was going to be a riot, ran to their vehicles and drove off in a cloud of dust without having said what they wanted.

After the dust had settled, to avoid confrontation with the Headmen, we (SWAPO) called a meeting under another tree nearby. We warned the people to avoid falling into the traps set for them by the authorities. If the authorities wanted to limit the number of cattle per household, it was better to fight it now rather than to try to disobey after it had been officially accepted, which could lead to penalties or loss of cattle. Also, how would people identify their cattle if they were all to be placed in designated and fenced-off cattle kraals? We warned people to be wary and to resist the treacherous designs of the authorities.

As far as water problems in the region were concerned, we encouraged people to form themselves into groups to dig wells or invest in bore-holes to provide water for their livestock. We also asked people to make consistent demands for the independence of the country from South Africa. We told them that many countries in Africa and elsewhere were fighting for their freedom and independence and were succeeding. The time had come for us to demand the right to rule ourselves. They were also told that SWAPO and other political organisations and leaders were going to petition the UN to take appropriate action to force South Africa out of Namibia. Emphasis was also placed on the lack of schools and hospitals: South Africa was not doing enough to promote the well-being of Namibians.

There was unity in the meeting and our message was well received, especially by cattle-owners but even by those on the side of the authorities. The majority wanted immediate action on the points raised. It was decided after the meeting that a delegation should be sent to talk to the Headmen about those points and to ask the Headmen to take them up with the Commissioner. Tuhadeleni and Erastus Kashikuka were appointed for the task.

In the summer of 1961, the authorities in the north embarked upon four major projects: building dams, building schools, intensifying the cattle vaccinating programme, and fencing the Namibian-Angolan border. All four projects met with strong opposition from the community because they were political rather than economic. Dams were deep and fenced and no watering troughs were provided; nobody could get in and draw water for whatever purpose. Thus they were useless to the people for whom they were ostensibly provided. School buildings were built near missionary-run schools and no one wanted to make use of them. There were no staff to run them – they ended up occupied by birds and goats! They were no asset to the community.

Cattle vaccination against foot-and-mouth disease, which started in the 1950s, intensified in the early 1960s. Because it was introduced at a time when the authorities were advocating the seven-cattle limit, many cattle farmers in the north were suspicious of their intentions. People suspected that the authorities were intending to kill their cattle in order to reduce their herds. Thus the vaccination was unpopular and people only took their animals to be vaccinated because they were compelled to do so by law.

Wire fencing along the Namibian-Angolan border was accompanied by restrictions on cattle farmers – any cattle found grazing on the good pasture grounds in Angola were not allowed to be taken back to Namibia. The Portuguese authorities in Angola, in collaboration with the authorities in northern Namibia, confiscated thousands of Namibian cattle. People responded by removing the fences (odalate) every time they were put up. This resulted in confrontations with the authorities, and gave us further ammunition with which to fight the system.

Whereas the police used to call on me once a week, they now came twice a week. They did not seem to know what they were doing because they never asked me anything besides how I was doing. This became a familiar pattern which did not hamper me from carrying on with my political work. Like many of my colleagues, I was determined to work relentlessly. We organised meetings everywhere and whenever we could to expose the intentions of the authorities. The people's response was fantastic.

Our work in the north was, however, not always plain sailing and it was hampered by some undisciplined elements amongst us. Most of us were disrespectful towards Headmen, referring to them as ignorant idiots and empty-headed fools who obeyed everything the authorities said without questioning their legitimacy to rule over them. Instead of trying to win them over to our side, we drove them right into the camp of the oppressors. They turned against us. Some people felt that we were 'lions' wanting to take over from the 'wolves', an expression used to demonstrate two similar characters trying to outdo each other for the same position.

Towards the third week in November 1961, I was again sent to the south. As before, I had no difficulties getting travelling papers for Windhoek. The police kept a low profile this time but they made it clear to me that they were watching me. In Windhoek I had a few meetings with the comrades. A big rally, addressed by both SWAPO and SWANU, was organised at the Herero II School in the last week in November. Jason Mutumbulwa was the main speaker for SWAPO and Gerson Veii spoke on behalf of SWANU. Speakers stressed the need for unity among the Namibians and to stand firm in the face of an 'enemy' determined to force people to go to the new township Katutura. Concerted action on demands for freedom and national independence was the theme of the meeting.

Police in uniform and civilian clothes were out in full force at the meeting. They took notes and photographed all those who spoke and some of the audience. Though I was due to address the meeting, I was advised not to speak as I could be arrested. My name was then removed from the speakers' list. After I left, Gabriel David, Wendy's policeman boyfriend, came to tell me that they had been watching and waiting for me to speak. They would have pounced on me immediately had I gone to the platform. They wanted to keep me in for Christmas, he said. It is a common practice in Namibia for the authorities to arrest people indiscriminately around the Christmas period, to prevent people from enjoying Nativity festivals. After a few days in Windhoek, I rounded up my affairs and headed for the north, expecting to be arrested at any time.

It was now obvious to me that the police were watching my every move. The game of cat and mouse was beginning to unnerve me. When I got home Captain Ackermann of the Ondangwa Police resumed his twice-weekly visits. On his first visit, he demanded to know where I had been for a fortnight. I said I had not been anywhere, which he clearly knew not to be true. He wanted to know where I was at all times, he told me. Did that mean I was under house arrest I wondered? He refused to clarify the position and left.

During the months of November and December 1961, and in the new year, we decided to challenge the authorities over the restrictions on movement and employment placed on many of our colleagues. We demanded that those restrictions be removed and that everyone be allowed to take up employment and be given freedom of movement within the whole country. Many deputations headed by Tuhadeleni and Simon Kaukungwa were sent to Oshikango to talk to Strydom on this issue and other related aspects. Strydom denied having placed restrictions on anybody's movement or blacklisting anyone wanting to take up employment. Delegations were also sent to the Ondangwa Native Commissioner to plead for Ya Toivo's house arrest to be lifted. He also washed his hands of the cases in question and placed responsibility on the Chiefs and Headmen.

The night of 11 May 1962 was just like any other night. I was just about to go to bed when I heard the familiar cricketty-crick of Tuhadeleni's bicycle at the front of our house. He was on his way to Ondangwa to meet the UN delegation, he shouted to me, and wanted me to go with him. I would follow in the morning, I told him and went back to bed. We had received information a couple of weeks previously that the UN would send a fact-finding mission to Namibia led by a Mr Victor Carpio of the Philippines. They were to study whether Namibians were 'ready' for their independence. They had spent a few days in South Africa and had now arrived in Namibia, our sources said. They held discussions with our comrades in Windhoek after which they flew to Rundu, in the Okavango region in the north-east, where Senhor De Alva, in the Carpio delegation, reportedly 'fell' into the Okavango River - there was a persistent rumour that he was pushed by a South African agent. They then arrived at Ondangwa on 11 May 1962.

I set out at 5 o'clock the next morning for Ondangwa, to join my colleagues in the SWAPO Northern Region delegation which was to meet the UN mission. When I arrived at Ya Toivo's place outside Ondangwa at 7 am, I found that everything was ready for the day. Many people had gathered there for a demonstration and rally. Placards to welcome the delegation and to demand independence for Namibia, and denouncing the South African regime, were readied. We set off in a convoy of open trucks and thousands of people on foot for the Native Commissioner's Offices where we expected to meet the UN mission.

On our arrival at the Native Commissioner's Offices, we learned that Carpio and his delegation had been taken to Oshakati by the Commissioner. The development of Oshakati, about 25 miles from Ondangwa, had just begun under the government Odendaal Commission's bantustan development scheme. The aim of the Commissioner in taking them there was to demonstrate how the South African Government had 'developed' the northern region. At this stage we did not realise that Carpio did not actually want to meet us and a SWAPO contingent was sent to Oshakati to trace him. It consisted of Helao Vinnia Ndadi, Immanuel Shifidi, Erastus Kashikuka, Benjamin Petrus, myself and two others. We were stopped by the police several times on the way, but we were determined to press ahead. When we got to Oshakati, he had already left for Okatana, a Roman Catholic Mission two miles away. He had been taken there to be shown the only well-equipped hospital in the area – the government had no hospitals of its own to show them and, to avoid embarrassment, it showed them the missionary one instead.

We caught up with them two hundred yards or so from the missionary premises but we were stopped by the police who wanted to take our photographs. By the time we got into the missionary grounds, Carpio was being pushed into his car by the Commissioner, who was apparently annoyed by the failure of his police to prevent us from getting near his guest. We managed to get a word to Carpio through the car window that we were a SWAPO delegation and wanted to see him. He was not given a chance to reply but was driven off under police escort back towards Ondangwa. Because we could not drive into the missionary grounds, we had left our car where we were stopped by the police, and by the time we got back to it we were ten minutes behind. Then the race to Ondangwa started.

The gravel road from Oshakati to Ondangwa was rough and dusty. All police cars in the north were four-wheel drive and did not find it difficult to negotiate the sandy roads. Our three-ton truck was no match for them. We wanted to catch up with the Carpio motorcade, but every time our driver tried to overtake the police cars, we found our way blocked. They even tried to push us off the road. We found ourselves blanketed in a heavy cloud of dust made by the police cars. Our driver could not see more than a couple of yards in front of him. But we took a side road and before the police knew it, we were through and in front. We put up a huge cloud of dust and the police found themselves engulfed in it. We caught up with Carpio's cars in the Ondangwa vicinity. His entourage was stopped by a huge crowd of people led by Ya Toivo, Tuhadeleni, Kaukungwa, Homateni and many others in the northern SWAPO leadership. It was the biggest rally I had ever seen in the north. We all went on to the Commissioner's offices at a snail's pace.

Carpio held separate talks first with the Commissioner and then with Tribal Chiefs and Headmen. All that time, people were demonstrating and singing freedom songs outside. More and more arrived to join the mammoth crowd. It became evident that Carpio did not want to meet our SWAPO delegation. He only agreed to meet us after demonstrators threatened to picket the buildings and to allow nobody out. When later challenged on this, he denied it and said there might have been a misunderstanding between himself and the Commissioner.

When our SWAPO delegation of about twenty men was eventually allowed to meet him, Ya Toivo was our spokesman. The UN mission consisted of four people. Carpio outlined the task of his mission. He said he thought it was a breakthrough for the UN to be allowed to enter Namibia on a fact-finding mission for the first time. They were there to listen to our problems and see for themselves the conditions prevailing in the country. They would then report back to the UN in New York.

It was obvious from the start to me, though not to all of us present, that nothing was going to come out of Carpio's visit. His questions and answers to our delegation lacked sincerity, enthusiasm and commitment. He wanted to know how many political prisoners were in jail (there were none at the time) as if that was all that mattered. 'Why do you not want the South African Government?' was one of his questions. He also wanted to know what sort of government we desired in Namibia should we succeed in removing the South Africans. Were we 'ready' for our independence, he wanted to know.

He was told in unambiguous terms that, as a people, we wanted to exercise our rights to govern ourselves and run our own affairs. He was also told that South Africa was a foreign power whose rule over us was not of our own making. We, therefore, did not want foreigners to rule over us indefinitely. The fact that there were no political prisoners in Namibian jails at the time was irrelevant. What mattered most to us was the desire for self-determination and freedom in every sphere of life in our society.

He responded by saying that he hoped that the UN would co-operate with the South African Government in bringing about Namibian independence. Was he really serious in suggesting that the South African Government would co-operate with the UN, I wondered to myself. What made me doubt him more was the fact that he did not even want to talk to the people gathered outside to greet him. He only went out to say a few words after we persuaded him to, otherwise he would have left Ondangwa without having seen them. I was convinced that he would present a negative picture of events in Namibia to the UN.

It was later alleged that he got drunk in a hotel somewhere in South Africa and that someone 'stole' his briefcase containing his report on Namibia. Rumours were circulating at the time that he never reached New York to submit his report to the United Nations but ended up in Cairo. In short there was no favourable outcome from his mission to Namibia. In my opinion, much of what subsequently happened, that is South Africa's intransigence, its defiance of the UN's resolutions on Namibia and the delaying of the territory's independence, can partly be blamed on his failure to accomplish what he was sent to do and to deliver his report. South Africa had discovered a weak point in the world body. It grabbed the chance and took advantage of that weakness at the expense of the disadvantaged, exploited and suffering Namibian people.

After the rally at the Commissioner's offices, we moved to Ya Toivo's where people were briefed on the meeting between the UN mission and the SWAPO delegation. We had some difficulty, however, in explaining to them what precisely Carpio meant by UN 'co-operation' with the South African government. Many people left that briefing very disappointed at the outcome, having come with such high hopes.

In spite of everything we felt it was significant that the UN had visited Namibia at all, and we appreciated it. Many people attributed the failure not to the UN as such but to Carpio as the leader of the delegation.

South Africa wasted no time in discrediting the UN. Before the Carpio mission, it used to tell the people that it would never allow the UN to set foot in Namibia. Now that it had, the powerlessness of the UN had been amply demonstrated. The South Africans went on a propaganda campaign against the UN, telling the people: 'You see! The government told you that the UN was nothing. The "Boers" are still ruling you. Where is your UN? Gone back to New York. It did not bring you mielies (maize). You should not have listened to those SWAPO communists and others telling you that the UN could help you. You would do better to co-operate with the South African Government. Who would give you mealie meal if the whites were to leave Namibia?'

But the people were familiar with this kind of propaganda and became almost immune to it. Carpio's visit and subsequent failure did not demoralise us. SWAPO and other parties, such as SWANU and the Herero Chiefs Council, did their level best to counter the South African propaganda campaign after the UN had left the country.

Although SWANU and the Chiefs Council were to some extent regional organisations, the three parties used to share platforms at their meetings, especially in the south.

SWAPO, which had membership all over the country, was continually faced with the problem of restrictions on movement and free expression. Its members in the north or in the south were not free to go to other parts of the country to organise, hold rallies or address meetings there. Thus we were left with no choice but to organise in the areas of our residence or employment. For example SWAPO was unable to operate properly in the so-called Herero Reserves. Likewise no other political groupings operated in the north, in so-called Ovamboland where SWAPO had the monopoly. This could be the reason why many people tend to portray SWAPO as an 'Ovambo' organisation. The truth is that the divide-and-rule system was forcibly in operation; the majority in SWAPO were Ovambo people. This could be attributed to SWAPO having had been born out of OPC and OPO, both of which represented migrant contract labourers from the north.

We nonetheless managed to gain some access to the rest of the country. The migrant contract system, though repressive, indirectly helped the spread of the movement. Contract labourers took up employment throughout the country and, being the victims of repressive laws, were more than ready to spread the political gospel. They were able to reach people from different social backgrounds and make them aware of SWAPO's aims and objectives. In this way, SWAPO succeeded in reaching many households in our divided society. We managed to break down regional, ethnic and tribal barriers and came to be the largest and most effective organisation in the country.

7

Windhoek – new identity

Though the Carpio visit in 1962 did not achieve much of significance in terms of the UN's role in Namibia, a few changes did follow. Ya Toivo, for instance, was able to move about the northern region. He was not officially unbanned but could express himself more freely than before the visit. He was able to meet influential people outside our SWAPO ranks and was in turn able to influence events. A number of blacklisted people, including myself, started taking out contract employment. The authorities appeared to turn a blind eye to certain people. Many others, however, remained blacklisted. There was also a slight relaxation in the authorities' attitude to the enforcement of cattle restrictions. It remained unclear whether these changes were due to the UN visit.

In the second half of 1962, I received a message from Ya Toivo that he wanted to see me. When I got there he told me that he had been approached by Haikukwafa, a male nurse in the recruiting clinic at Ondangwa. Kombat Copper Mine, a subsidiary of the Tsumeb Corporation Limited, wanted someone who could speak English and Afrikaans, he told him. He (Haikukwafa) had gone to Ya Toivo because he thought it would be a good thing for our movement to be represented there. Ya Toivo agreed with him and that was why he called for me: he thought I would be the right candidate. I would be working as an interpreter between the work manager and the workers. I agreed that it was an opportunity not to be missed, but I would have to go back home and wind up my affairs first. Ya Toivo suggested that before I left I should write and put in an application for the vacancy.

I did as advised but instead of posting the application, I delivered it by hand. That was a mistake because they interviewed me there and then, offered me the job and wanted me to start immediately. I reasoned with them that I was not ready yet but would return in a week's time. They agreed to give me five days in which to sort out my affairs and promised that they would keep the vacancy open for me.

However I was disappointed when I returned five days later to find the place was gone. It was taken up by Phillip

Namholo, also a SWAPO member. They offered me a clerical job with CDM (Consolidated Diamond Mines) at Oranjemund in the far south as an alternative. I declined because I had been looking forward to working in Kombat which, although hundreds of miles away from home, would mean that I could visit my family – people working in Oranjemund could not visit their families once they had taken up employment there. I went to tell Ya Toivo what happened before I went back home. We were both disappointed but he thought I should have accepted the CDM offer. I thanked him for his services and bade him goodbye.

I was still desperate to go abroad. I received some information that Tarah Iimbili, also a SWAPO member, was going to take up Bible Studies in Basutuland. I contacted him and he sent me some forms with which to apply. I filled them in and they were back after two weeks – I was accepted as a candidate in Bible Studies. I was pleased and went to tell Tarah about my success and to finalise our preparations. On my arrival I unexpectedly found Tarah's fiancée whom he had invited over for their wedding arrangements. He told me that he was not prepared to go as yet but promised that we would go immediately after their wedding. He would take his wife with him, he said.

That was another spanner thrown in to wreck my plans. Why do things not always work out as we wish them to? I did not want to go alone. I wanted company but not of someone who had just got married! I left his place a devastated man. I went unwillingly back home to make some other plans. Time was running out. I must do something or I would never go abroad, I told myself.

Back home, I found that the financial situation had deteriorated. I decided to take up one more contract, preferably in Windhoek. I planned not to honour the contract but break it when I got there and go and work for Mr Keian, the manager of the Kashmir Bakery in Windhoek, with whom I had made earlier arrangements. So in October 1962, I once more said goodbye to my aunt and headed south. At Ondangwa I had the misfortune not to acquire an 'A' classification – I got a 'B' which was not good enough to land me a 'good' job. Instead I was given a domestic job in Windhoek – I would work for a Mrs Geiger in the suburb of Klein Windhoek. Nevertheless, I was happy to be going to Windhoek.

I contacted Mr Keian immediately I arrived in Windhoek.

He came to meet me at the station but we were both disappointed when he looked at my contract papers. He had agreed to disregard the papers and to take me into his employment, but he could not do so because Mrs Geiger was his sister-in-law. He could do nothing but take me there.

I hated domestic work and I and my employers were soon at each other's throats. I started my day at eight o'clock in the morning, had a one-hour lunch break and worked in the garden until six o'clock in the evening. The housework consisted of sweeping, washing, scrubbing, polishing and shining the floors. In addition to that, I had to wash dishes three times a day. I also looked after their two children aged two and eight. I was earning £1.5s. per month.

The arguments over pay started in January 1963, when I told them that I was doing too much work for too little money. They would not listen, and told me that I was getting what was prescribed in my contract plus free lodging. Mrs Geiger went as far as to suggest that I would probably be better off in the USSR. She understood that my views and those of the Soviets were similar and that I would feel free there! I would prefer freedom in my own country, I told her.

Things came to a head when they went on a holiday for two weeks. They left me no food nor any money to buy myself food and I had nowhere to cook my meals because they locked the house. I therefore used my own money for provisions and presented them with a bill when they came back. They refused to refund me and I thought I would enlist the support of the law. I then went to report the matter to the Native Commissioner in Windhoek, hoping that he would be sympathetic towards me.

I presented my case twice to the Native Commissioner. Instead of taking action against my employers, he called the police to come and arrest me in his office, allegedly for desertion. A misuse of power and miscarriage of justice, one would think – not in Namibia, where a black skin counts heavily against one. I was taken to the Windhoek Central prison where I spent five days before my case came to court. Before I was taken away, I managed to send a word to my cousin Kapulwa. He brought me a change of clothes and some food and I told him that because my arrest was not political, they should not take political action against it. In prison, I was lucky to meet Julius Shilongo who had been brought there a week earlier from South Africa.

Shilongo was one of many of our members who had fled Namibia because of repressive apartheid laws and persecution. He headed for Tanganyika, which had become independent in 1961 and was one of the few countries which offered refuge to our earliest exiles. He met comrade Sam Nujoma and others who had left before him in Francistown, Bechuanaland - they had come down from Dar es Salaam to meet those arriving from home. He had also met Maxton Joseph who later became SWAPO Representative in Bechuanaland. Shilongo and Maxton left Bechuanaland sometime in 1963 to travel to Dar es Salaam. They wanted to pass through the Rhodesias but were arrested in Bulawayo, Southern Rhodesia, because they had not been given leave to enter the country.

After their arrest they were handed over to the South African Police and taken to Pretoria where they were badly treated. I particularly remember Shilongo telling me that water was poured over them while they slept in the cells. Maxton was not sent back to Namibia – he had earlier acquired South African citizenship while working in Cape Town, and was thus detained in South Africa. Shilongo had no papers but told his captors that he was a Namibian. The South Africans could not therefore try him in a South African court and they returned him to Namibia to be tried for allegedly leaving the country without valid travel documents.

This was how he came to be in the Windhoek Central Prison when we met. He told me that he was still determined to find his way abroad. The encounter with him sharpened my own ambition and determination to keep on trying until I succeeded. I had a burning desire to get out of prison and start preparing for the journey ahead. I, however, would not like to follow the same route he and some others had taken when they left the country, through Rundu, Maun and Francistown. It was now well known and closely watched by the authorities and a number of our men had been arrested attempting to use the same channel. I wanted to find a new and safer route out of the country.

My desertion case came up in the Windhoek magistrates' court. The prosecution called in my employer, Mrs Malga Geiger, as its chief witness. The Native Commissioner and the policeman who arrested me were the other witnesses. I represented myself because I could not afford a lawyer.

Mrs Geiger gave evidence that I failed to turn up for work seven days previously and that she had reported the matter to

71

the police. The Native Commissioner in his evidence admitted that he had seen me twice at his office complaining about money owed to me by my employers. He also admitted that he did not call in my employers for arbitration as I asked him to do. At the same time he told the court that he had called in the police to come and pick me up. When asked by the presiding magistrate whether I was arrested in his office, he replied: 'Yes, your Honour'. The policeman in his evidence destroyed that of the Native Commissioner. He said that he arrested me in the street where he found me loitering!

The magistrate found me guilty on evidence presented to the court before he even asked me to plead, and sentenced me to 30 days in prison or £30.00 fine. But I objected, was allowed to plead not guilty and told the court that I had not run away from work but had gone to complain to the Native Commissioner's office after I had done a day's work. As for my employer, she was aware of what I was doing, I told the court. On the two occasions I went to complain to the Native Commissioner, I asked her to accompany me there so that the case could be resolved. I further told the court that I had written her a note of explanation the day I decided to go to the Commissioner's office. As for the policeman's evidence, it could be treated as an untruth because he found me in the office, I concluded in my defence. Then all witnesses were called back to the witness box for cross-examination.

Mrs Geiger acknowledged that I did not run away without her knowledge and that she had seen the note I left her. She had submitted it to the police. The magistrate was not aware of the note and demanded that it should be handed in to the court. I told the court that I would like the Native Commissioner to be called to the witness box. When he came I asked him why he had found it easy to call the police to come and arrest me in his office but difficult to call Mrs Geiger to his office to settle our dispute before him. He could not give a convincing response.

Then the policeman was called. I asked him where he had found me loitering in the street when he arrested me. He could not say where, and when I suggested that he had arrested me inside the Native Commissioner's office, he replied that he could not remember.

I had destroyed all the evidence laid against me. The witnesses contradicted one another, the magistrate said, and dismissed all their evidence. I was jubilant when the magistrate pronounced me not guilty. But in reality, I lost the case because I was never reimbursed. I did not press the case against my employers or take them to court over the money they owed me – I was satisfied with my performance and did not want to push my luck too far.

At the end of 1963 I finished my contract with Mrs Geiger. I decided to stay on in Windhoek and went to live with my cousins Wendy and Sackie in the Old Location. I did not want to go back to my aunt because I had not saved enough money to take home – mainly due to the fact that I had not earned much. I could not bear the prospect of going empty-handed to my relatives who expected me to bring them something. But life in Windhoek did not become any easier. I was faced with a number of problems.

At the end of my contract, I no longer had valid documents to live and work in Windhoek. The expiry of my contract papers left me without any rights. This made it difficult to get a job anywhere: employers could not take me without risking their own business rights. I could not obtain employment papers without a residential permit. I could not receive a residential permit without a work permit. Catch 22. I therefore ended up as a 'shondoro', an alien, without residential rights or job prospects.

In order to survive I started doing some odd jobs here and there and slept rough at my cousins' place. Regular raids carried out in the Location in the middle of the night by the Municipal Police to arrest shondoros made it impossible for me to sleep peacefully. Life was tougher than I had at first imagined.

For six months from November 1963 to April 1964, I worked in a restaurant – cooking, washing dishes and serving at tables. After that, I worked in a soft drink company and ended up as a window-cleaner. I witnessed the appalling living conditions of the Location residents. They had to put up with regular midnight disturbances by the Municipal Police out to arrest people in rent arrears, or making home-made brews, or those found harbouring shondoros. At times doors were broken down by police when those inside were not quick enough in answering.

As a shondoro, my situation was worse than that of residents. Every night I had to lie half-awake listening for any police entering the Location on their raids – I would then rush out of the house to find a place to hide in. But there were no safe hiding places in the Location. One had to be on the alert every minute and ready to make tracks as the police came closer. On more than one occasion I found myself cornered after I had dashed out of the house. To escape capture and under cover of darkness, I climbed up a tree and found safety there. I was close to being caught on two occasions and wondered how much longer I could escape capture. I often had a feeling that one day they would take me in. However, they never succeeded in arresting me.

Then one of my distant cousins, Emily, stepped in. He had lived and worked in Windhoek for several years. To beat the system he suggested that we share his residential documents. He gave me his batch and he went for a new lot of papers. It was so simple but it helped me tremendously – I was now able to lead a near normal life, although I had to adopt a different identity. I was able to close my eyes when I slept and did not jump up and run every time the police entered the Location on their raids.

Meanwhile the political atmosphere in the country had taken a turn for the worse. The authorities became more ruthless, especially against SWAPO activists. Maxwilili, the SWAPO acting President, and Brandon Shimbwaye, the SWAPO Vice-President, as well as Reverend Theophilus Hamutumbangela were in detention for political 'offences'. Others such as Mutumbulwa and Ya-Otto received threats of arrest. SWAPO's rallies were disrupted by police and political opposition parties were threatened with banning. We were working under difficult conditions and the situation was highly charged – it only needed a little provocation to spark it off. On SWAPO's part, there were whispers of a revolution; there was muted talk of military training abroad. The authorities understand only one thing, the whispers went: meet like with like, meet force with force. These were popular whispers, especially among the youth. And for SWAPO to meet the challenge, it needed militarily trained cadres.

One problem was still prevalent, however. Communications with the north had become difficult again and to get or send information was almost impossible. As someone who had northern connections, I was able to meet people coming from or going to the north. It was decided at an executive meeting that I should be charged with the task of liaising between the northerners and the southerners within the movement. It was a task dear to my heart, but because I was planning to leave for abroad I told everybody at the meeting that I could not do it for long. They nevertheless wanted me to stay on as long as I was still in the country. I was thus appointed the secretary of the northern region known as 'Ovamboland'. I then started to build up contacts with many contract labourers in and around Windhoek. I had to operate clandestinely and tried to keep my membership of SWAPO secret. My work proved valuable and I was able to disseminate information satisfactorily in both directions, but after a very short period the time came for me to leave for abroad.

Before I left I had a brief encounter with the postmaster who had tried to turn me in to the police at Oshikango. It happened when I went to collect some of my mail from Miguel Neves at the main post office, Windhoek. I was standing at the end of a long queue when I heard a shout, 'Hello SWAPO!', coming from the counter. It was my 'friend' from Oshikango post office. I said 'hello', and all heads turned towards the rear of the line. Jason Mutumbulwa and John Ya-Otto were also in the line a few people in front of me. Who could be SWAPO? they must have thought to themselves.

'Where is Sam Nujoma, is he still in Cairo? Are you still in touch?' the man continued.

I said he was and we were still in touch.

'How are things inside the country?' he wanted to know.

I found his behaviour irritating and wondered what he was leading up to. I thought maybe he was trying to show off to some of his friends that he knew something about SWAPO.

At the counter, I told him that I had gone there to collect my mail and not to discuss politics. He knew damn well how things were and if he wanted to find out for himself, he would do better to attend SWAPO rallies to hear and see for himself how things were and not shout at me in public places like the post office. That seemed to amuse rather than annoy him for he held up his hand as if to calm me down. He said he knew that he had behaved badly towards me when he was working at Oshikango and now he wanted to make some amends and for us to be friends. I stared at him in disbelief. I asked him to give me my mail before I pulled him through the counter bars.

Outside, Jason Mutumbulwa and John Ya-Otto were waiting for me. They wanted to know who the man was and they were surprised by the whole episode.

'Why did he refer to you as SWAPO?' they asked.

I told them all about my encounters with him.

As time went by and I still received and collected my registered mail from Neves at the counter, I found that the man really had changed his attitude towards SWAPO. He would not even let his colleagues open and read my letters when they demanded to do so. He later told me that he wanted to join SWAPO but was not sure whether he would be accepted. I told him that SWAPO's membership was open to every Namibian and that he would be welcome like anybody else. But how serious he was about that I was not to find out before I left the country.

8

Across the desert to Bechuanaland

In March 1964 I and five friends, Jacqueline, Jason
Mutumbulwa, then the SWAPO secretary for Information and
Publicity and a teacher at the Herero School in Windhoek, the
two Shilunga brothers Nicholas and Bomba, and Adelaide
Ndjavera, also a school teacher at the Herero school, met one
evening to discuss plans to leave for abroad. Although, as
SWAPO members, we were increasingly harassed and
pressurised by the authorities, we were not leaving the country
for these reasons, and we did not regard ourselves as political
fugitives. We were, rather, academic refugees, people thirsty
for education which was denied us in Namibia. We wanted to
take up education from wherever it was available.

Despite political harassment and victimisation of our
members by the authorities, more SWAPO public rallies were
organised throughout the country. Most of them were disrupted
and broken up by the police on the grounds that they were
revolutionary gatherings. Several people were detained as a
result. Now whispers of military training were growing louder
and many people wanted to go abroad. Their aim was to return
to rid Namibia of the South African administration and its evil
system of apartheid and replace it with a non-racial and
democratic government.

Before our group left Windhoek, we organised a number of
music concerts to collect some money for our venture. We had
plotted our route through the Aminius Herero Reserve in the
Gobabis District, east of Windhoek, an area bordering the
Kalahari desert. Our way would then take us via Bechuanaland.
To go to the reserve from Windhoek, we needed some travel
papers. There was no way of obtaining such papers
individually. We therefore organised a bogus football team to
go and play in Gobabis and even arranged a game against a
local team. Our 'team manager' was charged with organising
passes for the team as a whole. Though only six of us were
leaving the country, the team was completed by other 'club'
members and supporters.

We hired a truck and a driver and left Windhoek on the eve
of 14 April 1964. I was very nervous, as were many of my
colleagues. We feared the prospect of something going wrong,

and facing possible jail sentences. We were, however, well coached and were told to behave rowdily – apparently the universal characteristic of footballers – in order to overcome our nervousness and as a cover with which to deceive the police. We were stopped by police at several roadblocks, often manned during weekends, before we entered the Gobabis district, but due to the foresight of our 'manager', we went through them all without any difficulties.

We arrived in the small town of Gobabis in the early hours of the morning of 15 April 1964 and we spent part of the day observing the situation. We could see that the atmosphere was a bit tense and a number of people were suspicious about our presence there: many did not believe that we were a football team. In the afternoon, however, we played against a local football club, as arranged, while waiting for the cover of darkness to drive to the border.

Unknown to us, NUDO (National Unity Democratic Organisation), formed by some Herero traditional leaders disenchanted with the radicalism of the Young Turks within SWANU, had also planned to send people abroad for military training. Although NUDO was opposed to SWAPO, and narrowly based, it too wanted to get rid of the South African occupation. At the time we were trying to leave, a group of about 150 NUDO men were in passage through Bechuanaland. Clemens Kapuuo, one of the NUDO mentors, had just joined forces with Mburumba Kerina who had left SWAPO. Kerina was the chief organiser of NUDO in Bechuanaland at the time and had engineered the exodus.

When darkness fell, we drove towards Aminius, about a hundred miles south-east of Gobabis. We expected to find a number of roadblocks to the reserve but fortunately there were none. Our driver dropped us at a homestead in the morning and he drove off back to Windhoek. Unbeknown to us the owner of the house was a strong supporter of NUDO and when we enquired about the prospects of crossing the border into Bechuanaland, he said he would go to consult someone who could help us.

The someone he went to consult was high up in the NUDO hierarchy. Because they were in the process of channelling their 154 men through and did not want to jeopardise their plan, they would not let us through and instead fed us with a lot of wild stories. They first told us that the border was sealed off by South African troops who would not let anybody through. Later they said that the border was cordoned off as a result of foot-and-mouth disease. Though we did not believe them, there was little we could do as they refused to provide us with a guide to the border. Thus we found ourselves stranded and utterly sickened by our circumstances. What was most annoying was the fact that our driver had only just left when we learned all these things but there was no way of calling him back.

Maybe we had expected too much in believing that our plan was infallible - we certainly had not expected this. We had no other car to take us back to Windhoek. There were no telephones anywhere nearby to contact our driver in Gobabis before he drove off to Windhoek. Our unpreparedness was now evident and frustrating. We had no choice but to look for a vehicle to take us to Gobabis. After a long and exhausting search throughout the Reserve, we came upon a dilapidated old Chevrolet truck with flat tyres and no lights. We struggled to get it on the road, paid the owner for the hire and hired a driver.

We set out in diminishing twilight. Knowing that he had no lights, and racing against the few remaining minutes of daylight, the driver went through the gears like someone possessed and stepped flat on the gas pedal. The engine, despite the unpromising appearance of the truck, responded surprisingly well. Winding and twisting his way along the bumpy, narrow, dusty road, the driver kept the truck firmly on the ground, but we in the back could hardly manage to keep hold of the open sides and stay on board. Rolling this way and that and covered in a red blanket of Kalahari dust we arrived safely in Gobabis, happy to be alive. We were disappointed at our failure to go through. To my friends this was their first failure to find their way abroad; it was my fourth failed attempt.

* * *

We caught a train back to Windhoek. Our absence had been noticed by everybody in the Location and I found it difficult to convince my cousins that we had only gone to play football in Gobabis. My story was unconvincing and full of holes.

'Why didn't you tell me?' Wendy demanded, 'You must have had something to hide.'

In the end I admitted that I was planning to flee the country.

79

I don't know whether Wendy told the police about me, but they took a renewed interest in me. As well as her policeman boyfriend, Gabriel David, three other policemen from the Windhoek Special Branch became regular visitors at our place. To avoid detection, they did not come in a group but singly, at intervals. Although they tried to keep a low profile I knew that they were watching me.

Wendy used to make and sell home-made brew and the policemen came to buy drinks – a good cover for keeping an eye on me. She had now gone on holiday and left me to take care of her three children and the house. I continued to make and sell the home-made brew. One evening I had a surprise visit from one of the policemen who came in to buy some beer. My cousin Sackie was present as well as a number of other people. Because the policeman did not know me, or who was who, he gave himself away by going to Sackie and asking to discuss something with him in private – preferably in his bedroom. Knowing that he was a policeman, Sackie told him to wait for a while and came to tell me. When we returned together the policeman had posted himself by the bedroom door. Sackie told him that I was the owner of the house if he had something to discuss.

The man put his hand on the bedroom door, ready to enter. I stopped him and told him that if he had anything at all to discuss, it would be safe with my friends. Not in public, he insisted, but in the end he explained that he worked in the Civic Centre, where identity cards and passports were issued. It was therefore not difficult for him to obtain passports for people wanting to leave the country. He himself was planning to leave and was now looking for someone to go abroad with him. Would I go with him? he asked. I had expected this trap to be laid long ago. Now here it was. I told him that such an idea had never crossed my mind, but he persisted until I said I would think about it and arranged to meet him again.

When he came back on the appointed day, I told him that I had given his proposition careful consideration and had felt very honoured that he had thought of me as a likely candidate but most unfortunately I could not meet his request. He asked if I could refer him to someone else. I said I could not. He left after that and I did not see him again.

By now people were leaving the country en masse and the police intensified their surveillance along the routes to the borders. And in Windhoek, there was no let-up by the police on SWAPO activists. They placed almost all our prominent members under observation. Reinforcements were brought in from other places – that could have been the reason why they brought in Naata Angula from Walvis Bay and Hamapindi from Tsumeb, both of whom were notorious. What they did not realise was that I knew them both – Naata while I was working in Walvis Bay, and Hamapindi was pointed out to me in Tsumeb by our activists there. Naata was the first to call and I surprised him by inquiring how things were in Walvis Bay. That took the wind out of his sails and he never came back. I did the same with Hamapindi when he came but he told me that he had quit the police force and was now looking for a new job. I said I was sorry for him, but I could not offer him one. He too never returned, but I used to see both in town and at our political rallies.

By May 1964 our new plans to leave were far advanced. When our first attempt to go through Bechuanaland failed, Jason, Adelaide and Jacqueline became disenchanted with the idea and subsequently withdrew from the plan. The Shilunga brothers and myself were, however, determined to see it through. We saved a little more money and made a resolution that our plan would not fail this time and if it did, we would never try again to leave the country. We were later joined by Joseph Katjindee, a SWANU member. Now that Jason, who had been the leader of our group, was no longer going, I took over planning responsibilities.

We hired a car to take us to the border on 14 May 1964, the day of a big concert and barbecue organised by SWAPO's Windhoek branch to collect money for bailing Maxwilili out of jail. We put in an appearance at the concert to fool the police and then set off for the border.

Instead of going east through Gobabis, we went south via Rehoboth and then south-east to the Aminius area – a route never travelled before by anyone leaving the country. We arrived safely in Aminius early in the morning. People there were more sympathetic and friendly than those we had met on our first attempt. We inquired about soldiers at the border but were told that there had never been any soldiers – it was a hoax. We were informed that the border was a twenty-mile walk away, so we rested the whole morning and hired a guide.

We set out for the border in the early afternoon and got there at dusk. As a precautionary measure, we surveyed the border area and waited until it was dark and safe enough to cross.

Having been born and bred in the Kalahari Desert, our guide was an experienced man. Before we crossed into Bechuanaland, he lined us up in a single file, then led the way and told us to step in his footsteps. We made the momentous crossing in the pitch dark – though the border consisted only of two wire fences 10 yards apart, it seemed to have taken us years to cross.

We could not relax our vigilance – we did not know what dangers were lurking in the dark and we wanted to get away from the border area as fast as possible. Our progress was, however, made difficult by the darkness and by the fact that there was no road or footpath to follow: our guide led by geographical direction and experience. We waded our way through the tall elephant-grass and thorn bushes of the Kalahari Desert. It was so dark that we could hardly see our own noses, but with an experienced guide, and the fear of being caught, we covered the distance quickly. Our guide called for a halt after three hours' non-stop march and told us that we were safely across the border and could make a fire and have something to eat. It was only then that we were able to breathe a sigh of relief and felt that we had succeeded at last. We celebrated our success with sausages, bread and beer which we had carried and then had an hour's rest. Our festive mood was soon to be dampened by the thought of the uncertainties ahead and we asked ourselves a simple question: where to from here?

The Kalahari, like any other desert, is treacherous: we were ill-prepared for our trip and it nearly cost us our lives. We carried no water and had eaten most of our food in celebrating our success and by midday we had nothing left to eat or drink. The Kalahari sun beat down upon us mercilessly; we gasped for air and prayed for rain to give us water; we chased after desert mirages thinking they were water. It seemed we had succeeded in leaving the country and evading the South African Police, only to die a slow death in the desert.

But death was still a long way off. We staggered, fell, picked ourselves up again and carried on once more. We shed some of our belongings and gave others to the guide but we never gave up hope nor the struggle to survive. Our lives were saved only by our guide who dug up some water supplies he had stashed away in the desert during the rainy season for his future use. By nightfall, we managed to make it to the nearest village which was roughly 100 miles from the border.

Exhausted, thirsty and hungry, we tumbled into the first homestead we found. Bechuanaland was in the grip of a severe famine and the people in the house had nothing to offer us except water. The log fire they lit for us helped to keep the cold out through the night and in the morning we were able to proceed on our way.

We found a village with a shop and bought some provisions. We also bought a goat, slaughtered it and prepared ourselves a huge meal. Afterwards we made enquiries about transport to Francistown on the other side of Bechuanaland, where we had our SWAPO representative. However, the local people would not let us proceed, but took us to their King, or Chief, to seek his permission. The King, for his part, would not let us go without the permission of the District Commissioner (DC) who lived in Ghanzi, over 150 miles away. So we waited for messages to be sent and permission to be given before we could proceed further.

The King took us in and gave his daughter, Babe, the responsibility of looking after us. Babe had worked in Windhoek and spoke Afrikaans well, which helped to overcome the language problem – she acted as interpreter between ourselves and the King. In our discussions we told him that we were only passing through and had no intention of remaining in the area. He listened to us attentively and he told us that, even though he understood our situation, he would not let us through until certain transit formalities were cleared by the DC. We waited for three days and on the fourth day, 20 May 1964, the DC arrived.

The DC was accompanied by police from Mamono, a border post between Namibia and Bechuanaland. He wanted to know who we were and where we were going. We told him that we were SWAPO members, and only wanted to go through to Francistown where SWAPO had its representative. He and the police appeared sympathetic towards us as SWAPO members but they wanted documentary proof, which we had not carried for fear of being arrested by the South African Police. Our reasoning and supplications fell on deaf ears. They were only prepared to let us through if we could show them permits to go through to Northern Rhodesia. The DC then instructed his police to take us to Mamono while they investigated whether we were part of the group of 154 NUDO members which by then had been detained in Ghanzi. The DC alleged that they had been detained because they were going to undergo military training and planned to overthrow the South African administration in Namibia by violence.

We told him that we were not part of the group of 154, nor did we intend to undergo military training, our intentions were to study mechanical engineering and driving. He said that he would see to it that our case received favourable consideration. He and the police spent the night in the village and in the morning they bundled us into the police van and drove us to Mamono.

At Mamono police station they took our personal particulars and tried to lock us up. We refused to go into the cells and asked them to allow us to sleep in the yard behind the police offices. They agreed, as we were not criminals, and after a few days' waiting we managed to slip out and catch a transport truck to Dacar, a village near Ghanzi and over 100 miles from Mamono. From there we tried to catch a lift to Otjihitwa, a village near Maun, over 150 miles north-east of Ghanzi, where we knew a SWANU member, Daniel Munamava.

Unfortunately we could not get a lift in Dacar and after about six hours' waiting the police arrived and demanded our papers. When we could not provide them with any, they asked us who we were and where we were going. We told them that we were SWAPO members and were on our way to Francistown where we had our representative. We were so naive and ignorant of immigration regulations - we thought that SWAPO was recognised everywhere and that, as SWAPO members, we had a right to pass through any country without hindrance.

The police asked us to accompany them back to Ghanzi so that arrangements could be made to enable us to proceed to Francistown. We argued that we had no intention of staying on in Botswana and since we were only passing through, there was no reason for us to go back with them to Ghanzi. We told them our SWAPO motto: 'Forward Ever! Backward Never!' They realised our naivety and only laughed and ordered us into their Land Rover. Frustrated and angry we had no option but to go with them back to Ghanzi.

In Ghanzi the police warned us not to try to escape or they would be forced to lock us up with the 154 other Namibians in the local prison. They detained us in a policeman's house for the night. The following day we were given our orders: we were to be taken back to the border at Mamono to wait for further arrangements to be made for us to pass through

Botswana. Presently a police van drew up and we were ordered in and driven back to Mamono. We were really furious that the Botswana authorities were treating us in the same way as we were treated by the Boers.

The corporal in charge of the Mamono police station gave an order that we should be locked up since we might try to escape again. We refused, and challenged them to return us to Namibia instead. When he realised that we were not ready to compromise the corporal proposed that we should sleep inside one of the cells which would not be locked. We would be allowed to come and go as we pleased. With suspicion, we agreed to his proposal.

Two days later we smuggled Joseph Katjindee, one of our party, onto a lorry bound for Ghanzi. He was on his way to Otjihitwa, where he was to arrange our escape with Daniel Munamava, who had a car. Katjindee never returned. He later wrote us a letter from Francistown telling us that Munamava had advised him against returning and said that he himself would have been arrested if he had ventured near Mamono. He told us to make our own escape or we would rot there. It was now June and terribly cold. We had no blankets or anything to keep us warm. We depended on a log fire outside the prison where we used to cook our meals.

One evening, we were shocked by the arrival of South African Police (SAP) and felt so insecure and that we thought it might be safer if the prison door were locked after all! On the other hand, how were we to know that the SAP would not gain access to the prison keys? They might even have sympathisers within the Botswana Police. We would stay alert!

We kept bombarding the DC with letters of complaint and demanded to be allowed to proceed to Francistown. One day the DC, tired of our complaints, sent us a telegram saying that he would let us through if we could show him permits to pass through Zambia. All telecommunications in Bechuanaland were controlled by the police, but the police at Mamono were semi-literate, with the exception of the radio operator. When they received and handed us our telegram they misunderstood it to mean that we were allowed to proceed to Francistown. We tried to tell them that was not the case. 'Do you want to go or not?' they asked us. Since we were planning to escape anyway, we took the opportunity.

The transport lorries from Dacar had passed there that morning for Gobabis and were due to return in the afternoon.

The police did the talking for us and got us onto the trucks. When we reached Ghanzi, we asked the driver to drop us there because we planned to see the DC in the morning and make our presence there legal. Because we did not know anybody, we went to the policeman's house where we had been detained previously. We told him that we had been given permission to travel through the country.

In the morning, we went to report to the DC. He was surprised and angry to see us in Ghanzi.

'What the hell are you doing here?' he demanded.

We showed him the telegram he sent us and explained that his police told us that it was alright for us to proceed to Francistown. He gave an order for us to be detained at the policeman's house and later be sent back to Mamono. But we escaped the following night and spent about ten days walking to Maun, north-east of Ghanzi.

To avoid recapture, we made it a rule to run for cover every time we heard or saw a car coming. One dark night, however, we had a close shave with the South African Police. They roamed as freely in Bechuanaland as they did in Namibia or South Africa itself. We were coming round a bend and, fortunately, they had their headlamps on and we saw them before they could see us. We scrambled for cover and, well hidden from their view, we could read their SAP number plates.

In Maun we made contact with Daniel Munamava, the SWANU member, who warned us that we should stay in hiding to avoid capture. We hid in the wilderness 10 miles north of Maun, near the Okavango Delta where the Okavango River disappeared into swamps. We spent three days there waiting for the transport from Francistown to pick us up. Daniel visited us every day and brought us some food. On the third day the transport trucks came. One of the trucks stopped and out jumped Daniel. We dashed out of our hiding place and got onto the truck for Francistown.

Maxton Joseph, our representative in Francistown, met us at the transport terminal which was only a few yards from the SWAPO office. He took us into the office and suggested that we assume false names to hide our true identities from the police. He then drove us to the White House, a building conspicuously placed in the centre of the township. There we found many others who had fled from South Africa, Lesotho and Namibia. From South Africa there were members of the

African National Congress (ANC) and Pan African 1st Congress (PAC), and from Lesotho members of the Basutoland Congress Party (BCP). SWAPO and SWANU members from Namibia made up the rest of the White House community. We were a sociable community whose members shared a common goal; freedom and independence for our respective countries. We all wanted to be free from foreign domination and persecution and yearned to be independent and to run our own affairs.

Maxton took us new-comers to the police station to register the following morning. My assumed name was Patrice Jackson. In the course of our stay at the White House, we were visited several times by the Francistown police. They wanted to establish whether the people who had 'escaped' from Ghanzi had made their way to Francistown. None of them could identify any of us as the escapees – we were safe as a result of our assumed names. We stayed at the White House from June to July 1964, waiting for our permits to pass through Northern Rhodesia – which was shortly to become independent Zambia. We were visited by Seretse Khama, leader of the Bechuanaland Democratic Party and the future President of Botswana, and Matanta, his opposite number of the Bechuanaland People's Party – they were both staunch supporters of the Southern African liberation movements. British Labour Party MPs also paid us a visit. They were interested in our health as well as in the form of government we wanted for independent Namibia.

Whereas some of these visits were welcome, we had some unwelcome visitors – South African agents. Some of them posed as journalists who claimed to have received permission from the police to interview us. Some were later arrested after we pointed them out to the police. Others posed as refugees and wanted to travel with us to countries offering us safe refuge. Some succeeded in blowing up two planes which were about to take refugees to Dar es Salaam, Tanzania. One was blown up at Francistown aerodrome and the other at Kasane, 300 miles or so north-west of Francistown, before they were boarded.

The refugee authorities were building a new house for the Southern African refugees in Francistown, very near the existing White House. The new building was located directly on the main road to Johannesburg from Bulawayo, Southern Rhodesia, which passed through Francistown. The completion of the new house was scheduled for August 1964. At the end of July we received a visit from the Botswana Police. They were interested to know when we were moving to the new house. It was a Friday afternoon and Maxton told them that we were moving in that same evening, but we did not make the move.

That night I was woken by a huge explosion. The floor beneath me shook violently and I was sure the roof would collapse. It was dark and I could not see my hand. There were about 10 – 15 men in the room, but I felt alone and thought everybody had gone. I struggled to my feet and tried to run, but I stumbled over others who were also in the process of getting up to find out what was happening. We all managed to find our way to the door and rushed out of the house. 'What was that?' everybody wanted to know when we met outside. The bang was so loud and sudden but now everything was quiet again. I thought maybe it was an earthquake but others spoke of a bomb. I had never heard one before and had no idea what they were talking about.

The police arrived an hour after the explosion and told us that the new refugee house had been destroyed by a bomb. They had come to check if everything was well with us. 'Who did it?' we asked them. They did not know yet. They were investigating.

In the morning, we went to have a look at the house. Debris was strewn over hundreds of yards. Half of the house was completely destroyed but the other half was intact. It certainly made me wonder at the wisdom of the authorities in locating a refugee house 15 yards from the main road leading to Johannesburg and Bulawayo, from where dangers to refugees would come.

9

'We are travellers'

Our stay in Francistown was almost unbearable. Though we were supposed to be out of the South African regime's reach, we experienced an atmosphere of lurking danger – made more real by the bomb blast. The Bechuanaland authorities seemed powerless to deal with the South African agents, if some elements within were not already collaborating with them in carrying out their terroristic activities. We were determined to head as soon as possible for the only independent Southern African country – Tanganyika, which had been independent since 1961 and had just become the United Republic of Tanzania. To get there, we had to travel through Northern Rhodesia.

Fortunately for some of us, permits to pass through Northern Rhodesia came towards the end of August 1964. But that did not mean the end of our problems. Our young movements were unable to raise enough funds to transport everyone and there were no institutions willing to help us financially. Eventually, enough money was raised to hire a five-ton truck to Livingstone, in Northern Rhodesia. SWAPO members footed the bill, but because of strong co-operation amongst the Southern African liberation movements, non-SWAPO members were also eligible to travel by the same truck. Even so, only 50 out of the group of 200 were able to travel.

I was given the responsibility of leading our group, but Maxton decided to accompany us to Livingstone, just in case. We left Francistown at midday and arrived at Kasane the following afternoon – just in time to register with the police. We spent the night at Kasangula, a border post on the Zambezi River at the point where the borders of what were then Bechuanaland, Northern Rhodesia, Southern Rhodesia and South-West Africa meet. We could see Southern Rhodesian police patrols on the other side of the border and were terrified that they might come down at night and kidnap us.

I was busy supervising my colleagues through the Bechuana immigration and Maxton went to check on the pontoon taking us across the Zambezi River into Northern Rhodesia. Suddenly, there was a brief commotion amongst my colleagues outside the immigration office - some of whom were heading for the river crossing. A man dashed through the wire fence separating Bechuanaland and Southern Rhodesia. He mixed with our men and ran to the river, saying that he was an activist of the ZAPU liberation movement in Southern Rhodesia. He introduced himself to Maxton. Maxton was a man of action – he paid the ferry driver to take the man across.

The Southern Rhodesian police burst into the immigration office, claiming that they were pursuing a criminal who might be hiding amongst the group gathered outside. Could they be allowed to look around for him? The immigration officer asked to see their permits to enter Bechuanaland. They had none. They were liable to arrest for entering the territory illegally, he said, and ordered their immediate departure. By that time the pontoon carrying the pursued man was in the middle of the river and approaching the Northern Rhodesian side.

We experienced no difficulties crossing the river but our problems began at the immigration offices in Livingstone, some 40 miles from the border crossing. There, we were told that some of our permits had not arrived and we had therefore entered the country illegally. Maxton himself was a wanted man in Northern Rhodesia for 'misconduct'. He fled to avoid arrest – before he had seen us all through immigration. About 25 SWAPO, 16 ANC and 8 PAC members were bundled into a police truck and, under a heavily armed police escort, we were driven to jail.

From our cells we wrote a petition to the authorities denouncing unfair 'imprisonment'. The next morning, the ANC members' permits came and they were allowed to go through, but the rest of us were bundled into a tomb-like truck to be taken back to Bechuanaland. It had no windows or ventilation and was only open at the back. Escorting us were four police Land Rovers with police armed to the teeth.

At the border, they loaded us onto the ferry but its engines failed to work when they were switched on. We disembarked and were loaded back into our tomb-truck and taken to a prison in Livingstone. The next day we were taken back across the Zambezi into Bechuanaland. I was now faced with a new problem. When we had gone through the Bechuanaland immigration two days earlier, Maxton's driver, Nghatanga Mukamba, had not registered with them. When Maxton left he had not taken Nghatanga back with him.

I was now faced with the problem of getting him through

immigration. I let everybody go through so that Nghatanga and I were last. The immigration officer could not find Nghatanga's name in the registration record book and threatened him with deportation. I argued Nghatanga's case by telling the official not to try and shift blame onto us for his own failure to record Nghatanga's name when he had passed through. We got away with it and he let him through.

We spent about two weeks sleeping in the open and waiting for our permits through Northern Rhodesia to come. At the same time, we kept up our communications with both Dar es Salaam and Francistown through telegrams.

Our finances ran low. We urged Dar es Salaam to advance us some money but nothing came and we were again faced with transport problems when our permits eventually arrived. It was a morning in September 1964 when the last man in our group went through the Bechuanaland immigration procedures. We boarded the ferry singing freedom songs, one of which was:

Fie ovaendanandyila
Dyeni po tu pite po
Tu henehalo oku shuna
Ha tu fiki ko, Okefikilo.

We are travellers
Give way for us to pass
With no desire to go back
We will reach our destination.

Because we could not afford to hire a vehicle to Livingstone, we walked all the way from the border to the main road. I travelled at the rear to see that everybody was accounted for. A few of us managed to get lifts from passing motorists and a refugee official, a Mr McKay, passed us by chance and took our luggage. But I and some others walked the 40 miles to Livingstone.

Some of my colleagues who arrived ahead of me organised some transport to meet us but by that time we had already reached the edge of the town. They told me that Mr Cunningham, the director of the refugee programme in Zambia wanted to see me. He gave me directions and instructions as to how to get a train to Lusaka but he could not help with our transport. It was SWAPO's duty to transport us. In a way he was right, but I found it odd for an organisation charged with taking care of refugees not to be able to transport them.

We found our way to the train station where we spent the night. In the morning, while I was busy buying all our tickets, a truck load of the UNIP (United National Independence Party) Youth Brigade pulled into the station. They encircled my group and tried forcibly to sell them UNIP membership cards. My colleagues told them that they were members of SWAPO of Namibia, and therefore could not buy UNIP cards. The Youth, who had not heard of SWAPO, threatened and harassed them, saying that they would not allow them to get on the train unless they bought the cards. Their political fanaticism made us all angry. We found it odd that people who were about to achieve their independence were behaving like lunatics towards foreigners.

I took the leader of the youth aside and told him to order his gang to leave my friends alone. I showed him our tickets, adding that we needed to get on the train and nothing would stop us. He called his gang away and they headed for the train where they continued to coerce people into buying their cards.

We arrived in Lusaka safely at about 11 pm. McKay and Cunningham came to meet us at the station and in a column of taxis we streamed out of the station, stopping at a big farmhouse roughly 20 miles outside Lusaka, now turned into a refugee centre. Here for the first time we met refugees from the Sudan, Mozambique and Angola. After dinner, we were shown our rooms and told to fit in with the rest of the community.

McKay took me and two of my colleagues to the refugee office in the morning to make phone calls to Dar es Salaam and Francistown. I told Peter Nanyemba, our representative in Dar es Salaam, how many we were and that we needed travel funds.

Nanyemba sent enough money for our group but the day I went to collect it, McKay told me that a Mr Ndadi, who claimed to be a SWAPO member, had arrived direct from Namibia and was coming to the office. Did I know him? Oh, yes I knew him, but as I was travelling under the assumed name of Patrice Jackson, he had not known who I was when asked. However, he recognised me as soon as he saw me at the office. I took him to the immigration office in Lusaka where he faced tough questioning by the chief immigration officer.

After he had satisfied the official, he was given a week's transit visa.

When we got to the office, we found Mishake Muyongo and Muronda had arrived from the Caprivi. They were both members of CANU (Caprivi African National Union) which was negotiating to join SWAPO at that time. Sam Nujoma and other SWAPO officials were in the Caprivi for discussions with CANU officials. Muyongo and Muronda needed transit visas and travel funds to Dar es Salaam. I could not help them because I had already accepted Ndadi against the wishes of many in the group, I told them. To take them on would eat deeper into our already diminished funds, which could have resulted in all of us being left stranded. I advised them to ring Nanyemba and ask him to advance them some money.

Ndadi and I met others and together we went to buy our bus tickets for Mbeya, Tanzania. Unfortunately we caught a wrong bus which was bound for Ndola. It dropped us in Brokenhill where we were left stranded for some time. The bus to Mbeya took about two days to arrive and 36 hours to reach there. By then we had made inroads into our finances. We had no money for provisions while we waited in Mbeya and were unable to get any more from the SWAPO office in Dar es Salaam. I was thus forced to seek aid from the Mbeya police. They were sympathetic and took us to a general dealer where we borrowed provisions.

On the day we were about to catch buses to Dar es Salaam, Ndadi took ill and we took him to the hospital in Mbeya. He was found to be suffering from malaria and ordered to stay in hospital for at least three days. We left him there and caught our buses to Dar es Salaam the following day.

Rahemisa Kahemise, a member of staff at our office, came to meet us at the bus station and took us to the office in a combi (minibus). There we were not only welcomed by Nanyemba, but also by a number of top SWAPO officials, among whom were Sam Nujoma, our President, Jacob Kuhangwa, the then Secretary-General, Louis Nelengani, the then SWAPO Vice-President and Paul Smith, our representative in Algeria. And for the first time we met some of the trained SWAPO guerrillas under the command of Tobias Hainjeko. Later on Comrade Nanyemba welcomed us and told us that he would take us to Onheleiwa, which would be our temporary home, for at least a week's rest, before we discussed the scholarship question.

We had heard much talk about Dar es Salaam while still in

Namibia. It became every Namibian's dream to one day see Dar es Salaam but we had thought that we would never get there. Dar es Salaam is one of the most densely populated cities in the world and one of the most beautiful. It was made up of various sections: the old city (some houses hundreds of years old) with its mainly Indian and Arab speaking communities; the ever-present slums; and the harbour area with its modern offices, hotels, banks, railways and warehouses. The harbour area was the centre of trade and its population was mainly affluent foreigners; many vestiges of the colonial era were in evidence here. New suburbs were coming up around the city which were mainly settled by the up-and-coming affluent black population, who were newly employed in the civil services or had found their way into private as well as public sector occupations for the first time. The Presidential Palace stood majestically at the entrance to the harbour, like a sentinel on guard, overlooking the beach.

10

Armed struggle

The December 1959 Windhoek massacre and the subsequent failure of the United Nations to take action against South Africa created resentment, frustration and anger amongst the black population. The massacre came on top of many other atrocities and crimes committed against black Namibians by white settlers.

With the founding of SWAPO and other black Namibian political groupings, the resentment and anger towards the oppressive system of divide-and-rule grew. Battle lines began to be formed. The lines were drawn according to the division and classification of the community and the devices used by the system. Against many people's wishes and principles the struggle was inevitably based on the conflict between black Namibian inhabitants and white settlers and colonialist oppressors.

Despite the anger and resentment expressed by Namibians against what they saw as an oppressive foreign elite, all black political organisations showed a degree of restraint and pursued non-violent political struggle. But the oppressive system intensified its repressive machinery: people were detained, some were deported to Angola and others fled the country. Black Namibians were still denied basic human rights; they were denied the right to live where they pleased, and the rights to free expression, freedom of association and freedom of movement; they could not earn a decent wage or lead a decent settled life.

After the bungled Victor Carpio UN mission in 1962, SWAPO was forced to reappraise its strategy and line of action. Its passive resistance to the system had been met with an iron fist. Questions began to be asked: could SWAPO afford to continue its non-violence? Was it worthwhile for SWAPO to continue banging its head against a concrete wall of repression? Was it wise to continue talking to a system deaf to reason and which answered with bullets? What answers did SWAPO have to these crucial questions? There was widespread but muted talk amongst many about a revolution. Could SWAPO afford to embark upon such a difficult road without risking lives? A crucial and difficult moment had been reached.

Actions to match the oppression were needed. Alternative strategies to passive resistance had to be found. Difficult decisions had to be made, and quickly.

It was thus at the eleventh hour and at a time of desperation that SWAPO, with difficulty, decided upon an armed struggle. The Namibian population was less than a million people at the time, as compared to the much larger white South African population with its economic and military power. But the Namibian people had something important: determination and the will to be free and to reclaim what belonged to them – human dignity and the right to exist as a people. Before it embarked upon the revolutionary path, SWAPO read and understood the feelings and desires of the people.

It was against this background that SWAPO decided to mobilise the Namibian youth in preparation for a day of confrontation. Though the decision to embark upon an armed struggle was made in the early 1960s and SWAPO had trained guerrillas as early as 1962, it did not immediately execute the option but continued to pursue the path of peaceful political struggle, hoping against hope that the system would eventually come to its senses. There was another reason for holding back. In 1960, Ethiopia and Liberia – the only two African member states of the United Nations – had taken the Namibian case to the International Court of Justice (ICJ) at The Hague. It was hoped that South Africa's occupation would be declared illegal and that the international community would bring about Namibia's independence. Despite the increase in acts of violence against Namibians by the South African administration, SWAPO did not therefore see the military option as an end in itself, but a means of contributing to the solution of the Namibian problem. It was to be held in reserve and to be used only if and when the need arose.

This, then, was the situation in 1964, when I arrived in Dar es Salaam. After a week of rest, we were briefed on the prospects of obtaining scholarships. We could choose between academic or military training. However, our choice depended on our qualifications and our ability to speak English. Many countries who offered SWAPO both academic and military training scholarships wanted people under twenty years old who had a minimum Standard VI academic training. No one in my group was under twenty and not many had received any formal education. Given our Namibian academic background, we were a disadvantaged lot. I was the only one in my group with Standard V education. The rest were between Standards III and IV or had no formal education at all. It was therefore difficult for most of us to meet the requirements, particularly for academic training, although some countries offered military training to unqualified people.

The office gave us time to think things over and to inform them of our preferences. The applications were then studied and people were allocated to courses according to preference, suitability and availability. Academic prospects were open to me but not to many of my colleagues, to whom I had became very attached during our sojourns in Bechuanaland, Zambia and then Tanzania. I still had a yearning to follow academic education but as a young man of 30 and after five years in politics, the excitement of military training was too tempting for me to resist.

Military action appeared to be the only way of removing the South African apartheid administration from Namibia. After strong consideration, I found that I could not reconcile myself to facing the same discriminatory system after completion of my studies. The experience of Kerina, Dr Abrahams and others, strengthened my decision to opt for military training. Kerina, after he had finished his studies in the US, applied for a job in the medical services in Namibia, but because he was black he could not be recruited. The same thing happened to Dr Abrahams. One either has to work under the apartheid system and face all the humiliation it metes out to anybody with a black skin or one has to fight it and face its wrath and retribution. I chose the latter.

A week after I and others had handed in our applications for military training, we were told that we had been offered military scholarships in Ghana, West Africa. I was then placed in charge of a group of 12 others. Because SWAPO did not have passports of its own at the time, we were issued with Tanzanian travel documents to enable us to travel through the length and breadth of Africa. We boarded an East African Airways plane bound for Nairobi, Kenya.

We spent the night at the Ambassador Hotel in Nairobi. With the mentality of everyone brought up under colonialism where blacks were taught to respect everything white, two of my colleagues in one suite did not sleep in their beds. They thought that the beds were for some whites who might be arriving later in the night. In the morning, the hotel staff could not wake them when they took coffee to them. Nobody could

97

get the key in the keyhole because they had their key there and they would not answer the telephone.

I managed to raise them and when I asked them why they had barricaded themselves in, they told me that they had heard people knocking at the door and they thought they were criminals trying to break in. They did not answer the phone because they did not expect anyone to ring them! We quickly ate our breakfast and left to catch an Ethiopian airliner to Addis Ababa. From there we caught a plane bound for West Africa via Khartoum. It was in the middle of October 1964 and as there was civil war in the Sudan we did not disembark when our plane landed at Khartoum airport. It was terribly hot and the temperature in the fuselage soared beyond 60 degrees centigrade as the ventilators were not working. We were relieved when at last the plane took off.

We flew much of the breadth of Africa westward, passing over the Nile and chasing the sun. We overflew several West African countries and refuelled in Lagos, Nigeria. After many hours of flight, we finally landed at Accra airport where we were met by African Centre personnel. They saw us through the immigration as quickly as they could and took us to the city centre where we were given a warm welcome by a number of African students. Jacob Kuhangwa, who was visiting Ghana at the time, came to see us in the morning. He wished us good luck and success in our training. After our passports were processed, we were picked up by officials who drove us about 500 miles northwards to the Province of Ashanti.

Under Ghanian instructors, we followed customary military training procedures. We also had political training. At the end of every course intensive competitions for speed, expertise in handling and maintenance of arms, discipline and observance of army rules were undertaken. These helped to determine candidates' suitability for specific jobs within the army. After training, we all returned to base where we would meet and exchange training experiences with others who had done their training in other countries.

Before I took up my training in Ghana I did not realise that English could be spoken in other accents. In West Africa they speak a special English so, at first, we could not communicate properly. But in the end, we mastered it. When they want to ask where you are going they say: 'Where you de go? Me de go wagga wagga.' ('I am going for a walk.') (My own spelling – but that is how it sounded.)

Our training took six months and then it was back to Tanzania. Before we left there had been fewer than a hundred trained guerrillas, but by the time we came back, our numbers had increased almost threefold. There were even more waiting to be trained.

We immediately went to work and started two programmes of training and retraining. A system of passing on knowledge was found to be important since we were trained in different countries and in different weaponry. Our system helped to acquaint cadres with all kinds of arms and all sorts of military activities. It also helped to weld together an otherwise unco-ordinated Liberation Army.

We knew that our enemies would try to get at us. Security measures were taken to ensure that they would not find it easy to penetrate our defences. The location of our base near Dodoma in central Tanzania was one of strategic importance and it proved to be impenetrable although some enemy agents, using unsuspecting locals, managed to come as close as the gates of our encampment. Many were apprehended and handed over to the authorities before they could cause any damage.

After two months in Tanzania, I was made the third secretary of our armed forces. It was during this period that some rifts between commanders and the grassroots emerged. Leonard Philemon Awala, nicknamed 'Castro', who was second-in-command of SWAPO's armed forces, and some of his junior officers, were of the old school, believing in a rigid military hierarchy. Apart from being strict in military discipline, they were corrupt and embezzled funds destined for the use of the army as a whole.

The rules were that everybody, irrespective of their ranks, should be back to base at 1800h after an afternoon out. Castro and his elite group slept out and came back to base early in the morning. This led to resentment by the grassroots who believed that rules should apply equally to rank-and-file and commanders alike. There should be no privileged few at the expense of many. The grassroots demanded the removal of the elite group as well as a general overhaul of the top army command. The political office was opposed to this and in turn it was accused of encouraging corruption within the army hierarchy.

On top of this there was growing restlessness within the trained cadres. They had not been trained to be based in

Tanzania or anywhere else far from the battlefront. Many wanted to go home and fight. They did not want to go for refresher courses. I, as one of the young radicals, was part of this group. We wanted to go and engage the enemy in battle and to rid Namibia of an evil system. We were yearning to unite our people and to be recognised as a nation among other nations of the world. We hated to be kept in camps far removed from Namibia. We felt that we could liberate our country within a month or so if we were allowed just to get nearer the enemy. We did not understand many aspects of diplomacy – all we wanted was arms and the right of passage through countries neighbouring Namibia.

11

Mission G2

In early February 1966 a group of top SWAPO political officials from Dar es Salaam came to see us at our camp near Dodoma. They told us that the time had come for us to begin moving homeward. They made it clear that such movements did not mean a start to the fighting, but were preliminary to a possible launching of guerrilla warfare in Namibia if things did not go well at the hearings into Namibia at The Hague.

The selection of cadres to be sent home was left to the army executive committee, which presented the names to the political executive office for approval. People were selected from different army departments and sorted into groups. Four groups, each of ten men, were told to be ready to be sent home in the first half of 1966. Further selections were to be carried out as time went on.

I was selected to be in the second group (G2); the first group (G1) was already operating. G2 consisted of the second-in-command of our armed forces, 'Castro' Awala, Lazarus Haidula Zacharia who was chief of our Military Police, myself from the Secretariat, Elia Ndume from the Medical Corps, Julius Shilongo from the Reconnaissance unit, Eino Kamati Ekandyo from the Demolition Squad and Jonas Shimweefeleni, Festus Nehare, Nghidipo Jessaja Haufiku and David Hamunime, all from the Gunners.

Things started moving fast. We made our final preparations to leave during the first week of February, and on 14 February, on a rainy night, we left Kongwa, central Tanzania, for Namibia. Castro, despite his rank, was not our group leader. This task was given to Lazarus Zacharia (known as Shakala). We got into our Land Rover and headed west towards Zambia, which had become independent in October 1964. Our plan was to pick up weapons and equipment in Mbeya, and then enter Namibia through the Caprivi Strip.

We experienced some problems at the Tanzanian-Zambian border. Our names had not been submitted in time to the border post. Peter Nanyemba, our representative in Tanzania, who was supposed to see us through the border, had not come. We therefore spent three days waiting to get through. When our names eventually came through and Nanyemba arrived to see us across, we witnessed one or two strange things – at least they seemed strange to us.

The first was a young Portuguese-speaking fellow who was at the border post the whole time we were there and whose presence baffled us. He seemed to have no intention of actually crossing the border in either direction and had no obvious function either – indeed it seemed unlikely that a Portuguese-speaker could have any official business on a border post between two English-speaking countries. I later came to connect him with information which was used against me during my interrogation – a document containing all our particulars was sent from the Zambian border post to Luanda and from Luanda to Pretoria.

The second was that the Zambians manning their border post showed open hostility towards us. One even made an open and insulting remark, saying: 'The cowards! They must go and rot in Verwoerd's jails like we have been rotting in Sir Roy Welensky's prisons.' I failed to understand the bearing of his remark until I entered the interrogation chamber in Pretoria when a document was placed in front of me by Captain Swanepoel of the South African Security Police.

The border incidents apart, we travelled at a time full of danger. Southern Rhodesia, under Ian Smith, had made its Unilateral Declaration of Independence (UDI) in 1965. British troops were 'assisting' Zambia to prevent an invasion from its powerful southern neighbour, and there was an oil shortage because Zambia's trade links were cut. As a result, oil was transported by tankers through Tanzania on the route we had taken, a mountainous and difficult road with a thousand dangerous bends. Many tankers failed to negotiate those bends and lay littered at the bottom of gorges. It was dangerous driving on that road.

In both Angola and Mozambique the Portuguese were fighting off wave after wave of determined guerrillas. The Pretoria regime was having nightmares of returning guerrillas. Though the timing seemed right for us, the circumstances were inappropriate to our cause. All the combined forces of the minority regimes in Southern Africa and their friends elsewhere converged in and around the independent front line states supporting us. All these forces wanted information on guerrilla movements southwards. They conspired together for our destruction. Also, in hindsight, I can see how ill-prepared we were for the journey and all that lay ahead. We had little logistical support and made many mistakes, sometimes through ignorance, sometimes through lack of any real alternative.

To beat the oil crisis and to be self-sufficient we carried two barrels of fuel. Our Land Rover was an unusual one-ton type – it was conspicuous and easily identifiable. The British troops we passed along the road to Lusaka turned their heads and pointed to our vehicle. By the time we arrived in Lusaka, we found a thousand eyes trained on us and our hotel became the focus of unwelcome attention. There was nowhere safer than the parking lot in the street where we could leave our vehicle. We put the matter to our high command but there was nothing they could do. We were sitting ducks in a sea of international agents, with nowhere to hide.

We made several blunders when we went shopping in Lusaka. Against our better judgement our group of 15 men went from one shop to another buying equipment for our mission, which was then paid for by our representative in Zambia. In one of these shops, a trader pointed out a customer wearing a straw hat as someone he suspected of being a Zambian government agent. We did not pay much heed to him, although he had seen us buying radio receivers. The man was in fact a South African spy who later identified himself to me during my interrogation in Pretoria.

We rang up Zambezi River Transport (ZRT) to enquire about our departure from Mamboa, near Livingstone, to Sesheke near Katima Mulilo, on the Zambian-Namibian border, and whether it was possible for our Land Rover to be transported. This proved dangerous because the Zambian telephone and postal services were still run, to a large extent, by elements sympathetic to the minority and racist regimes in Pretoria, Luanda, Salisbury and Lourenco Marques. Our conversations with the ZRT provided them with vital information. We also picked up our weapons from our SWAPO contacts in Lusaka, but we were bitterly disappointed. Instead of rifles, we were issued only with pistols and knives, which we carefully concealed in our Land Rover. Once we had established ourselves inside Namibia, and recruited more people, we would be provided with heavier weapons to take on the Boers, and more trained combatants would join us.

We left Lusaka on a pitch-black night. It was pouring with rain and we hoped that we would be able to avoid watchful eyes but we were wrong, and after two miles' drive, we learnt that we had company. We first thought it was somebody in a hurry who wanted to drive past. We gave whoever it was every chance to pass but it was never taken. We slowed down, they did the same. We accelerated, they followed suit. We only managed to shake them off when, around a bend, we pulled off the road, stopped, switched off the lights and waited. We did not have to wait long before whoever it was came zooming past. We got back onto the road, retraced our tracks in the Lusaka direction and then went to Livingstone by a different road. However, before long we were landed with an albatross, the spy we never suspected. We picked him up, or rather he picked us up, in Mamboa.

We got to Mamboa in the early hours of the morning, and tried to doze off in our Land Rover. A village in the swamps of the Zambezi River, Mamboa was the cradle of mosquitoes found along the river. Although the back of our vehicle was tarpaulined and we thought it was impregnable to mosquitoes, they managed to get through to us and made sleep impossible. After sunrise, we went to what had been the UNIP command post prior to independence, to find a place to rest. It was now delapidated and it was here many 'volunteers' came to offer us their 'free' services. Amongst them was Peter, a Zambian. He claimed to have been the district UNIP official and volunteered to see us through to Sesheke, two days' cruising up the Zambezi River. We tried our best to vet him but he was too cunning to be found out.

We spent two days waiting for the river boat and when it arrived early one morning, there were many eyes on shore eager to see us depart. Our Land Rover on the boat was like an elephant in a herd of calves. It could be seen miles away on either side of the river. Thinking back, I could not understand the reason why we had even bothered to take the vehicle with us on the river, because we never used it again.

We docked at Mwandi, a half-way station on the Zambian side, where we spent the night. On the other bank was the Caprivi, part of Namibia. Peter was accused of being a spy by the Mwamdi local police as well as by the Elder Counsellor of the village. The police warned him that if anything happened to us, he would find it difficult to find somewhere to hide. We still did not suspect him and thought he was unreasonably accused. We left our Land Rover at Mwandi and continued our journey up the river the following morning, with our weapons and equipment concealed in our baggage. It was a beautiful sunny day. The river was calm and the breeze was nice and cool. At around midday, a South African army patrol boat, on the Namibian side of the river, passed us going down the river.

The boat was scheduled to dock at Sesheke in Zambia, where we would disembark and arrange to cross secretly into Namibia. But the boat suddenly changed course and went straight towards the Namibian bank to make an unscheduled docking at Katima Mulilo. The action was so sudden that we did not know how to react. Before we docked, we could see that there were again a thousand eyes on the shore watching our approach. People disappeared quickly in the bush as soon as we got close. Were we hijacked? was the first thought that came to my mind. The atmosphere was electrified in expectation of an attack by the South Africans. We braced ourselves for the encounter silently, and mixing with other passengers on the boat, stepped ashore. We did not fit in with the rest of the passengers. We were different. We were conspicuous and presented easy targets. We went to sit down under trees a hundred yards or so from the river, together with other passengers waiting for the bus.

At Katima Mulilo the Zambezi cuts north through Zambia, so we could catch a bus back across the border. We waited and waited for the bus. Maybe because we were so anxious to get away, the bus seemed to take ages to come. It was beginning to get dark and we expected South African soldiers to come in shooting at any minute. Instead, a four wheel-drive van arrived with GG (Government Garage) number plates, the standard South African official number plate. It was driven by a man in shorts who went straight to the boat. Peter, the Zambian, went up to him and seemed to pick a quarrel with him on the 'Africa for Africans' political slogan. However, Peter's harangues sounded rather hollow. All the time he was talking to the man in shorts, they both looked in our direction, as if we were their centre of discussion.

Peter came back to us and sat down with his knees raised, his arms folded and resting on his knees, his head tilted towards the river and resting on his arms. He appeared to be passing on sign language messages to the man in shorts next to the boat. It was getting increasingly dark but the bus arrived in the end. People scrambled to get on board, but Peter remained seated and pretended to be asleep. We called to him to get on board but he pretended not to hear us and would not look in our direction. Hainyeko got down and pulled him up onto the bus. Peter's odd behaviour, together with the suspicions of the people of Mwandi, made me seriously question his loyalties.

The bus turned slowly and headed north-west. After continuous heavy rains, the gravel road was almost destroyed by water rushing from high ground on its way to the river. The water had uprooted a number of small trees and shrubs and had eaten deep furrows so that the bus found it difficult to negotiate the uneven and muddy road. Its engine laboured heavily and complained of the heavier load it now carried. Its wheels bit deep and tried to find their grip in the soil. The bus slid this way and that, with us swaying like puppets in a puppeteer's hands. Progress was really slow.

We eventually arrived at the border post. It was only manned by the Zambians, and we crossed without difficulty, but we still felt uneasy because the South Africans were just a stone's throw away. They could get in and out of Zambia at will.

Joseph Nawa, our SWAPO contact in the Eastern Caprivi at the time, met us at the border post and took us to a friend's house. We briefed him on our mission and gave him a list of our needs. Because there was still a lot to discuss with him, Peter, the Zambian, was delegated to go and get provisions for the journey. He was given money and because it was dark, he was also given a flash light. He disappeared and we waited for him for what appeared to be an eternity. My own suspicions were confirmed and my colleagues now agreed with me for the first time.

Someone else was sent to get the provisions we required. Nawa, realising the danger of keeping us all in the same place where Peter had left us, moved some of us to a neighbouring house. Three of us, Hainyeko, Shakala and myself, remained behind to see what would happen if Peter returned. The others were told to make final preparations for the road.

When Peter eventually came back, he had brought a stranger with him. The stranger was dressed in a heavy army raincoat and a hat; the typical dress of the South African secret police. Peter did not introduce the man to us. Instead, he said to him: 'There they are!'

The man, not knowing how to deal with the situation, just grunted, 'Mmhh!'

We demanded to know who he was – I don't remember what sort of answer he gave us. Hainyeko was a man of action and he wanted the two men to be disposed of there and then. Shakala and I intervened and instead ordered Peter and his friend to remove themselves before anything happened to them. We reached the others with just time enough to grab a few morsels of food. Nawa saw us off in the dark of the night towards the unknown.

Because we had been detected, we had to revise our original plan of travelling through the eastern Caprivi. We decided to head westwards through Zambia, skirting the Namibian border, crossing the Cuando River into Angola and then entering Namibia further to the west.

In training, we had practised operating as guerrillas by night – in total darkness and in downpours, but with no real threat. Now everything was real enough. It was complete darkness and the rain never let up, even for a moment. It was madness to travel under such conditions in normal circumstances. But our situation was not normal. The enemy were close. We had a mission and a commitment to carry it out in whatever circumstances, come rain, come darkness.

Despite the discomforts of being wet to the skin, and not being able to see where we were putting our feet, we felt relatively secure, ready to face any dangerous situation if the need arose. We were as battle-ready as anybody in our situation could be. We were a special breed and felt great! As a team, we had a marching song, which went like this:

I was standing at a corner then I heard
the freedom fighters in the dark,

I was watching in the dark when I heard
the freedom fighters on the march,

They were marching! marching! marching!
in the rain to the war!

We travelled by night most of the time, especially in populated areas, and rested during the day, well hidden from view. We avoided all traffic, whether by day or by night. However, we approached the locals for provisions and directions when we felt it was safe enough and really necessary. Our nocturnal companions came to be the lions. Though they never attacked us, their presence was always evident and they never stopped roaring. This again was comfort to us as no one would dare to venture near lions' dens unless they had a special mission like ours.

After heavy rains, March being a rainy month, all rivers in the Zambian/Angolan regions of Cuando Cubango broke their banks and were impassable. No matter how prepared we were, we were not equipped for floods. We depended on local people to take us across the rivers, but they, with their little canoes, would not risk it. Due to flooding, we were unable to cross the Cuando River into Angola. We were forced instead to spend a week following the river up north, on the Zambian side, looking for a ford and people willing to see us across.

On the eighth day we arrived at Caunga, a village on the Zambia-Angola border. Here the locals were experienced canoeists – they were prepared to take us across the Cuando River for £1 each. To cross the river here would mean we would cross it into the Angolan territory, inviting the possibility of encountering Portuguese troops rather than the South Africans we were prepared for. But we did not care any more. They were all the same and whoever we met, daggers would be drawn. The Portuguese colonialists in Angola, too, regarded all freedom fighters as one and the same and they would not have hesitated to fire at anyone they thought of as their enemy. We were therefore ready for whoever we encountered, despite our instructions not to engage anyone on foreign soil. Self protection was our priority.

We set out for the river while it was still dark and landed on the Angolan side at around 1700h. The Cuando was not an ordinary river where we crossed it, it was like an ocean. It had many islands, some of which were inhabited. We crossed the centre of the river and the border at noon. The centre was marked by strong whirlpools which went the whole length of the river. The canoeists, however, saw us safely over and fortunately we did not leave one of our comrades in its churning waters (many people drowned there, we were told). The twelve hours we spent crossing the Cuando River convinced us that we had reached a point of no return. Life or death, we would never retreat until we had set foot on Namibian soil and executed our duty.

A Portuguese man was one of the people in the welcoming party when we finally reached the other side of the river. He wanted to take us to do some 'shopping' at nearby Portuguese shops. Were we interested? No, we were not, we told him. But we knew that he had already achieved his objective and got what he wanted – to report to his superiors that he had seen us crossing the river into Angola and that he had talked to us and seen whether we were carrying weapons openly (our pistols were hidden in our coats). To hide our real identity, we tried to tell everybody that we were Angolan or Namibian mine workers returning home after a period at the mines in South Africa. Few people believed us. We did not look like mine workers nor did we speak Fanakalo, the lingua franca of the South African mines.

Vast areas of south-eastern Angola are sparsely populated. We found them ideal and travelled uninterrupted day and night for a couple of days, although it rained continually. We were now running out of provisions and needed to replenish our stocks. The locals in these areas were not sophisticated enough to be manipulated or used as spies by the Portuguese colonialists. When we asked them where we could find some shops to buy some food, they told us that there was a Portuguese shop several days' walk away – they themselves could not satisfy our needs. So we set out for the Portuguese shop.

After three days' march, we arrived. The shop keeper 'Mandevu' (a nickname meaning 'beard') was a young unmarried man in his twenties. Immediately we arrived there, I knew that he knew who we were. Because it had never stopped raining, we had our raincoats on – all identical – and we resembled priests in their dark robes. These had an ill effect on him – he looked like someone who had seen a ghost. Nevertheless, he put on a brave face and allowed us into his shop and sold us what we wanted. Shakala, our group leader, who understood and spoke the local language, acted as our interpreter. Mandevu offered to put us up when we asked if we could spent the night under the trees in his yard.

There were several sheds in the yard, one of which was occupied by his staff. He told them to share it with us. To satisfy himself that we were the group he had heard about, he came round to have a 'friendly' chat with us towards midnight. How were we settling in, he wanted to know. He also wanted to know if we had any radios to sell as he was in need of some! Were we the right people, or had his source of information let him down? I could see those questions going through his mind. In the end, he left, still wondering.

Although we were aware of the risk in staying at Mandevu's we felt safe in the knowledge that the shop was many miles from the nearest town and that we were surrounded by deep bush.

12

Never follow the wolf

There was only one track from Mandevu's place, mostly used by wild-life hunters. It went onto the Luiana River, to a compound owned by one Shipinya, an elephant hunter and trader. The area was virgin jungle where few human feet had trodden and where animals still roamed unperturbed and enjoyed peace in their wilderness kingdoms.

We left Mandevu's place early in the morning, and followed the track. A wolf (or hyena) preceded us: we did not know where he started from or where he was going. When we first saw his footprints on the ground, we thought he was an inhabitant of the area near Mandevu's place, as most animals are known to have defined areas of residence. Not this Mr Wolf. We marched for at least five days non-stop without losing his tracks. He seemed to lead us, heaven knows where!

In some traditional beliefs, wolves are thought to be unlucky creatures, especially when they cross one's path. We did not know whether this superstition also applied to following a wolf's tracks. Though none of us said anything, we all felt we should change course. But to have done so would have led us either down to the Caprivi which we now wanted to avoid at all costs, or further north, which would have taken us into more populated areas with a possible presence of Portuguese soldiers. We needed to head west, in order to enter Namibia across the Okavango river, and we decided to stick to Mr Wolf's track, come what may.

The downpours on day six from Mandevu's place were the heaviest. They made our travel by night impossible. We knew that we were no longer far from Shipinya's compound and because we did not want to stumble upon it in darkness, we called a halt and planned to reconnoitre the place first thing in the morning.

Shilongo, our intelligence cadet, and myself were sent out to scout the place after we had made inquiries from the locals as to how far it was. The camp, a cluster of wooden buildings, was strategically situated on a bend on the Luiana River and well concealed from all approaches by tall trees. The track we followed, which skirted the river, and another road from the north-east, crossed the river over a wooden bridge and converged fifty or so yards from Shipinya's encampment. There were no side-roads skirting the camp and the jungle around the area was as thick as a sugar-cane field.

Mr Wolf's prints led right to the entrance of Shipinya's camp and there they disappeared in the thicket.

Shilongo and I spent several hours trying to find a way round Shipinya's place. In the end we gave up and decided to go in and look around the camp. Because we did not have any other excuse to put forward we told Shipinya that we had run out of salt. Could he sell us some? 'Of course!' he said.

I watched his behaviour the whole time he was selling us salt. I wanted to find out whether he knew something about us in advance and whether he would give himself away in one way or another. He eventually betrayed himself in discussions with his assistants which he thought we could not overhear. He asked them if we had told them who we were and how many we were, and he told them to ask us to bring our friends to come and buy from his shop tomorrow. 'How did he know that we had some friends?' was the first thought to strike me.

When we got back to the others, we gave them the details about the difficulty of avoiding Shipinya's camp. Not to alarm everybody, I told our group leader what I had overheard from Shipinya and asked him not to say anything to the others in case it was not correct.

When we returned the following morning to buy our things, I could see the excitement in the shopkeeper's eyes. He counted us and was satisfied that we tallied with the number he had been given. Before he opened his shop, he went into a radio transmitting room. He left the door open and with his face beaming with delight and eyes fixed on us, he started transmitting to Dirico, a Namibian border post, on the Okavango River. At Dirico there was a pontoon that carried traffic between Angola and Namibia.

Having overheard his discussions the day before, I was more interested in his transmission than in anything else. I had my back to him so he did not suspect that I was listening. He began thus: 'O Dirico! O Dirico! Bon Dia O Dirico! Eu resebei as minhas desas coisas! (Good morning Dirico! I received my ten things!)' It was clear to me that Shipinya hoped that we would use the road to Dirico and be apprehended before we got there. When he finished, he hung up and came out with glee written all over his face. Rubbing his hands together, he opened the shop and ushered us in. He said he had a limited number of supplies but hoped we would find what we wanted. When we had finished our shopping, he locked up and called us to his quarters.

He left us standing in the yard and went inside. He reappeared on the balcony and, speaking fluent Oshikwanyama, he told us that he was Omukwanyama himself and well understood the problems facing travellers. They often forgot to carry water containers or cooking utensils. He had therefore sent a member of his staff to bring us a 5 litre 'galfao' (bottle) for water. From his balcony, he dropped down to us a sack. 'You might need this as well', he said. We definitely needed it very badly – not for carrying anything but to give us a very important clue. The sack originated from Durban in South Africa. It was a commercial brown sugar sack sold mainly in South Africa and Namibia. Before we left, he instructed one of his men to show us the road to Dirico. We must not follow other roads otherwise we would get lost, he instructed.

Three hundred yards from Shipinya's place, the road split into three. The track on the left led to Dirico and the one in the middle to Nyangana near Dirico. The third led to Nkurenkure, about 150 miles to the west of Rundu in the Okavango region. Shipinya's man put us on the road to Dirico and said goodbye. After he left I told Shakala, our group leader, what Shipinya had said in his transmission. Shakala immediately called a halt and a council of war with Castro and myself. I gave them all the details of the coded message and what I understood it to mean. They agreed with my assessment and after a brief discussion, we decided to inform the others and to change course.

Now everybody was convinced that Shipinya was dangerous and sympathised with the racist regime in Pretoria. When we entered Angola it was decided that, no matter what happened, we should avoid engaging ourselves in any activities on Angolan territory which could jeopardise our mission and compromise the route to Namibia. Shipinya was a great danger. His removal and the clearing of the way was considered to be of paramount necessity. Shakala wanted him killed immediately and all of us concurred with him. But how far would his removal compromise our mission and the missions of those following us? How would it be interpreted by both Luanda and Pretoria after they had received a message from him that he had received his ten items? These were the questions we asked ourselves. The Portuguese or South

Africans might be on their way to Shipinya's camp already.

We decided against going back to kill him and left the job to the next group to come that way. We also decided to radically alter course and take the road leading to Nkurenkure, two weeks' march.

We had just changed course when two low-flying helicopter gunships appeared over treetops above the Dirico road. Their markings were clearly of the South African Air Force. We dived for cover and waited until they landed at Shipinya's place. When we were satisfied that there were no more eyes in the sky, we hastened our departure. Under cover of the thick surroundings we made our get-away as invisibly and as quickly as we could. By the time the choppers took off again, we were miles away. Each chopper followed one of the three routes, but the one on our road turned away before it came close to us. They spent the whole day scouring the bush. We could only see them from afar and all the time we were increasing the distance from them.

The route we had chosen was exceptionally safe. The area was uninhabited and our now daily tactics of leaving the road and changing course, made it impossible for the South Africans to trace us. But we did not drop our guard, and having seen the choppers scouring the bush, we prepared ourselves for battle. We had now run out of provisions and were desperate to find somewhere to buy something to eat. On the morning of the third day from Shipinya's, we came to a settlement. We reconnoitred the settlement to make sure that there was not a 'welcoming party' there.

Shakala, who speaks the language of the area, and myself were sent to go and get some provisions. Others covered us with a 'fire jacket'. We cautiously approached a homestead which turned out to belong to the King. We checked all the approaches to the house and found that everything was as quiet as a tomb. As it was early in the morning, there was nobody in the house because the people had gone out to tend their corn fields.

We returned to the others and suggested we look elsewhere for provisions. The others were listening to the radio from South Africa. Prime Minister Verwoerd came on the air: 'We want to tell the Russians and others supporting and sending the insurgents to come and attack South Africa, that they are sending them to their deaths and that their graves are already dug! To the Afrikaner nation I say, the struggle continues!' he concluded, or words to that effect. To us, this was a clear indication that he was referring to our group. The news about our movement southwards was now public. We did not, however, mind that the enemy had got wind of us. We were ready for them.

After the news, we headed off in another direction and met several people returning from their fields to their homesteads. Some of them came from the King's household and we could tell that they knew who we were. We found out later that the South African and Portuguese security forces had been there for the last two days waiting for us and had left a message with the King to apprehend us if we turned up there. But we were not to be caught that easily. We changed course again and, to the King's men, seemed to have disappeared into proverbial thin air. Soon afterwards, we met a lone old man coming from his field, and asked him to sell us some omapungu (corn on the cob). He invited us to his field. He did not know anything about us as yet, we deduced.

We bought everything we wanted from the old man and said goodbye. He instructed his son to show us the way. We had gone just two hundred yards or so, when the old man started calling back his son. 'Come back as quickly as you can! Those people are criminals wanted dead or alive!' he shouted, evidently suddenly realising who we were. The boy, who was 15 years old or so, had a mind of his own. While shouting to his father that he was turning back, he still continued to show us how to get to the road. We thanked the boy, gave him a tip for his troubles and ordered him to get back to his father.

When we got to the road, we found it thoroughly ploughed down by horses' hooves. By examining the hoof-prints we deduced that the King's cavalries had been chasing about at full speed trying to track us down.

At the next homestead we came to, we found terrified people. Some, through curiosity, climbed on the fences to have a good look at us. We saluted them amicably and must have managed to allay some of the fears they had got from the stories about us being criminals wanted dead or alive. They followed us with their eyes until we disappeared into the Angolan jungle and safety. Once in the bush, we changed course and headed directly north, where nobody would dream of us heading. We travelled for another three days without encountering a human being and then turned west before we again turned south. It was still raining continuously.

We came to a place known as Makulungungu (vast emptiness), two days' march from the Cuito River. From a young man we came across we received information that the river crossing, a pontoon near the junction of the Cuito and Okavango Rivers, and just north of the Namibian border, was guarded by Portuguese soldiers. He said he could lead us to a safer crossing to the north of the principal one.

The young man worked in the South African mines and as we told him that we had come from there, there was some affinity between us and, like any black Angolan, he understood our reasons for wanting to avoid contact with the Portuguese.

After two days' passing through empty bush, we arrived at our crossing point on the Cuito River at midday. Time and tide wait for no man, Shakespeare once said. Here, we found that the river was in flood and we could not cross. We had to spend several hours waiting for it to ebb.

We had crossed many beautiful rivers but none were as striking as the Cuito. The canoeist drew our attention to the beauty of its waters which were crystal clear and green. Fish and other underwater creatures could be seen deep below; its rock formations were spectacular. It was a pity that it was not part of our mission to observe and enjoy beauty. I would have liked to have spent some days just sailing up and down the river.

We had again run out of provisions and we decided to find a place where we could spend the night. We were now in an inhabited area and we found a house just yards away from the main road to the north. The owner said we could sleep there. However, we needed to stock up at shops in a nearby village, although we ourselves could not venture there. As strangers, we would easily be picked up and we requested the owner of the house to help us by going to the shops for us. Though we had only known him for a couple of hours, we thought he was an honest man. He too had worked in the South African mines – we were brothers and trusted that he would not betray us to the enemy. At the same time, we were prepared to react to any situation if he did give us away. He agreed and we gave him some money for our purchases.

The man had not returned by the afternoon and we became worried. We dug ourselves in under a thicket near the house and remained alert, prepared for whatever might turn up.

At about 1500h a Portuguese army jeep full of armed soldiers came hurtling along the dusty road. It stopped about

300 yards from the house. Our immediate thought was that our new friend had given us away and had been brought back to point out where we were. We tensed ourselves in our positions, ready for action, and waited for the soldiers to jump out and storm the house before we opened fire. But the soldiers were only dropping off the owner of the house as they had given him a lift.

We left the place within an hour of the man's return, heading south towards the Namibian border. By now we had given up our plans to reach Nkurenkure – our main aim was to get into Namibia as soon as possible.

We came eventually to a settlement near the Okavango River. It was the first heavily populated area we had come across since entering Angola. The first person we met suggested that it was customary as strangers to spend the night at the King's house. Arms at the ready, but keeping them well concealed so as not to attract suspicion, we agreed. As was customary for their tribe, the man said, we were also expected to give something to the King as a gesture of goodwill.

The man took us to the gates of the palace but refused to enter when we asked him to take us inside. The King welcomed us nicely. He was in his mid-forties and was surprised when we offered him a 'goodwill' present. Contradicting his subject, he told us that it was customary to put up strangers without expecting something in return.

The King enjoyed cracking jokes and in a conspiratorial whisper he said he knew the person who told us such nonsense. To suggest that strangers spend the night at the King's house was a tactic used by those working for the Portuguese authorities. If we had refused, we would have given him an excuse to take us to the authorities. The 'customary' goodwill present to the King was another way of demanding a bribe, if we did not want to go to the palace or be taken to the authorities. In our conversations with him, we learnt that the King was a man of the people and did not tolerate individuals who spied on others. He was pleased with us and praised our actions. He ordered that we be given food and he would see to it that we had a nice place to sleep. In the morning, he sent us breakfast before we proceeded on our way along the Okavango River.

Namibia was on the other side – so near yet still very far. The river had burst its banks and only experienced people dared challenge it in their little canoes. It was the first time I

116

had seen the Okavango River, as was the case with most of us except Shakala, who had grown up in the area.

There was no river crossing nearby and we travelled for miles before we came to one. The bush had thinned and trees were fewer. But there was one place on the river bank with a crop of large trees and some undergrowth. We went to inspect it and found it ideal and decided that we would remain concealed there until we could find someone to take us across the river. We sent two of our colleagues to go and negotiate a crossing with local people. Suddenly three Portuguese army jeeps appeared: all had heavily armed soldiers and were apparently tracking us down. All the soldiers' eyes were trained on the river, possibly hoping to see us crossing and to eliminate us there and then.

Had the King misled and betrayed us? Were the soldiers on our scent? They appeared extremely alert, but because their attention was focussed on the river, they did not see our colleagues going to look for a canoeist. Our colleagues had their backs to the soldiers and did not see or hear the jeeps until their attention was drawn to them by people at a nearby house. Fortunately they did not panic or they would have attracted the soldiers' attention.

Meanwhile, we on the river-side where the soldiers had concentrated their attention, thought that they might have seen some movement. We immediately prepared ourselves for what would have become known, should it have taken place, as the battle of the Okavango. The soldiers, however, did not seem to have an inkling of our presence. We were well hidden under the shrubs and did not make any movements to attract their attention. They went their way without stopping and we relaxed. When our colleagues returned, they told us that there was nobody who could take us across at that moment but the people would let the canoeist know as soon as he returned.

We waited for almost an hour before the canoeist appeared. Lying low on the river bank in anticipation of being discovered and perhaps killed was a harrowing experience. We could not relish the beauty of the Okavango River which, because of the incessant rain, was surrounded by lush greenery. We could not see beyond our personal safety and the anxiety of what awaited us on the other side.

We braced ourselves for what was to be our last river crossing. The dugout was so small that it was only able to take two passengers at a time and we would have to make five trips.

The river was about three-quarters of a mile wide where we crossed it and there were no reeds to provide us with cover. If the enemy had been waiting for us on the Namibian side, or appeared on a river patrol, we would have been sitting ducks! We were able to cover our comrades on the first crossing from behind, but we did not know what awaited them on the other bank so we were much relieved when they landed on the other side without incident. After they had reconnoitred the bush near by and found no threat, they set up defences and gave an all-clear sign for the other groups to proceed.

Castro and I were the last to cross. He nearly caused the dugout to overturn due to his clumsiness. The canoeist told us to sit down on the floor of the dugout to help stabilise the craft. Castro, however, chose to squat and clung to the sides, which made us rock from side to side. He panicked and nearly fell overboard. The boat went completely out of control. I felt anger mounting in me after I tried to calm Castro down to no avail. I was ready for a swim, if things went any further wrong. But the pilot remained calm and, being an expert, he did not struggle but let the canoe drift downriver. At the same time he manoeuvred the craft, now powered by the current, towards the Namibian shore. We were about one and half miles downriver from the crossing and in thick reeds before the pilot regained control and at last landed us on the Namibian shore.

I heaved a huge sigh of relief when I found myself on firm ground. This was the land I loved so dearly and had left two years ago. This was the country I had deserted because it could not offer a bright future for me or my descendants. I returned to you, my Namibia, fully prepared to liberate you from the abhorrent system of apartheid perpetuated by the racist regime in Pretoria. I was prepared to pay the supreme price for your freedom and independence. These were the thoughts that ran in my mind as I struggled up the bank and tried to find my way through the thick bush that grew along the river.

We made it to the others, and because it was not yet dark enough for us to proceed, we made final preparations and wished one another luck. We divided ourselves into four groups – two groups of three each, and two of two each. I was again, as on the river crossing, landed with Castro, and when darkness fell, we were the first to set out. Thirty minutes were to be allowed to pass before the next group followed. All groups were to report to Eliaser Tuhadeleni at Endola, about 300 miles to the west. To get there, we had to head for Rundu, the nearest town, where we had a SWAPO contact.

Here we go, I thought to myself as I heaved my rucksack onto my back. It was 23 March 1966, a date I was to remember as the day when, as a returning guerrilla, I was prepared to play the game according to its rule of kill or get killed. Similar liberation wars had been fought and were now being fought in other parts of the world. Our struggle resembled many national liberation struggles such as that of the Algerians against the French colonialists, or the Angolans and Mozambicans against the Portuguese. It also bore resemblance to historic revolutionary wars fought before ours, to the French Revolution, the American war of independence, the October Revolution in the Soviet Union and the Chinese revolution. Our struggle was in essence a national liberation struggle against a colonial power, South Africa. A war of deprived, exploited, down-trodden and oppressed and expropriated people. We were fighting to regain what had been taken away from us – our country and our freedom.

I did not regret, not for even one second, having undergone military training. It was essential in our liberation struggle. The time had come and it was now imperative that my training should be put to the test. Here, on this soil, I was prepared to shed my own blood for the freedom of every Namibian, and to shed the blood of the enemy. I felt strong and full of courage now that I was no longer on foreign soil but in my own country. I was ready to meet the challenge. The rain, to our surprise, had stopped when we crossed the river.

We arrived in Rundu at about 0200h and because we could not find our way through the town, we decided to rest and have a little snooze. It was too dark to see farther than our noses, and we did not realise until dawn, when the first light appeared on the horizon, that we were only yards away from the Rundu police station. Though we were aware of car headlights going in and out of the yard, we did not bother to investigate and assumed that it was a garage or something commercial.

We moved away from the police station at first light and located the house of our contact in Rundu. He was not at home

119

but his wife, Helena, invited us in. She asked who we were and why we wanted to see her husband. Because we did not know her or her attitude towards SWAPO, we tried to hide our identities from her and fed her with false information. We left our bags with her and went to the shops. There was an acute shortage of transport from Rundu to the west, so we decided to buy bicycles to be self-sufficient in transport.

We met Shakala and Shilongo on our way to the shops. Shilongo told us that he and two others had managed to get into the compound used by SWANLA for recruiting contract workers looking for jobs both in Namibia itself and South Africa. The mission of Shilongo's group was to take up employment in the south with the aim of organising the southerners in political as well as military activities. Shakala told us that he and his two colleagues had met a SWANLA lorry driver who had agreed to give them a lift to Nkurenkure. From there they would march on to Oshikango and then to Endola where we were all going to report to Tuhadeleni.

Rundu was teeming with security police. The Ondangwa as well as Oshikango Native Commissioners were there. Uniformed police in four-wheel drive vans were patrolling everywhere in the dusty town. Police in civilian clothes and in unmarked cars were in evidence everywhere. It was clear that they knew we were in the area, but did not know who we were or what we looked like. We, however, had some idea of what kind of people they thought we were. SWAPO's trademark was known to be beards and most SWAPO members were thought to be in their mid-twenties. To beat these widely held beliefs we had all agreed to be clean-shaven. Dressed in tatters, I walked with a slight stoop like an old man. I had cut myself a walking stick in Angola and wore omukonda (a dagger) to complete the picture of an old man. The deception was perfect and nobody suspected us.

We bought everything we wanted except bicycles which were sold out but were expected in a couple of days, we were told. I nearly committed an unforgivable mistake in the SWANLA shop. One area of the shop was reserved for whites only and blacks had to point to what they wanted from a distance. Blacks could not hand money directly to the white saleswoman. They first had to give it to the black salesman, who would then pass it over to the white saleswoman after he had 'cleaned' it. People entering the shop were sprayed with fly repellent pesticide.

The whole practice infuriated me and, coming from abroad where I had not seen such disgusting behaviour, I just snapped. Speaking in fluent Afrikaans, I refused to leave the reserved 'whites only' area. With my elbows on the counter (which was even worse) I did my shopping there and only moved out after I had finished. Watching the white saleswoman out of the corner of my eye, I saw her pulling on the black assistant's sleeves and asking: 'Wie is hy? Miskien een van die SWAPO mense. (Who is he? Maybe one of the SWAPO people.)' It was then I realised my big mistake. I had allowed my anger to overcome me and could have given us away. I withdrew from the shop before any further damage was done.

Outside the shop, I found Shakala surrounded by a group of security policemen asking him who he was. He had forgotten to change into tatters. Speaking in fluent Oshikwangari (the language spoken in the area) he beat off all their penetrating questions. Like an inquisitive old man, I stood outside their circle, leaned heavily on my walking stick and listened. When he emerged from the circle, Shakala ordered us to make tracks. He later met us at the house of our contact.

There, the cat was well and truly let out of the bag. Shakala and the lady of the house had been at school together. He desperately tried to deny that she knew him or that he had been abroad in Tanzania. In the end, he admitted that he was Shakala and confessed that we were coming from abroad. Helena told us that she already knew who we were and did not believe anything we had told her earlier. She was aware of everything because the Boers had been announcing on radio broadcasts that they expected a force of about ten guerrillas to enter Namibia. She pointed out many cars belonging to the police and Native Commissioners and their assistants.

She said it was too dangerous for us to hang around the house because of our contacts' position within the SWAPO leadership in the area. Besides, police now visited the house regularly because their first-born daughter had left for abroad a couple of weeks earlier. Helena was going to do her washing at the river. It would be better if we went with her, she suggested.

Spotter planes and helicopters were scouring the area around Rundu and flying low over the river. One chopper came to have a closer look at us: we stood gazing up at it like innocent 'curious' blacks. Satisfied, it banked away to follow the river's course. Helena told us that police surveillance had increased since the night before and that we should avoid hailing a lift because they were checking on everyone going west. They were also checking every car leaving Rundu for either Oshikango or Ondangwa. We briefed her on our mission and the reason why we wanted to see her husband, adding that we would be grateful if she could convey our messages to him.

We thanked Helena for her hospitality and at about 1300h on 24 March Castro and I headed for Mupini, about 10 miles west of Rundu. We were heading for the house of Stephanus Haundyange, Shakala's uncle, who lived there. Shakala in the meantime went back to his travel companions.

We arrived safely at Haundyange's. By now our disguise had changed: we were no longer mine workers returning from South African mines. Castro was now an ex-patient of the Uutokota Hospital east of Rundu, I was his cousin who had gone to collect him and we were returning back home to Oukwanyama. We did not tell the old man Haundyange who we were, only that we wanted a place to spend the night.

The following morning we set off down the road which followed the course of the Okavango River. We tried to hail a lift from a SWANLA lorry carrying contract workers back to their homes. Here it was safe to get a lift westward, but there was no room on the lorry. At about 1400h, a horseman came by: we slipped into the bush to hide. He stopped to talk to herdsmen who were herding their cattle nearby. From our hiding place I could see that he was agitated and I heard him asking the herdsmen whether they had seen three Ovakwanyama criminals on the road there. Immediately I heard the questions, I knew that it was a reference to some of our colleagues. Their group had had a skirmish with the police, I heard the horseman saying.

We decided to change course and we travelled for the rest of the day in thick bush two miles away from the road and the river.

Helicopters and spotter planes were now scouring the woodland along the river and it was difficult for us to approach the river to drink – it being the only source of water. Because the fields were ripe with corn and water melons, however, we helped ourselves to everything we could get. When it was dark and safe enough for us not to be seen by anybody using the road, we ventured closer to the road. We were then able to survey the movements of police vehicles.

Herd-boys in northern Namibia

Helao Shityuwete as a young man

Shityuwete in Windhoek during SWAPO's election campaign, 1989

Katutura, the segregated black township outside Windhoek

German colonial influence in Windhoek

*me of the accused in the 1967 Terrorism Trial: (Top, left to right) Eliaser
ιhadeleni, John Otto Nankudhu, Julius Shilongo; (Centre) Lazarus
ιchariah, David Hamunime, Kaleb Tjipahura; (Bottom) Abel Aluteni, John
ιipponeni, John Ya-Otto*

The Terrorism Trial sketched in a South African newspaper, 1967

Robben Island – prisoners breaking rocks in the courtyard

Andimba Toivo Ya Toivo, Secretary General of
SWAPO

Sam Nujoma, President of SWAPO and first
President of independent Namibia

We had just got onto the road when suddenly we saw the powerful headlights of a police vehicle approaching around a bend. We dived into a hedge nearby and then crawled through a corn field away from the road. Fortunately, they didn't see us and passed us lying low in the corn field. When it was safe enough, we left the field and went back to the road. We walked for the whole night and only rested for three hours towards morning. Castro was dead tired and was snoring before he hit the ground.

13

Arrest

Five o'clock in the morning of 26 March I got up and checked my equipment. Everything was alright. We had slept under a hedge because we did not want to be run over by horses, which were numerous in the area. It seemed the horsemen there never stopped riding, even in the middle of a pitch black night. I used to be a horseman and I would not have ridden in such darkness. I was terrified at the speed they rode without seeing where they were heading.

I looked down at the figure of my companion curled up in a ball on the ground. Castro was still fast asleep and appeared lifeless. I shook him to wake him so that we could resume our march westward. He grunted and did not make any effort to get up. It was our third day in the country and Castro was too tired to move. He wanted to wait for the sunrise, he mumbled, half asleep. He added that we should try and get a lift as it would alleviate his sore feet. We had had serious arguments the previous day. His feet were covered in blisters and he could not walk properly. He was prepared to hail a lift, even from the police. I was against any kind of a lift because it would give us away. Now we were having the same argument all over again.

The worst thing was that now he did not even want to make an effort to get onto his feet. I was left with a big dilemma. I could not leave him behind, yet I could not drag him along. He was a liability rather than a companion. In the end, I pulled him up onto his feet and showed him the direction we were going. I then let go of him and he dropped to the ground like an empty bag. I decided to leave him because I felt that I could not help him if he did not want to help himself. Dawn was fast approaching and I wanted to make my way to the woods before the world woke up. He must get his lift without me, I concluded, and left him.

The sun rose at about 7 o'clock that morning, and because it was open country, though it was not yet clear, I could see far in the distance. Three miles away in front of me was a wood. I undertook to get there before it was light enough for my movements to be detected. When I reached the edge of the wood, I looked back to see whether Castro was coming. There was no sign of him. I then went into the wood and hid my rucksack and went back to look for him. I had by now realised that I could not leave him behind, whatever happened.

The sun had risen and the world had become alive with birds singing in the woods and people going to their corn fields to harvest and drive away the birds. I found Castro just a mile from where I had left him. He was making his way to the road, determined to get a lift. I told him that I could not leave him alone unless he wanted to give himself up to the police. No, that was not his intention. His only problem was that he was now tired and wanted to rest.

I took his luggage then placed his arm over my shoulder and we went slowly towards the wood where we rested before we resumed our march.

We were now walking between the river and the road but we wanted to make our way to woods on the other side of the road where it was safer. It was too risky walking in a confined space with helicopters and spotters flying low. It was while we were trying to do this that we noticed a short man jumping over a hedge. He was one of our comrades, Nghidipo Haufiku, from the group just behind us, and we called him to us.

Their group had indeed been involved in a skirmish with the police the previous day. They were stopped by the police who wanted to search their baggage. They agreed to it, believing that they had nothing to incriminate them in their baggage – their weapons were hidden in their clothes. They were wrong. Inside a briefcase police found a 'Political Lecture' by Maxton Joseph. This gave them away and before the police could do anything, Nghidipo and others scattered in different directions. The police fired at them but they fired back and that gave them time to escape unscathed. Nghidipo did not know where the others were but was sure that no one was hurt or captured.

After the clash with the police, Nghidipo said he had been chased by a mob of locals who were armed with rifles, assegais, omikove (a bigger version of assegai), knobkeries and sticks. He took refuge in thick bush, which the locals surrounded and set on fire, with the intention of burning him to death. They were so busy dancing in celebration of their success that they failed to notice him crawling out. Once he was at a safe distance, he turned and watched as they threw in melons to flush him out. When one melon burst in the flames a wild cry erupted from the mob. He said he felt sorry for them because they had no idea what they were doing.

The three of us went to cross the road. We had five yards left when a van came hurtling towards us from our right. We scuttled forward, jumping over hedges before diving for cover in the corn field. I was listening for gunfire but was relieved when I saw that the van belonged to the mission station near by. We made our get-away and reached the safety of the woods.

Meanwhile, the search had intensified and we saw a helicopter landing at the mission ahead of us. We knew that it was dropping some police there and it would be a matter of time before they caught up with us. The chopper was later joined by another two and together they flew sorties over the fields and the woods near by. We were trapped. In addition to the helicopters, there were police vehicles and foot security men on our trail. There appeared to be no escape and we could not make our way into the woods further from the combed area. They were getting closer and closer, much to our discomfort. We split up and agreed to find trees to climb with enough branches and leaves to hide us.

Though traumatic, it was interesting to see my pursuers, who were bent on my elimination, passing under the tree I was hiding in. I had found myself a comfortable place where I was hidden from my pursuers' eyes but where I could see all activities that went on around me. When darkness fell, and our pursuers had gone, we regrouped and resumed our march. But it was difficult to find our way through the thick bush. In order to make any progress at all we headed for the road, hoping that we would not be intercepted or find police waiting there.

Travelling by road was faster but full of dangers. Besides being wanted men, we faced the hazard of being run over by horses ridden at full speed by the locals in the pitch black darkness.

We had hardly reached the road when we were nearly run over by about five cavalrymen. They pulled their horses to a grinding stop. They were part of the tribal police force. Speaking in Oshikwangari, they asked us who we were and where we were going. Though this was only our third day in the area, I had learned their language faster than I had ever learned any language before. So I was conversant in their vernacular and told them that we were also Ovakwangari from the other side of Nkurenkure, returning from a visit to

Rundu.

They first would not believe me and demanded that we accompany them to their kingdom. Having collected and rehearsed all the names of the kings and queens in the area, I praised them for being nice to their subjects. I told them that I found it odd that they, of all people, wanted to defile the local King's good name by antagonising some of his loyal subjects. I threatened to take up the matter with the King next time I paid a visit there. Upon that, though they were still not sure of us, they apologised and allowed us to proceed.

We had just parted when another cavalry group came riding at full speed towards us. We did not wait for them to ask us silly questions and dived into the corn field nearby. The road here ran between the river and local residences and, not being able to see further than our noses, we ran straight into an ambush. It was laid by tribal police on either side of the road and we just walked into it like one puts on socks. They were armed with rifles and omikove (assegais). They took us to the house of the local foreman where we found other armed men waiting. They did not search us and we still had our weapons hidden beneath our coats.

The foreman came to talk to us. He told us that a new law had just been passed that nobody was allowed to travel by night in the Oukwangari area. I explained that we were not aware of it, and since we were not far from our homes we had not found it necessary to look for somewhere to stop for the night, adding that it would be a decent thing if he would let us proceed. This did not help because I was the only one who spoke their language and they were by now convinced that we were not who I said we were. Our features, again, were different from theirs. Speaking amongst themselves, they kept on saying: 'Ovakwanyama!' The foreman told us that we should spend the night there and that he would allow us to go our way the next morning.

We tried to see the foreman in the morning but he had made himself scarce. His men would not let us go without his permission.

'Are we arrested?' we wanted to know.

The answer was no, of course not.

'But why don't you let us go?'

'Because the foreman wants to see you before you go,' was the answer. When he at last appeared, he told us that he was taking us to see the King.

'What for?' we protested but to no avail. Like Jesus on his way to Golgotha, we too were led away on a similar road. The only difference was that ours ended on Robben Island, the Golgotha to black South African freedom fighters.

A force of about 50 tribal policemen led us to the kingdom. The King was a young man in his mid-thirties but his hair was as white as snow. He greeted us but never said a single word or asked who we were. We did not volunteer any information and that was where we failed, I thought. Castro, who was supposed to stand up and say something as a commander, never uttered a single word. Nghidipo and I were looking to him for leadership but he failed us. My thoughts were, if we had spoken out and told the King and his men about ourselves, they might have listened and possibly let us go. We said nothing but sat there like fools.

Eventually a force of police arrived. Nghidipo and I went for our weapons which were concealed under our clothes. Castro, however, stopped us from doing anything 'silly', as he termed it. We stopped dead in our tracks and the police immediately drew and trained their guns on us. Others came forward to search us. The King was shocked when he saw that we had guns and radios concealed under our clothes. He stared at us open-mouthed in disbelief. 'Oh! these are really dangerous people!' he guffawed loudly, though he was not amused. The police collected our weapons and other items then led us outside.

The police searched all our luggage but found no more weapons. They did, however, find some documents, but because we had dumped our things together they could not pin the documents to any one of us. They were interested in the suitcase where they found the documents. To find out to whom it belonged, they sat us down, mingled with some locals. Then they brought in Eva, a trained dog, to sniff out the owner. She stopped beside Castro, then sat down barking. She put her paws on his shoulders and barked again. The police reshuffled us and then sent in Eva once more. She did the same as before when she came to Castro. Castro tried to deny that the suitcase was his, but Eva had already incriminated him.

The police put leg irons on us, handcuffed us and threw us into their vehicles. I landed on my side in the back of the van and that was how I travelled. Two armed policemen got in with me then bang! the door was shut behind them. We set out on the long and bumpy journey back to Rundu. Now Castro has got the lift he wanted, I thought to myself.

They removed our leg irons at the Rundu police station but left the handcuffs on. I was led into a workshop where a car had its bonnet open. I was pushed in front of one policeman while another was busy fixing an electric rod onto the battery of the car. Pointing to the rod, the senior policeman told me to tell the truth. He wanted to know who I was and where I came from. I gave him my assumed name and told him that I was coming from Uutokota Hospital where I had visited a relative of mine and that I originally came from Oukwanyama. Without any warning, he grabbed the rod and poked me with it on my right hip, saying: 'I warned you to tell the truth!' A sensational pain swept through my body and I thought I was going to drop to the ground. Before I recovered he asked the names of my friends. He jabbed my right side. I screamed in pain – my head was now throbbing and I did not know where I was.

Before long, David Hamunime and Jonas Shimweefeleni were brought into the same workshop. They were part of the group which was to go to the south and they had been arrested in the SWANLA recruitment compound. Their arrival saved me from further electric shocks. I was led away to be locked up and they were taken through the same process.

When I had been arrested in Angola, I was able to stick to my lies because I was alone and there was nobody to contradict me. Here we were; a group with a common purpose. More than one arrest means giving everything away. One refuses to reveal the secret but the other confesses. Though we did not seem to have revealed our mission as yet, the police had an advantage over us. They were convinced that they had the right people. It was just a matter of time before one of us let the cat out of the bag.

Towards the evening of 27 March all five of us were taken into a yard between the workshop and the police cells. They asked us as a group who we were and what our mission was. They had by now established that we came from abroad as they had found a copy of the *Zambian Times*. After we looked at each other and gave them no answer, one policeman suggested that we be thrown into the river for the crocodiles to have a feast. This was a practice favoured by the Portuguese and I took it seriously when I heard it mentioned here by a South African policeman. They must have learned it from their neighbours in Angola.

After the long and fruitless group-questioning session, they decided to call the Portuguese who were at Calais across the river in Angola. They wanted to hand us over to the Portuguese and wash their hands of the responsibility, knowing that the Portuguese would deal with us ruthlessly – during the 1960s this was a common practice. After a while, a South African police helicopter brought the Portuguese police captain in charge of Calais. He brought an interpreter with him. The South African Police told him that we were Angolans arrested on Namibian soil and that they were officially handing us over to him. Through his interpreter, the Portuguese captain established that we were not Angolans but Namibians. Having realised the trick the South African Police wanted to play on him, he became angry and said he would be burdened with nothing Namibian.

Disappointed at the rebuff they received from the Portuguese captain, the police contacted Pretoria to send an aircraft to take us to South Africa. A Dakota belonging to the South African Police force arrived on the morning of 29 March, 1966. It took off at roughly eleven o'clock with the five of us on board: Leonard Shuuya Awala, alias Castro; Nghidipo Jesaja Haufiku; David Hamunime; Jonas Shimweefeleni; and myself.

14

Interrogation and torture

The Dakota touched down at No 1 Voortrekkerhoogte Air Force base, Pretoria. The door of the plane opened and looking down I saw two columns of uniformed South African Police, all armed with sten sub-machine guns (the scene reminded me of events in Lubango, Angola in 1961). Handcuffed and in leg irons, we descended the steps into waiting Special Branch cars. We sped through the Pretoria streets and came to a halt in front of a huge and ugly looking building. A Special Branch man got out and knocked on the outside of a gate. A flap in the door opened and after some discussions we were driven through a series of gates. In the prison yard they removed our leg irons but left the handcuffs on and ordered us to proceed towards yet another gate. Someone on the other side let us through. A big prison warder who had the face of a bulldog, thinking that we were South Africans, shouted to us in Zulu to run up the stairs. He herded us up the stairs of the first and second floors using his enormous stomach to push us and dishing out a stream of abuse as we went. 'Why do they bring this lot here? They should have shot them on the spot,' he shouted.

We had heard of Pretoria Central prison – where people are executed every Friday. I assumed we were there and already condemned to death. But we were later to discover we were in the Pretoria Local prison.

Pretoria Local was a very intimidating place. The dimly lit corridors were frightening and the heavy steel doors with peep-holes in the middle were a haunting menace to those locked within. The constant jingle of keys was a reminder that we were being watched all the time.

All five of us were bundled into one cell which measured about ten feet by seven feet with threadbare, filthy and lice-infested blankets. Beside two buckets, one containing drinking water, the other used as a latrine, there was nothing else in the cell. The peep-hole in the steel door was intimidating, especially when there was an eye peeping through – it felt as if someone was aiming a gun at your heart. The whole atmosphere was threatening and we saw danger everywhere, even in the blankets we were sleeping in.

We were not given any food our first night in Local – by then we had been given no food for over 48 hours. The next morning they gave us soft maize meal porridge. It was watery and tasteless and despite my hunger I could not force myself to eat the stuff. None of us had been in prison long enough to know all the written and unwritten prison laws and regulations. The mats and blankets we were given the night before were supposed to be neatly rolled up throughout the day which we failed to do, and when an officer came for the inspection, he claimed that our cell was dirty and we were to be deprived of our meals for a day.

We were also expected to clean our cell and stand to attention when the officers passed in front of our cell door. We were told that we could make complaints but these were hardly listened to. We had a lot to worry about in anticipating what was to follow. Any footsteps, jingling of keys, opening and closing of doors in our wing made us uncomfortable because it could mean trouble. Each one of us kept thinking to himself: Will they come for me? The Special Branch, however, did not turn up for about four or five days.

On the 4 or 5 April 1966 they came for their first quarry. It was in the middle of the night when I heard the now familiar but terrifying jingle of keys. The flap covering the hole in the door opened and a menacing eye peered through. The keys rattled in the door and it was flung open. I felt my heart pounding and thought the end had come. 'Staan op! Staan op! (Stand up!)' a Special Branch man in the doorway shouted, and we all scrambled to our feet, bumping into one another in the process.

'Wie is Castro? (Who is Castro?)' the man in front of the others in the doorway wanted to know.

'I am,' Castro answered from the far end of the cell. But for some reason they had it in their heads that Castro was a big bearded man, which he was not. We were all clean-shaven because we did not want to be recognised as SWAPO members. I had one disadvantage – I was the tallest man of the group and was thus very conspicuous. I felt nervous as I knew that I might be singled out.

'Wie is jy? (Who are you?)' asked one of them, pointing at me. Before I could answer, he grabbed my arm and pushed me towards the door. Others – they were about five or six – pushed me back into the cell. Falling backward I protested that I was not the Castro they wanted. 'Waar is Castro? (Where is Castro?)' another one asked. There appeared to be no one in charge of the pack and even after Castro stepped forward as an indication that he was the man they were looking for, they still were not satisfied. One of them went to Castro, measured him up, slapped him in the face, and then said, 'Jy lieg! (You lie!)'

How they knew the name Castro was a mystery to all of us because we all had assumed names and none of our real identities were known to them at that time. The Special Branch man turned away from him and surveyed the rest of us.

'That is Castro over there!' one of them said, pointing and beckoning to me.

'Hey you, what is your name?' he wanted to know from me.

'I am Joseph,' I told him. I was again pushed towards the door and pulled through. Four or so hands went for my arms while others went for my trousers. They frog-marched me through the dark corridors, down the stairs in the yard and then pushed me into a waiting car. 'What is your name?' asked a man in the car, who must have been their boss.

'I am Joseph,' I told him.

'You are not Castro?' he asked.

'No,' I replied.

He ordered them to take me back to the cell and to bring Castro instead. I passed Castro on the way to the cell. I did not see him again until the day I was taken to the interrogation chambers in May.

Days went by and the four of us, Nghidipo Haufiku, David Hamunime, Jonas Shimweefeleni and myself, were left wondering what had happened to Castro. We became accustomed to prison life. Every morning we would roll up our bedding, stand to attention for the inspection and wait for the medicine man to do his rounds shouting: 'Muti! Muti!' (Zulu word for medicine). Pretoria has a cold climate, yet we were made to shower in cold water and given only 15 minutes' exercise. We had nothing to do but wait for our turn for interrogation to come.

About a week or so after Castro had disappeared the Special Branch came for Hamunime. He too, like Castro before him, never came back. As we knew little about courts, let alone interrogations, we believed that they must both be dead and it was just a matter of time before they came for us. Having been born and brought up under the apartheid system and knowing a lot about its injustices and having already gone

133

through electric shock treatment at Rundu, we did not expect to get any fair treatment at the hands of the South African Police.

The three of us remaining, Haufiku, Shimweefeleni and myself, nevertheless decided to deny all knowledge of having done any military training and to say that we were returning home because we were starved and badly treated. We believed we had built a strong and watertight defence. After another week they came for Shimweefeleni. He never returned and Nghidipo and I used to joke between us that we would be the only survivors of the group. But towards the end of the first week in May they came for him too and I was left alone. I was left searching my mind why I was the last to face execution and wondering when they would come for me.

Before I went to prison I thought I would not survive a minute in jail. But after a month and a half in Pretoria Local prison I found myself still alive and determined to carry on living until the day they executed me. But I used to have horrible nightmares – I still do – of falling into bottomless pits, and I also lost all sense of time.

They came for me at the end of the second week in May. The jingle of the keys, the footsteps approaching and then the flap in the door being replaced by the eye – none of this worried me much because by now it was routine. But when the key rattled in the door, it rattled through my whole body and I thought my end had come at long last. The door was flung open and three men entered the cell. 'Hey! Staan op! (Stand up!)' I jumped up and waited.

'What is your name?'

'Shityuwete,' I said.

'Come,' they all grabbed me, pushed me through the door, frogmarched me along the corridor as before, on down the stairs, across the yard and then pushed me head first into a waiting car. Two Special Branch men got in, one on either side, and we drove out of Pretoria Local into the street. We passed the Union Buildings to our left and headed for the centre of Pretoria and the Kompol building, headquarters of the Security Branch.

Kompol has been the scene of many an interrogation. Before me had gone Bram Fischer, Nelson Mandela, Robert Sobukwe and many others. The sign hanging from the ceiling in the interrogation chamber read: 'The truth, nothing but the truth is spoken here!' This was brought to my attention before I was told to sit down on the chair reserved for me in the centre of the chamber. The time was approximately 10 pm.

Captain Cornelius 'Rooi Rus' (Red Russian) Swanepoel had just arrived for the evening session. There were comings and goings of policemen but there were always about 7 or 8 police in the chamber at any one time. The chamber was divided into two sections. The big chamber was where much of the activities took place. There were pipes for suspending people and maps of various countries and pictures of guns on the walls. The small chamber consisted of a table and two chairs, one for the interrogator, the other for the interrogated.

'Praat jy Afrikaans?' This was thrown in my direction by Warrant Officer Erasmus. When I did not answer he asked if I spoke English. I kept mum, as though I did not understand or speak the languages, because to do so would invite direct interrogation and the writing of my own statement, which would be difficult to deny later. They called in Eino, a black policeman from Namibia, to act as interpreter.

'Ask him when he last spoke to Sam Nujoma by phone.'

'I did not find it necessary as we were always together,' I told them.

'Then we will make arrangements for you to speak to him now,' said Swanepoel.

I could not understand what he meant. I was confused and asked where Nujoma was.

'In Dar es Salaam, where else do you think?' Swanepoel said, confusing me still further. I did not say anything but sat quietly to see what happened next.

A small table was moved beside me. A box with wires attached to either side was placed on the table. A basin of water with a cloth in it was placed in front of me. Eino, the black policeman, was ordered to blindfold me with the wet cloth. When he had finished I felt them tying my legs to the front legs of the chair and then my arms to the back of it. All of a sudden I heard piercing screams from the adjacent chamber. 'One of your friends is already talking to Nujoma,' I was told. Then they started fiddling with my ears, my fingers and my toes. Before I knew what was happening a sudden and excruciating pain swept through my whole body. I felt as if I was thrown high in the air and I tried to struggle free but I was bound tightly to the chair. When I came round I was lying face down with the chair still on my back. I do not know how long I had been there, but by now it was morning.

'How was the conversation? What did Nujoma tell you – to tell the whole truth, eh?' I heard someone in the group asking. Mockery before the execution, I thought to myself, and now I grasped what Swanepoel had meant by talking to Nujoma by phone.

Someone shouted that time was up for stage one. We were now ready for stage two. They picked me up from the floor, undid the blindfold and freed my arms and legs.

'Come over here,' a policeman who I had not seen before beckoned me to where he was. An expert at stage two, I wondered.

'Squat here kaffir!' he ordered, pushing me down.

A broomstick was thrust behind my knees through my squatting legs and tied to my wrists. He ordered me to get up, knowing well that I could not. In my effort to rise I fell forward onto my face. More laughter and cursing. They picked me up and I was placed between two tables. Suspended by the broomstick, I hung upside down. A little push would send me swinging and invite more laughter and insults.

'Hey, freedom fighter, how can you fight for your freedom hanging upside down? Guerilla tactics, eh? Where were you trained?' They clearly didn't expect answers to all these questions they were throwing at me.

'What is your mission – to come and kill Boers eh?' Another push and more abuse. I was left there for a long time – maybe six or seven hours.

'Het hy al gepraat? (Has he talked?)' demanded Swanepoel when he returned. 'Take him off and show him the pipes,' he barked, when he heard that I had not uttered a single word.

It was evening when the stage three experts took over and I was led to the pipes which were high up on the wall. A chair was pulled up and I was ordered to stand on it. Handcuffs were thrown over the pipes and click, in went my wrists. They removed the chair and left me suspended from the pipes. Fortunately for me I am six feet tall and my toes just touched the floor. Yet it was good fun for them – a free-for-all because any policeman passing by was free to give me a shove which would send me swinging to and fro. To some I was a punchbag, while others joined in with thick sticks. I found stage three unbearable. With electric shocks one does not know whether one is alive or dead. Here I was wide awake and could feel every pain they inflicted on me. Defenceless and surrounded by a bunch of bullies and sadists, after three or four hours hanging there I could bear it no longer and let out a powerful kick with both feet. It caught one unsuspecting young white policeman on the chest and sent him hurtling to the floor. Others scurried away, at least for the moment, before reassembling with shouts of 'Hy kan skop! Hy kan skop! (He kicks!)'

The young man on the floor got up fuming with rage, his face as red as a tomato. 'Jy sal kak kaffir! Ek sweer vir jou. (You will shit kaffir, I swear!)' he shouted and rushed forward like a raging bull to a matador.

I was to regret my action. Within a minute or so the chamber was full of policemen wanting to see how I kicked. They came at me like a plague of ants, with fists, sticks and anything they could find.

'Wat gaan aan? (What's going on?)' Swanepoel, unaware of what had happened, came in. 'Stand back!' he commanded and everyone moved away from me. Slowly the Rooi Rus made his way through the throng of silent policemen who were now standing in a semi-circle around me. Looking at him I could not help but wonder who nicknamed him the Red Russian. Red Devil would have been more appropriate, I thought. His cropped hair, his bulbous red nose and his tiny piercing serpentine eyes made him look like the Devil himself. The only difference between them was that the latter is depicted black with hooves.

He demanded to know what the policemen were all doing there. 'Out!' he ordered those who were not supposed to be there and immediately there was a jam at the door. He then turned to those guarding me and asked whether I had soiled myself yet.

'Nee Kaptein', he was told.

With arms akimbo he turned and surveyed me.

'Watch out Captain, he kicks!' he was warned.

'Jy kan skop eh?' he asked as he smashed one of his huge gnarled fists into my stomach, close to the diaphragm. Darkness fell over me. Voices became distant and soon everything became quiet. When I came to I was lying on the floor with my legs in irons. It was about six or seven in the morning and Swanepoel had gone home to Johannesburg.

I spent the day in leg irons on the floor of the big chamber waiting for the interrogation to begin again. Towards early evening the leg irons were removed and I was told to stand motionless in a corner. Although I had not eaten for 3 days, was desperate to sleep and was very weak, anxiety about what was to follow kept me alert. I passed the time by rehearsing what I would say under interrogation.

Late that night Warrant Officer Van Rensberg came. He had been given the task of conducting practical interrogation. Unlike the Portuguese Police, who are notorious for their crude torture methods, the South African Police use every trick in the book – from brute force and coercion to sweet talk. Van Rensberg used the sweet talk method – we came to nickname him the Priest for this approach. He told me he would help me if I made a statement – he did not want me to be handed over to the likes of Erasmus or Van Rooyen. The latter was the one I had kicked and would have been more than grateful to find me placed under his thumb. Van Rensberg knew this and tried to use it to his advantage.

When we sat down he started by asking me when and why I joined SWAPO, who recruited me, what SWAPO stands for, who recruited me for military training, when I left the country, who my instructors were, what kinds of guns we used and what my mission was. His approach did not impress me. He was clearly surprised by my resistance and could not hide his annoyance. 'You are either stupid or ignorant of what we do to people like you,' he said.

Eino, to support him, chipped in, 'People are killed here and no questions asked. You can fall down the stairs or fall out of the window and that is the end of the story.'

My indifference made them change their tactics. 'Your friends have already told on you. There is no point in not telling us all you know,' they said. I replied that I was pleased they already knew everything as it would save me the trouble of telling them. I repeated my refusal to give a statement. I was told that everyone before me had come in unwilling to make a statement but had ended up not wanting to stop talking, even when they were told to stop. 'They continued singing like canaries,' they said. I was told that they could make me talk and confess my sins, the only problem was they could not forgive my transgressions. Only the courts could do that.

The interrogation lasted three or four hours. Van Rensberg took a statement from me, in which I was careful not to incriminate myself or anyone else. I was made to stand in my corner again and the statement was taken to Swanepoel.

They spent five days trying to make me confess. Interrogations came only at night. I spent the days standing in the corner and often, towards evening, they would use one or the other softening-up methods to prepare me for the night ahead. I gave them nothing they wanted. All the statements were taken to Swanepoel for his scrutiny. Mine finished up in the waste paper basket. He wanted facts not bullshit. He decided to take over the interrogation himself and swore to elicit the information he wanted.

On the sixth night of mental torture and sleep deprivation I was back in leg irons. Swanepoel was conducting stage 4 of the softening up process. 'Now I want you to exercise, precisely as you were doing in Moscow, or was it Algiers? Oh no, I mean Cairo,' he said.

I was ordered to pick up a heavy chain and to pace up and down but due to the weight of the chain I only managed to hobble a few steps forward.

'Show him how to do it,' Swanepoel ordered one of his boys as he left the room.

Putting a stick in the loop of the leg irons, the policeman ordered me to move back and pulled me over. I landed on my back with a thud. Another policeman joined in to help hold the stick at the other end. They started running, pulling me round the room. Then the rest of the gang, some armed with broomsticks and hosepipes, joined in, chasing after me, hitting out wildly. Those who could not find something with which to beat me used their boots to kick out at me. Most blows landed on my hands and arms because I used them to protect my face – the only part of my body I could protect. But some kicks caught me on the jaw, sending my head rolling on one side.

'Come on! Get up and fight, Kaffir!' All were shouting, intensifying their attacks on the 'terrorist' on the floor. How I survived such beatings and came out without even a broken limb was a miracle, if there is such a thing. I would not have believed that my body could stand up to the beatings and torture meted out to me. The pain was unbearable at first, but as they continued it was as if my nervous system stopped registering their blows.

When they stopped I could hardly move. They left me lying for dead in a corner. The first thought that entered my head was a wish to die, there and then. But death eluded me. I remembered a story from the Bible – that when trouble came people would want mountains to bury them and the earth to open its mouth to swallow them up, but the mountains would run away and earth would disappear.

I was taken into the small chamber. Half walking and half carried I entered to find myself face to face with Swanepoel, the beast himself. A second captain and Eino the interpreter were also present. Having been dragged round the room and badly beaten I could barely sit unaided. The pain was severe, I ached all over and felt as though someone had thrown burning coals over me. I longed to dive into a pool of cold water to cool my aching limbs and wanted to tell them so, but to do so would indicate that I was weakening.

Swanepoel offered me a cigarette which I declined. He then began asking where I was militarily trained. I denied having been trained in any military activities. He picked up the statement I had made earlier, looked at it and slowly began tearing it into tiny shreds. With his piercing eyes fixed on me, he chucked the pieces into a waste paper basket. Leaning forward, like a cobra preparing to strike, he hissed then let out a terrifying growl. He grabbed me by the neck with both hands and began to squeeze me, swearing that he would kill me there and then. I began to see stars and when he let go my neck felt as if it was released from an iron grip. I no longer wanted to die and now struggled for air. His stare petrified me and now I wanted to tell him that I was ready to make a statement. But I could not utter a single word. There were debates going on within me, one side telling me to get on with it, the other saying no I must not give in to his brutalities.

Wasting no time, Swanepoel smashed one of his fists into my face. It caught me squarely between the eyes and sent me falling backward. Another powerful punch caught me from behind. It was thrown by the other captain who had placed himself behind me earlier. Back and forth I went, like some kind of punchbag. Again I began to see stars and everything in that small room reeled and swayed from side to side. Then the stars went out and the darkness fell. Everything was peaceful and presently I was flying over high mountains and beautiful valleys. And then, there down below was a sparkling, placidly flowing river. Splash, splash, splash! I went in. I was swimming peacefully and felt refreshed.

When I came round I was lying in a pool of water which had been thrown over me when I lost consciousness. They helped me back into the chair. On the table were stacks of papers. Some were statements from my comrades who were interrogated before me. Beside them was a bulging file. On closer inspection I could see it was my file. It contained my correspondence with my friend Miguel Neves in Angola. But I was struck by another document, marked top secret/strictly confidential. It had come from the Zambian/Tanzanian border post, was sent to Luanda in Angola and then to Pretoria. It contained all the particulars of my group when we crossed the border, including the type of vehicle we travelled in and its number plates.

Swanepoel did not try to hide these documents from me. His intention was, of course, for me to see them and believe he knew everything. He desperately wanted a confession from me and would get it at any cost. 'Look, Kaffir,' he said, patting the stacks of statements on the table, 'All your friends have finished making statements. You would also have finished yours but because you are stubborn and stupid you are making things difficult for yourself.'

I replied that unless they wanted me to lie, which I did not think was a good thing, I had told them all I knew.

Whack! went his fist in my face. Once again everything dimmed and I was out for the count. When I came round it was early morning. I spent the day in the corner as usual and the evening in leg irons. At night I was taken to the small chamber and given electric shocks to the ears, fingers and toes.

Then they brought in Castro, who looked the worse for wear and despondent.

'Tell him to tell the truth!' Swanepoel commanded.

Hesitantly Castro began, 'You must tell these bosses everything you know. I have told them everything I know.' He paused.

I was dumbfounded to hear this from our second-in-command. I asked what he had told them.

Before he could answer a heavy blow landed on the back of my head. 'You don't ask questions here. You do as you are told!' shouted Swanepoel.

I said I did not know what Castro was talking about and held my hands over my head, expecting another blow. It did not come. Instead more electric shocks were given and Castro was told to continue.

'I know that you don't understand, but I believe that these bosses want to help us,' he said.

'In what way?' I asked.

'No questions!' I was reminded.

'They will help us to prevent communism from coming to

our country and for us not to be prosecuted.' He paused. 'I told them that you know everything.'

'I know what?' Jumping up to go for him I was caught by several hands and pressed unceremoniously back into my chair, with a punch on the jaw from Swanepoel for good measure. Castro said that as a secretary I was privy to all confidential information and secrets. He was then asked to leave. At the door he turned and said that he had told them how many people had already penetrated back into the country and how many groups were to follow ours. With that he left.

Despite my physical pain and the vice-like grip that held me to the chair I struggled to free myself to go after him. I was appalled and enraged by his arrogance and irresponsibility. I could have wrung his neck there and then. How dare he endanger the lives of so many people and expose me to these brutes?

Swanepoel told me to relax so that we could get down to the business of confession. 'Mr Secretary,' he began, 'I want you to tell me whether you are now prepared to co-operate or whether I will have to make you talk.'

'If you mean killing me, get on with it,' I said.

'No, no, we are not going to kill you. What I mean is that we have methods of making people who refuse to co-operate change their minds. If you co-operate now we will not bring these methods into operation.'

I said I had nothing more to tell him and that if he thought he could make me talk, then he could go ahead. By now I had reached a stage of indifference to physical torture and mental agony. He stared at me in disbelief. He called for a recess, saying that I must have time to reconsider my decision. 'Triumph!' I shouted within myself.

That night – the seventh in the Kompol, and the second under interrogation by Swanepoel – my whole body ached. I had a bad cough and thought I had pneumonia. I felt very ill indeed. They later discovered that I had a temperature and a minor malarial attack. The room was spinning and everything was upside down. I felt as if I was lying on the ceiling and struggling to prevent myself from falling to the floor below me. The malaria bout saved me from further torture and further interrogation for the rest of the night. In my distressed feverish state I longed for comfort – someone to hold my hand and tell me that everything was alright. Instead I felt someone forcing open my mouth saying, 'This will help yòu go quickly to the Devil.' Something was popped into my mouth, followed by water. I must have passed out for the whole of the eighth day because I heard them say later that I was out for twenty-four hours.

Swanepoel was not impressed bỳ my illness. When he returned to the building he immediately ordered the resumption of my interrogation. I was still lying on the floor when they brought in Eino Ekandyo, who had been arrested two or three weeks after me. He said that he had come to tell me to tell the truth, as he had done, to save myself from further punishment. He, like Castro, appeared to have undergone very severe treatment. His legs were wobbly, his eyes were tiny blobs sunk deep in his head. Two white policemen held him on either side. Seeing me lying on the floor he must have thought I was dead. But when our eyes met he could see that not only was I alive, but I was very shocked that he should be brought there to tell me to tell the truth. I was picked up and carried to the chair where I was given more electric shock treatment.

'Tell him!' said one tall brute, prodding Ekandyo in the side. He told Ekandyo that I had refused to acknowledge the things Ekandyo said I knew about. Ekandyo hesitated then, to my surprise, said, 'What I told you was not true.'

The tall policeman grabbed him by the neck, squeezed it and lifted him off the ground. 'Why did you lie? Eh?' he demanded.

'To save myself from further electric shocks,' Ekandyo replied.

'Jou fokken Kaffir! (You fucking Kaffir!)' screamed the policeman. With the assistance of his colleagues they half-carried Ekandyo from the room.

Swanepoel looked at me with cold, venomous eyes. They freed my hands. He called for a black plastic bag to be brought. He pulled it over my head, tied it, then said: 'This is going to teach you how to tell the truth.' In my weak state I thought I was unable to move any of my limbs but immediately the bag was thrown over my head life returned to every part of my body. All the air in the bag was used in my first breath and I was choking. Like a beheaded snake I struggled and wriggled on the floor to free myself. I felt myself beginning to lose consciousness. In one last desperate effort I tore the thing off my head, coughing badly at the first breath before taking in

143

huge gulps of sweet fresh air.

Swanepoel did not give up easily, but he was running out of torture methods. As bullying didn't seem to be working, he changed tactics again. He and his men took me to a small room. He now pretended to be a reasonable person dealing with a stubborn child. He lit himself a cigarette and asked Eino, the interpreter, whether I had been given anything to eat. When the latter said that I had not, Swanepoel said, 'All you Kaffirs are the same. You can't think without a white man. You can't even think to give food to your brother.' Eino rushed off and brought me fish and chips. That was my third meal in eight days. I went for it hungrily and Swanepoel said, 'You came to kill the Boers, now you are stuffing their food. We are nice people, unlike your communist friends in Moscow.' I certainly wasn't interested in what he had to say as I eagerly carried on with my meal. Afterwards he ordered that I should be taken back to Pretoria Local prison. Although I had by then lost my faith, I found myself thanking God that I had survived. But most of all I thanked those who had trained us to withstand interrogation – training which we had taken so lightly at the time.

I believed this to be the end of my interrogation. However, it became their practice that whenever one of our cadres was picked up they were asked under interrogation if they knew anything about me and my position in the armed forces. If they admitted knowing anything about me I was taken to the Kompol buildings for further questioning. This went on until the middle of the fourth week in June 1966.

15

Detention at Leeuwkop

During April and June 1966, as detainees, we spent most of our time shuttling between Pretoria Local prison and the Kompol building for interrogation. By now, Castro had been released and was fully collaborating with the police (if, indeed, he had not been doing so before). They hoped he would be able to get Sam Nujoma for them and offered him a downpayment of R250, with a further R250 on completion! The four of us who remained from the original group had by now been joined by four others; Lazarus Haidula Zacharia (Shakala), Eino Kamati Ekandyo, Festus Nehale and Elia Ndume. We were never informed under what South African law we were arrested or detained. But after the interrogation which ended roughly in June 1966, we were all held under a 90 days' detention order. This was rescinded in September 1966, and replaced with a 180 days' detention order, which was renewed when it expired at the end of February 1967. This was done to enable the South African Parliament to pass a law known as the Terrorism Act, No. 83 of 1967, under which we were to be tried. It was made retroactive to 1962. The South Africans did not even make an official announcement of our arrests until June 1967, when Parliament was debating the Terrorism Bill.

While we were in detention events outside came to a head. In July 1966, by the casting vote of its President, the International Court of Justice rejected the case brought by Liberia and Ethiopia against the South African presence in Namibia, arguing that the two independent African countries had no legal right to bring the case. The SWAPO leadership in Dar es Salaam responded by formally declaring the armed struggle. The failure of the ICJ to decide on the case, declared SWAPO, 'Will relieve Namibians, once and for all, from any illusions they may have harboured about the UN as some kind of a saviour.' The statement announced: 'We have no alternative but to rise in arms and bring about our own liberation.'

At dawn 26 August, South African Security Police, led by Captain Swanepoel, and guided by Castro, attacked one of our newly-established military bases at Omgulumbashe, north-west Namibia. Eight helicopter gunships accompanied by a number of personnel carriers took part in the attack. The guerrillas were preparing for their breakfast when they found themselves under fire: it was a surprise and effective attack.

John Otto Nankudhu, the commander, after a brief engagement, realised the futility of withstanding a powerful enemy armed with high-powered weapons. His men were out-gunned and out-numbered. He gave an order to disperse and escape, and then made his own escape. Two guerrillas were killed and two injured and eight taken prisoner in the skirmish.

The eight combatants captured at Omgulumbashe in August were brought to Pretoria in early September 1966. To make room for the eight, and because of overcrowding in the Pretoria Local prison, our group was taken to Leeuwkop, to the south of Pretoria.

Leeuwkop (Lion's Head), was one of the most infamous prisons in South Africa. Its population was around 900-1,000 inmates – all of whom were common-law prisoners. Torture and sometimes murders were committed almost every month. Prisoners killed each other here at the instigation of the warders. They formed themselves into gangs, one of which I remember was known as B5. They had authority in certain cells where no one from other cells dared to venture.

There were no permanent political prisoners imprisoned in Leeuwkop, and those who found themselves there were usually in transit to or from Robben Island or, like ourselves, were temporarily accommodated there. We were there for about nine months and we tasted some of the harsh treatment meted out to common-law prisoners.

Leeuwkop experiences some of the coldest weather in the Transvaal. Its cells, 12 feet by 5 feet, were built with red bricks and no effort had been made to cover the walls with mortar. This made them like fridges as there was no heating. The only windows in the cells opened onto catwalks. At night and when it was really cold, warders opened windows and poured ice cold water from buckets onto sleeping and unsuspecting prisoners. Prisoners were called out of their cells naked and ordered to have cold showers in temperatures below freezing. Exercises were taken at the double.

Meals, which consisted only of maize-meal porridge in the mornings and evenings and boiled maize at lunch, were left for hours outside cell doors until really cold. Deprivation of meals at the behest of any warder was a common practice meted out to prisoners. We were held in solitary confinement, but we were able to communicate from cell to cell by shouting.

As political detainees, we were visited by a magistrate every week. He came to ask if we had any complaints or had been 'assaulted' in jail – he was only interested in assault complaints and not in our general mistreatment. During one such visit, we complained to him about our detention without trial. We should either be charged or be released, we told him to tell his government. On his next visit, he told us that we were not to be committed for trial but were detained as 'witnesses' for the state in 'protective' custody.

Protective custody; what was that? we wanted to know. To be protected from what? The magistrate found it difficult to explain this to us. But wait a minute! Was there any one amongst us who had agreed to give evidence? we asked one another. No! there was none. Then how dare they, without our consent, detain us as state witnesses?

We discussed the matter amongst ourselves. We found that we were unlawfully detained. We decided to press charges but we did not know how to go about it. We did not even know any lawyers or anybody courageous enough to take on our case. Many lawyers in South Africa were now frightened to defend political cases because they became assassins' targets. We asked the magistrate on his next visit if he could arrange something of that kind for us, but he could not. But before long, Dhlomo (not his real name), an ANC activist on his way to Robben Island, gave us the names of George Bizos and Ernest Wentzel, two Johannesburg lawyers renowned for their successes in defending political cases. They were members of the former Liberal Party of South Africa and good lawyers, Dhlomo told us. He offered to pass on our request to see them through his relative when she next visited. Unfortunately, he was soon taken away and we never knew whether or not he had conveyed the message.

On 16 September 1966, we learned that Verwoerd, the architect of apartheid, was dead, stabbed to death by Tsafendas, a parliamentary messenger. Rumours were that he was killed because he wanted to grant Namibia its independence. These rumours were never confirmed and Tsafendas was never brought to trial. The truth has never come out. John Vorster, the then Minister of Justice, renowned for his ruthlessness in dealing with his opponents (blacks knew him as Minister of Injustice), succeeded Verwoerd as Prime Minister.

On 27 September 1966, SWAPO guerrillas, in a retaliatory action for the attack on the Omgulumbashe base, attacked and burnt down government administrative offices at Oshikango on the northern border with Angola. From then on, guerrilla activities increased tremendously. South Africa responded ruthlessly by rounding up all SWAPO political leaders throughout the country. But guerrillas were pouring in from abroad and the authorities could not arrest them all.

The UN General Assembly finally took direct action on the Namibian question in October 1966, when, in Resolution 2145, it terminated South Africa's mandate and declared that the UN should administer Namibia until independence. But the Security Council – blocked by Britain and the US – failed to back up this stand, and South Africa was able to defy the UN.

Around April 1967, Lieutenant Erasmus of the Security Branch came to collect me and Nghidipo Haufiku from Leeuwkop. He took us to Pretoria, to the Kompol building, where among others waiting to greet us was Captain Swanepoel. He was pleased to see us looking well, he said. He introduced us to some of his new men as 'our best friends' and went straight to the point.

He began by telling us that we were intelligent and knew everything about SWAPO. He believed that it would be a good thing if we could co-operate with them. He said they knew very little about the activities of our organisation abroad and they wanted us to be state witnesses. In order to find out more, I asked whom were we going to give evidence against. We were to testify against our colleagues with whom we were trained. If the police knew little of their activities, why had they arrested them in the first place, we asked. They had arrested them because they were trained guerrillas.

Well, we were also trained guerrillas, and if the police thought we would be naive enough to testify against our comrades, then they were wrong, we told Swanepoel. And if they did not have enough information for convictions, then why should they bother to prosecute. We would not do the policeman's dirty work, we told him. He laughed loudly, his wolf-like laugh, and said that as the idea was new to us, he would give us time to think it over.

We were then moved from Leeuwkop back to Pretoria Local where we found about 150-200 Namibian detainees had been brought in. Among them were Ya Toivo, SWAPO's northern regional secretary; Eliaser Tuhadeleni, chairperson of the northern region; Nathaniel Maxwilili, acting president; John Ya-Otto, secretary general; Jason Mutumbulwa, information and publicity secretary; John Otto Nankudhu, commander of the Omgulumbashe Base; and many others. By shouting from cell to cell we found out that they had all been rounded up and brought to Pretoria for interrogation for their 'part' in the armed struggle. We were really disturbed to find the entire SWAPO internal leadership in detention. Other SWAPO members were detained in several prisons outside Pretoria. With Castro released and instructed to lure Nujoma to his capture or death we thought that the end had come for SWAPO as a liberation movement.

We learned from Rehabeam Olavi Nambinga that James Hamukwaya, alias Hangula Shoonyeka, who had been injured and taken prisoner in the Omgulumbashe battle, had been murdered by the police during interrogation at Kompol. His body was taken to the Pretoria Local where they hung him up in a cell and locked the door. He was 'found' the following morning by the warder on duty. The case, like many others in South African prisons, was treated as suicide.

Three days later I was taken back to Kompol and the interrogation chamber. Swanepoel, Lieutenant Ferreira and a new interpreter were waiting for me. Swanepoel repeated his proposition and I told him that my answer remained no. Before they could go any further Swanepoel received a telephone call from the state prosecutor who would take on our case, asking to see me. In their desperation for witnesses, and hoping to persuade me to agree to give evidence against my colleagues, I presumed the police must have told the prosecutor that I had already agreed to testify for the state.

Ferreira and the interpreter took me to see Oosthuizen, the prosecutor, whom they addressed as Colonel. Oosthuizen told the interpreter to 'ask' me. But what? The poor man was clearly completely in the dark. He vainly tried to say something but never managed to make himself clear and I responded vaguely.

'What did he say?' Oosthuizen asked the interpreter.

'He said nothing,' the interpreter replied.

'What do you mean, he said nothing?' asked Oosthuizen baffled.

'He said nothing because I did not know what to ask him,' the interpreter stuttered. I could not help but enjoy the communication break-down.

'Ask him if he has agreed to testify for the state,' Oosthuizen told the interpreter.

To his surprise, I said my answer to the police and to him was the same – no.

'Didn't the police tell you that?' I said mockingly. 'If they have not, I want to make it clear here and now that I have never agreed nor will I ever agree to give evidence for the state.'

Disappointed and angry at the snub, Oosthuizen ordered that I be taken back to prison.

Ferreira, exasperated, grabbed me, one hand on the back of my collar and the other on the back of my trousers. He frog-marched me out of the office and pushed me into the lift. Blows started raining on me in the lift and as we emerged from it. He frog-marched me to a different interrogation chamber occupied by a Captain Gericke, and told him that I refused to be a state witness and he thought it was time I was taught a lesson.

Captain Gericke showed hatred and venomous disgust – he had taken my refusal as a personal insult. He found my file, put it on the table and was about to go for my neck when a senior officer, Vial, in the prosecution team, came in. He had watched Ferreira frog-marching me out of the office and suspected that they planned assaulting me. Vial demanded to know what I was doing there and ordered that I immediately be taken back to prison. On my way back I passed Nghidipo who was clearly in for the same treatment. As we passed each other, I told him that I had not agreed to testify and asked him not to be turned into a state witness. I was pleased when he came back and told me that he had refused to become a turncoat.

Some days later, my cell door opened, and Lieutenant Ferreira came in with two colleagues. He had witnessed not only the scene with Oosthuizen but was also present the day Nghidipo and I were brought back from Leeuwkop when Swanepoel asked us to testify against our comrades. He hated my stubbornness and now he was making his last effort to persuade me to give evidence. I was standing with my back against the wall at the far end of the cell.

'Hello!' he greeted on entering. He had come to find out whether I had changed my mind, he said.

I told him that I had not and added that no amount of pressure would make me give in. At this he told his two colleagues to leave and close the door behind him. With clenched fists like a cat ready to pounce on its prey, he slowly came towards me. Like a cornered animal, I watched his every move. When he reached the centre of the cell, he charged at me. I jumped away from the wall and he crashed against it. He screamed with pain and rushed at me again. I avoided him and he again crashed into the wall.

His curses and screams brought in his colleagues. They wanted to get at me and teach me how to respect 'bosses' but he stopped them before they could do any damage to me. With a venomous look in his eyes, he said I was a fool and swore that he would see to it that I was hanged or got a minimum of 20 years' imprisonment. There were many of my brothers willing to testify, he said, banging the door behind him. Neither he nor anyone else from Kompol ever came back again. I was relieved that they had decided to leave me alone at last.

Many of my comrades were also approached to testify and like Nghidipo and myself refused to do so. We did not want to turn Judases and betray the principles we were fighting for. Nor were we prepared to sell out our comrades.

There was nothing as important as news and information in prison. And there was nothing as difficult as getting it. One had to devise means – despite insurmountable odds – to obtain information. We were all novices in these matters and were kept under even closer surveillance than the other prisoners. To make matters worse, we were only given one minute's exercise in the corridor of our wing, under the sharp eyes of warders. We were not allowed to meet or talk to anyone. But we managed to befriend the common-law prisoners who brought us meals and cleaned the passage, and who were sometimes ordered to shave our hair and clean our cells.

I befriended a young fellow whom we nick-named Nylon. Every time I was given my one minute exercise, he would pop into my cell as if he was cleaning it. He would then leave me a piece of a newspaper – at times advertisements and useless. In order to receive commodities with which I could trade for news, I started 'smoking'. Nylon, in addition to newspapers, also brought me zollos, hand rolled cigars. Thus I became a source of information, news gatherer and newscaster and my cell became known as 'Ombako P' – 'Radio P' (for Prison).

After lock up, Maxwilili's booming voice would vibrate

through the corridor: 'Helao!' he would shout, 'What's the news today?' I would then struggle to put up my broadcasting platform. My cell had two windows (standard for every cell) which were just below the ceiling . One window opened onto the corridor and the other overlooked the yard at the back. There was a little platform under the window facing the corridor, where I had my bucket of water. To reach the window, I had to put the sisal mat – part of the bedding – on top of the bucket. I would then add the blankets and the chamber pot to complete the platform before pulling myself up to reach the window.

Before I climbed up, I had to be given the all clear sign that there was no warder on our floor by our signal man near the entrance to our wing. Otherwise I would be in big trouble which would cost me a day's meal. Sometimes the signal man failed to hear a warder on night duty, who would creep stealthily to my cell door then shout: 'Thula! (Shut up!)' – sending me unceremoniously tumbling down to the floor, followed by my platform, chamber pot and all. For the rest of the evening, I would be busy mopping up the mess. After I finished broadcasting, Ya-Otto, who was in the adjacent wing, would then broadcast to other wings on our floor.

One day in June 1967, when I returned to my cell from my one-minute exercise, I found a piece of newspaper tucked away in my hiding place. Nylon had delivered. I had a quick look at it and there in two inch bold letters were the words: '37 South West Africans Face Death Sentence!' That was a scoop! I had picked up very important news! I wanted the warders to leave. I could not wait for Maxwilili to ask me what the news was! I wanted to set up my platform immediately. This was the news my colleagues and I needed and wanted to hear – that we were to be tried at last. By now, our numbers in Pretoria Local had swelled to over 200. Some of us, like Nghidipo, Hamunime, Shimweefeleni and myself, had spent more than 550 days in detention.

Due to the excitement of the news item I received that day, the afternoon seemed to drag on. I tuned my ears in order to hear the concertina gate leading to our wing closing. Grrrrrtch! It closed and my platform went up. I called to the signal man. The coast was clear, he declared, and Ombako P went on the air. I had special eenghundana (news) today, I announced. Everybody listened attentively. The news was shocking but was received with great interest. It also provoked a lot of anxieties as well as many questions like: How many were we in detention? Why was the number to be charged so small? Who were likely to be charged? and so forth. I was unable to satisfactorily answer all these and many other related questions as the newspaper gave no names or the date of the trial. We spent much of the night speculating.

16

The Terrorism Trial

After the news that only 37 of about 250 Namibians arrested and detained by the police were to be charged, there blew an air of suspicion amongst us. The feeling was that, if only 37 were to be charged, then the rest must surely be used to give evidence against the 37. To give evidence would be viewed as betrayal; not to do so was patriotism. Who were the 'traitors'? The question rang in almost everybody's mind. Almost everybody wanted to be one of the 37 patriots.

The morning of 27 June 1967 brought the answers to our questions. Immediately after breakfast, cell doors on our floor were flung open and, as expected of every prisoner, I jumped up, stood to attention and waited for the inspection. However, instead I heard names being shouted out in the passage and people answering 'Yes!' when they heard their names, and the warders shouting 'Haak! Haak!' to urge people to be quick.

I tuned my ears and listened attentively. 'Eliaser Tuhadeleni! Nathaniel Maxwilili! Hermann Ya Toivo!' the person calling out the names shouted. 'John Ya-Otto! Jason Mutumbulwa!' he went on. More names, then, 'Helao Shityuwete!' My heart jumped with elation – not because I wanted to be tried, but because that meant I was not one of the 'traitors'. 'Yes!' I shouted in response. Warders were going from cell to cell pulling out those who answered the call, with 'Kom! jou fokken terroris!' I was pulled out of mine and was passed from one warder to another towards the concertina gate at the end of the passage.

Warders and security men lined the stairs from our floor to the yard in front of the offices. I was pushed into a blue van with wire mesh. It was surrounded by armed men and barking dogs. Inside were a group of some of my comrades who had been called out first. Though I used to 'broadcast' to them, we had had no chance of meeting one another before – this was the first time we had ever met in Pretoria. What a place and circumstance for old friends to meet! Though we were heading for a trial that carried death sentences, the joy of meeting old and new comrades was overwhelming. It was a moment of laughter and tears. We hugged and shook hands despite the fact that there was no room to manoeuvre in the van. The greetings continued as more people arrived.

Before the van moved out of the yard, Maxwilili started a freedom song and everybody in the van joined in enthusiastically:

Nde mu lombwela, nde mu longela
Ota mu manguluka
Ota mu manguluka.
Ileni amushe! Ileni Vakwaita!
Ileni ko SWAPO nena
Opo mu manguluke.

I told you, I worked for you
You shall be free
You shall be free.
Come you all! Come you soldiers!
Come to SWAPO today
That you be free.

The van turned and slowly pulled out of the yard. Outside the gates, the sun greeted our emergence from the tomb with a huge smile. We responded by smiling back – thankful that after many days we were again able to see sunshine. The 'outside' world had just woken up and it appeared that everybody was racing in one direction or another.

Immediately the air was filled with sirens. Police cars screeched all around us. Three motorcycle outriders and two police cars preceded the van, there were riders on either side of the van and three police cars brought up the rear. The convoy turned towards the city. We followed the road along to the Kompol building, passing the Union Buildings, the administrative seat of South Africa. The sirens continued whining. Private cars were forced off the street. We inside carried on with our freedom songs. People on their different errands stopped to look at what was happening. We raised our clenched fists in greeting to those close enough to see us inside.

Our escort turned into another road and stopped in front of a high wire fence. A gate opened and our van drove past two lines of armed policemen and barking dogs. It stopped and reversed into a dimly lit basement under a huge building. The steel door opened before the van stopped. 'Haak! Haak!' we were unceremoniously pulled out of the van and led up steep winding dark stairs, emerging into a corridor with cells on either side. Each of us was pushed into a cell. The steel doors were banged behind us and we heard the screech of keys as the cell doors were locked in turn.

A few moments later, the doors were opened and we were issued with indictment papers. I, like many of my colleagues, did not understand what they were for. They were written in both English and Afrikaans. I looked at mine and found it unintelligible, folded it, put it on the floor beside me and waited for something exciting to happen.

I did not have to wait long. The cells were opened again and we were dragged out and pushed up some steps. The steps led into a chamber packed with people – we were in the magistrates' courts. Our entrance caused a flurry as people jostled for places to have a better view of the 'terrorists'. Cameras flashed, journalists scribbled in their notebooks. Police stiffened and held their sten guns as if ready to shoot. Had we already been sentenced to death? I wondered. This could be the firing squad, but why inside the building? My mind raced here and there. Instead of being frightened, I was curious and watched almost every movement in court. I wanted to take note of everything taking place there before I died. No, it was not the firing squad. It was the 'preliminary' hearing, I was told. What was that? Rituals before the shots were fired? No, it was the first hearing before one was committed to be tried in a high court.

Those who came to the court room to get a glimpse of real 'terrorists' were not disappointed. We looked awful. Many of us were all in tatters with no shoes and dressed in shorts. My shoes and those of many others had been taken away the day we were arrested and we never got them back. All our belongings were confiscated and were to be exhibited in court as evidence of our wrongdoing.

A bench was reserved for us in front of the gallery facing the magistrate's chair. A security policeman ordered us to line up along the bench. He arranged us this way and that way until he satisfied himself. We stood there shivering and waited for the magistrate to enter. The state prosecutor and his team sat on our right in their dark robes. We had no defence.

Another flurry of activity heralded the magistrate. I watched him walking in and sitting down on his bench while the court stood up. He had a smile of satisfaction on his face and an air of arrogance about him. He made a quick survey of us and asked the prosecution to present its case. The prosecutor stood up to read out our names and the charges against us. I recognised him as Oosthuizen, the man I was taken to in the Kompol buildings who wanted me to be a state witness. What was the relationship between the police and the prosecuting team? I wondered. Were they one and the same? If so, it was certainly a rotten system of 'justice'.

He began by reading out our names followed by charges and the 'terroristic' activities each one of us had allegedly committed. The case was known as:

The State v. Tuhadeleni and 36 Others.

Accused No 1 Eliaser Tuhadeleni (Kaxumba Kandola);
Accused No 2 John Otto Nankudhu;
Accused No 3 Simeon Shixungileni (Kambo);
Accused No 4 Julius Shilongo (Kashuku);
Accused No 5 Lazarus Zachariah (Shakala);
Accused No 6 David Hamunime (Keenogoya);
Accused No 7 Helao Joseph Shityuwete (Kandindima);
Accused No 8 Eino Kamati Ekandjo (Maquestions);
Accused No 9 Festus Nehale (Ndengu);
Accused No 10 Nghidipo Jesaja Haufiku (Kambwa);
Accused No 11 Immanuel August Shifidi;
Accused No 12 Kaleb Hanganee Tjipahura (Day by Day);
Accused No 13 Rudolph Kadhikwa;
Accused No 14 Abel Shuudeni Aluteni (The Great);
Accused No 15 Bethuel Nuunyango;
Accused No 16 Michael Nghifingilwa Moses;
Accused No 17 Mathias Elia Kanyeule (Shimbungu);
Accused No 18 Malakia Shivute Uushona;
Accused No 19 John Shipponeni;
Accused No 20 Petrus Kamati;
Accused No 21 Andimba (Hermann) Toivo Ya Toivo;
Accused No 22 John Ya-Otto (Waniipupu);
Accused No 23 Jason Mutumbulwa;
Accused No 24 Nathanael Gottlieb Maxwilili (Kayala);
Accused No 25 Matthew Joseph (Jo'burg);
Accused No 26 Jonas Nashivela;
Accused No 27 Nathanael Lot Homateni;
Accused No 28 Philemon Kakwalindishi Shitilifa;
Accused No 29 Simeon Namunganga Hamulemo;
Accused No 30 Shinima Niilenge (Harakatyi);
Accused No 31 Ndyaula Tshaningwa (Manghono);
Accused No 32 Sakeus Philipus Itika (Oshiveva);

Accused No 33 Efraim Kaporo;

Accused No 34 Simeon Iitula;

Accused No 35 Naftalie Amungulu (Kombadyele);

Accused No 36 Petrus Simon Niilenge; and

Accused No 37 Rehabeam Olavi Nambinga.

With others unknown by the state, we were charged with conspiring to overthrow the South African Government and the South West African administration by violence to replace it with a SWAPO government. We were charged under the Terrorism Act, as well as other legislation such as the Suppression of Communism Act.

The proceedings were conducted in Afrikaans and did not make any sense to me but no efforts were made to either switch to English or to allow the proceedings to be interpreted into Namibian languages.

Since I could not follow what was happening, I concentrated my attention on those in court. I observed that the majority of those present were men and all were white. Most had pot bellies. No black faces were to be seen anywhere except those of black policemen. All those in court looked hostile and intent on seeing our blood spilt. Hatred was written all over their faces. Why did they hate us? There certainly must be something more than our alleged terroristic activities. Perhaps they were concerned about their privileges. They did not want us to have equal privileges with them. They did not want to share anything with us; they did not even want us to have pot bellies or to be fat as they were. Our desire for freedom, peace, justice and equality and to rule ourselves was a threat to them.

Our names were followed by a list of 83 names of our alleged 'co-conspirators', headed by Sam Nujoma. I did not know how long it took the prosecutor to read out all the charges but it must have been about two or three hours. When he finished, he sat down and the magistrate began in Afrikaans: 'Accused No. 1; do you plead guilty or not?'

Tuhadeleni, like many of us, did not know what was going on and did not know what to say when he heard his name mentioned. He stood there helpless. Jason Mutumbulwa, who understood both English and Afrikaans, realised the desperation of the situation and went to his rescue. He raised his hand to draw the court's attention.

'Yes, you! What is it? Are you Tuhadeleni?' the magistrate screamed at Jason.

'No, my Lord, I am not Tuhadeleni, but, my Lord,' Jason began hesitatingly, though determined to have his say, 'we refuse to be tried in Pretoria hundreds of miles away from our country. We have all been held in isolation for months. We have not seen a lawyer to represent us and we ourselves know nothing about the law. Could we postpone our pleas until we have consulted some legal experts?'

Ya-Otto added, 'Your Lordship, we may consider pro deo defence if that would be permitted. But we need some time to consult before pleading.'

The magistrate appeared lost and he looked to the prosecutor for an explanation. They conferred briefly and he agreed to the postponement. Journalists raced for the exits to have their latest news in for the evening newspapers. Our escorts marched us out of the court and packed us again into our waiting steel box and took us back to prison. Back in my lonely cell, I looked at the English version of the indictment. I tried to read in the hope of understanding what was contained in it.

Beside being retroactive to 27 June 1962, the Terrorism Act provided that any person who committed certain specified acts shall be guilty of the offence of participation in terroristic activities. A terrorist was defined among other things as:

Any person who –

(a) with intent to endanger the maintenance of law and order in the Republic or any portion thereof, in the Republic or elsewhere commits any act or attempts to commit, or conspires with any person to aid or procure the commission of or to commit, or incites, insitigates, commands, aids, advises, encourages or procures any other person to commit, any act; or

(b) in the Republic or elsewhere undergoes or attempts, consents or takes any steps to undergo or incites, instigates, commands, aids, advises, encourages or procures any other person to undergo any training which could be of use to any person intending to endanger the maintenance of law and order, and who fails to prove beyond a reasonable doubt that he did not undergo or attempt, consent or take any steps to undergo, or incite, instigate, command, aid, advise, encourage or procure such other person to undergo such training for the purpose of using it or causing it to be used to commit any act likely to have any of the results referred to in subsection (2) in the Republic or any portion thereof;

or

(c) possesses any explosives, ammunition, fire-arm or weapon and who fails to prove beyond a reasonable doubt that he did not intend using such explosives, ammunition, fire-arm or weapon to commit any act likely to have any of the results referred to in subsection (2) in the Republic or any portion thereof, shall be guilty of the offence of participation in terroristic activities.

Subsection (2) was extremely wide-ranging and vague and left it to the accused to prove that he or she was not guilty.

The harder I tried to grasp what the Act implied, the more confused I became. There were too many clauses, sections and subsections. I could not understand why some people should go out of their way to make things so difficult and complicated. It was as though they had woven a web that was impossible to escape from. There appeared to be no way of escaping the main charge of the Act. Besides, even if one could have escaped it, there was another web of alternative charges under the provisions of the Suppression of Communism Act of 1960 (as amended by the General Law Amendment Act, No. 62 of 1960). Convictions under the Terrorism Act carried a maximum death penalty and a minimum of five years in jail. Under the alternative, the convictions carried prison sentences of one to ten years.

In frustration and despair, I threw the indictment across the cell and then went across to kick it, as if to kick its authors and the whole system of South African 'justice'. After a while I felt better and went to sit down again.

Mutumbulwa and Ya-Otto had told us in the truck that we were going to get pro deo counsel. Everybody concerned should think about it and we should have a unanimous decision the following day. So I started thinking about the implication. How could we know that the state would not just appoint a policeman in the guise of a pro deo counsel? To win its case, the state would certainly go to any lengths to get hold of information the police had failed to elicit from us at interrogation. That in turn would compromise our chances of getting a fair hearing. The pro deo could just feed the prosecutor the information he gathered from us. At the same time, I felt helpless because I could not afford a lawyer. But I decided I would rather hang than give away, to a pro deo policeman, information I had refused to divulge during interrogation. I would not give them the noose with which to hang me!

I put up my platform and asked Ya-Otto to explain in detail how pro deo defence worked. He explained that the counsel could be any lawyer from a law firm. The only difference was that the state had to pay for his/her services rather than the accused. How would we know that the pro deo counsel was genuine, I asked. It was unlikely that the state would appoint someone not qualified for the job, Ya-Otto replied. I took his word for it but remained sceptical and hoped for the best.

Those who were not indicted were concerned and wanted to know what would happen to them. Why were they not charged with us? Who decided who would be charged and who would not? If they were not to be charged, what would happen to them, they wanted to know, because they did not want to be seen as state collaborators. We could not answer them, except to assume they might be charged at a later date. Some were indeed later charged while others were released without charges being brought against them, and some were used as witnesses.

After lunch the next day, Ya Toivo, Mutumbulwa, Ya-Otto and Maxwilili were called out to meet someone in a small room next to the prison reception. When they returned to our block, they told us that they had met a Mr. Joel Carlson, a solicitor from a law firm in Johannesburg. He had been instructed to come and represent Ya Toivo in court, he told them, and had received the necessary funds. Carlson had also handed them a letter from Sam Nujoma with ten names of those to be defended by him. They thought the letter from Nujoma seemed authentic enough. It seemed that he would consider representing all of us. We agreed to accept his services and hoped that he would not betray us.

The following day, I joined the other four, Ya Toivo, Ya-Otto, Mutumbulwa and Maxwilili to meet Carlson – the five of us were the only ones who could speak a little English and Afrikaans. He assigned us to take down accounts from the rest of our comrades, and gave us exercise books to write down particulars.

Fearing that the police would try to get hold of the information, we asked Carlson to secure a guarantee from the prison authorities that they would not raid our cells and take away the exercise books. We were still kept in solitary confinement and we asked him to request the authorities to remove restrictions preventing us from talking to each other.

We requested further that the solitary confinement order should be removed altogether to give us free access to our co-accuseds' cells for gathering information. He secured all these conditions and for the first time we were allowed to meet in the communal hall – a huge cell with a capacity of 50 inmates. The prison authorities undertook not to interfere with our work. Carlson collected the books every day and after three or four days he had gathered all the information he needed.

In addition to the tedious task of compiling information from the 37 defendants, Carlson also had the hard task of reconciling several factions amongst us, factions which had arisen only as a result of the prospect of death sentences.

After a long and arduous arbitration by Carlson, an uneasy understanding was reached and peace restored between the parties involved and after intensive consultation with all our co-defendants, we managed to complete our defence. Carlson was pleased, but pointed out that since he was not licensed to argue a case before the Supreme Court, he would have to assemble a team of licensed lawyers and that could present some problems. He also said that for us to have any chance at all, he would need to know the full truth and would need our full confidence and co-operation. We had come to like him and thought that we could trust him, so we accepted his conditions.

He worked tirelessly and selflessly. He was a hard task-master and drove us hard in producing a well compiled defence. He wanted the personal experiences, views and beliefs of every one of us and nothing of a 'sloganeering' nature would do. He wanted to know the views of each of us on the need for undergoing military training and waging the armed struggle. Did we understand the dangers involved in war? How did each of us feel about the South African occupation of Namibia? He never appeared despondent, even when he thought we stood no chance of winning the case. He wanted us not to be sorry for what we had done but encouraged us to put up a fight. That was how we were united.

Carlson told us that the judge who was appointed to try us, Justice de Vos, was notorious for handing out death penalties as if he was handing out sweets to small children. He also showed us the newspapers with such headlines as '37 South West Africans to Hang!' The Terrorism Act itself, he said, gave him little room to manoeuvre but he intended putting up a tough fight provided he could put together a strong defence team.

He promised to select a team of respected barristers. He was not as successful in this regard as he wished but managed to find one Senior Counsel, Nick Philips, and three junior barristers: George Bizos, Ernest Wentzel and Denis Kuny. They, especially the junior advocates, were a formidable team. But they faced a shrewd prosecution who had all the inside information from the police and were armed with an armoury of laws made to measure and without loopholes. Carlson took our statements to his team. They ironed and polished every statement and when the trial began they were as ready as they could be. We had a preliminary hearing on 7 August before an Acting Justice, because Justice de Vos was ill. He died later that month and the trial proper began under Justice Ludorf on 11 September 1967.

The Supreme Court was an old synagogue converted into a courtroom. On the morning of 7 August it seemed as if the whole of Pretoria was there waiting to witness the scene. Trams which passed in front of the court and all other traffic came to a standstill. Journalists and camera crews all jostled for places. One camerawoman had her camera seized and the film ripped out by the police when she tried to take a close-up photograph of us inside the van. We found our steel box engulfed in a sea of faces and hands outstretched to touch it as if it contained life eternal despite the cloud of the death penalty which hung over those inside.

The entrance to the yard behind the courtroom was blocked by people wanting to get into court, who joined the multitudes around our van when they realised that we had arrived. Police dogs were brought in to help the police to clear a way through the yard to a metal cage which had been built to accommodate us. Carlson tried to come to greet us immediately after we got into the cage but he was prevented from doing so by the police who had cordoned it off. He went back and returned accompanied by our barristers.

In their dark robes, the barristers looked sinister, people out to harm us rather than save us from the noose, I thought. I was beginning to feel uneasy with them and to lose confidence in Carlson himself. How was he sure that these people would defend and not betray us? I was, however, put at ease by Ernest Wentzel, one of the junior barristers. He must have been the youngest of them, at least he appeared to be. He was full of life and liked to crack a joke or two. Before long we were all roaring with laughter at the way he impersonated the warders and the police. He would also ask them provocative questions and when they got angry he would walk around them measuring them up and down or would poke his finger in their big stomachs.

The cage gate was opened to let us into the court. We marched between two lines of heavily-armed policemen who were supported by a dozen or so dogs. A group of journalists and photographers who had been hiding behind the courtroom broke through the police cordon. Cameras started clicking and flashing. They retreated behind the court with the same speed they had arrived and before the police could confiscate their cameras.

All entrances to the court were guarded by policemen lining the four walls – all armed with French automatic weapons. People of all colours and from all walks of life filled the court throughout the trial and diplomats from missions in South Africa attended the proceedings every day. There was no standing room left in the gallery and people were jammed in the doorways, all struggling to get inside. We, of course, had our way cleared for us by the police and were ushered into the dock according to the pre-arranged order in which we were to appear for the six months of the trial.

The dock was made of two long boxes facing the judge's bench, with hard wooden benches in each. Our lawyers had their chairs in front of us. The state prosecutor had his chair on our right. To our left sat the media, behind the witness box. Court messengers and clerks had their places in the centre of the court. The judge's bench was on a podium overlooking the dock, with the two assessors, one on either side.

Before we sat down, a number of court attendants came to stand in front of us. Then someone at the door behind the judge's chair shouted: 'Staan reg Hof! Court Stand Up!' and the judge walked in followed by the two assessors. The prosecutor stood up to read out our names and the charges against us. As he read out each name, an attendant came over and pinned a numbered placard around our necks. These were to become our 'names' for the duration of the trial. I was Accused No. 7. From where I was standing, I could see that Judge Ludorf was looking at us keenly. The prosecutor was reading the terrorism charges with due drama, to the judge's obvious satisfaction.

The prosecutor went on and on cataloguing our 'crimes'

and the laws that we had allegedly contravened. All pointed, it seemed, to us being criminals of the highest order. The prosecutor thundered on: Accused No. 1 had conspired, together with accused Nos. 2-37 and others unknown by the court, to overthrow the administration of South West Africa by violent means and had incited, instigated and recruited people for the purpose of engaging in terroristic activities. An interpreter was provided at this stage after we complained that we could not follow the charges levelled against us. When the prosecutor finished presenting his case, he sat down with an air of satisfaction. Clearly he felt the state's case was watertight and he had left no chink in the armour.

Advocate Nick Philips, the leader of our defence team, however, stood up with an air of self confidence. He immediately went to the attack. He questioned the right of a South African court to try us, pointing out that we were Namibians and that the alleged activities had not taken place in South Africa itself. The Terrorism Act had been extended to Namibia after South Africa's mandate had been revoked by the UN. In this context, he argued, no South African court of law had any jurisdiction to try us. Therefore he would ask for the charges against us to be dropped and for us to be repatriated to Namibia with immediate effect.

The judge conferred with his assessors then looked over his glasses at the prosecutor for a counter-argument. But Oosthuizen, the state attorney, had none. Clearly he had not expected this kind of argument to come up and was totally unprepared. He applied for a postponement of the case to gain time to study the issue. The judge granted him a postponement to September.

To discredit our defence team and to throw the whole trial into disarray, the pro-government press alleged that our defence was funded by the Defence and Aid Fund, which had been banned in South Africa towards the middle of the 1960s because of its financial support to the victims of apartheid. It was illegal for a solicitor defending the victims of apartheid to collect funds for his clients and to receive funds from a banned organisation. It was clear that the pro-government papers wanted us to be left with no legal advisers of our choice. They were trying to force the government to order the court to throw out our lawyers and substitute them with a government-appointed pro deo. This would have made it easier for the state to find us guilty and pass the maximum penalty. Our defence was actually funded by a British aristocrat, Lord Campbell of Eskan.

Later other newspapers, to the left of the government, decided to expose our plight as paupers. They pointed out that we were dressed in tatters. Some of us had been given clothes from the prison stores which were either too big or too small but with no shoes. We did not like the way we looked but there was nothing we could do about it. The exposures sent the police running for our personal belongings which they had confiscated. They even gave back my radio which I had managed to smuggle into prison.

Our lawyers also called for help and were generously rewarded for their efforts. They were given bags full of clothes. To avoid complications, and before they gave the clothing to the police to distribute amongst us, they removed all the labels to make sure nothing could be traced back to the original owners. When we next appeared in court, the newspapers were intrigued at our transformation and we saw such headlines as 'Terrorists Smartly Dressed'.

Carlson busied himself by collecting information and particulars of those of us who were assaulted by the police during interrogation. Our defence would argue that the statements we had made to the police should not be admissible because they had been made under duress; in fact the prosecution made little reference to our statements for fear that our defence would raise the issue of torture.

When the case resumed in September Justice Ludorf quickly dismissed our defence case. He ruled that a South African court had jurisdiction to try us and that he as a judge was empowered to try anybody brought in front of him, providing parliament had legislated for it.

Philips entered a not guilty plea on our behalf. The prosecutor then started calling the state witnesses. South African officials from Ondangwa and Oshikango and 'Rooi Rus' Swanepoel – now promoted to Major – were the chief witnesses for the state, the first two because the alleged battles were fought in 'their' areas. Swanepoel was the chief of operations against 'insurgents'.

Many of the witnesses were, however, ordinary rural peasants brought from Namibia to come and testify for the state. Some of them had spent several months in 'protective' custody. Because they had given water or food to the guerrillas, they were held as accomplices. They were liable for prosecution if they failed to give 'satisfactory' evidence. They, like many of us, suffered the traumas of solitary confinement and feared the death penalty or life imprisonment on Robben Island, the most feared place in the whole of South Africa. Many who gave evidence were coached by the police as to what to say in court if they wanted to avoid prosecution and many gave evidence against their own free will.

We felt that it was pointless for our lawyers to cross-examine many peasant witnesses who were mere pawns in the legal farce. We were unhappy with the way they conducted some cross-examinations even though we were pleased with the manner they vigorously cross-examined Major Swanepoel and the two commissioners and other officials from the far north.

It was interesting to see one official when asked under cross-examination if he knew what we were fighting for. He replied that he had heard that we were fighting for 'freedom'. He found himself admitting that he valued freedom, adding that it was good to be free. Why then did he call the South African Police and soldiers to go to Namibia to arrest, fight and even kill the people who he said were fighting for freedom, our lawyers pressed him.

Swanepoel, on the other hand, was stubborn and arrogant. He used to get out of the witness box to confer with the state prosecutor after which he would refuse to answer certain questions. We protested to our lawyers but they did nothing to prevent it happening. They knew he was lying most of the time but they let him off the hook and said that they were more keen on vigorously cross-examining Castro about his role in betraying his former colleagues to the enemy. Unfortunately he was never brought in to give evidence. The police were too busy using him to inflict more damage on our organisation – he was too precious a commodity to be exposed to the tough questioning of the defence counsel.

Castro was not only responsible for the attack on the Omgulumbashe base but was also behind the arrests of many people like Ya Toivo, John Otto Nankundhu, Nathanael Homateni and many others in the north. He was set up by the police to approach Ya Toivo to procure some dynamite to be used for bomb-making by the guerrillas. Ya Toivo reluctantly approached a worker at Tsumeb Corporation Limited for explosives. This incident led to his arrest, trial, conviction and imprisonment on Robben Island.

As if the damage he had already caused to the liberation movement was not enough, Castro made several trips to Zambia to entice unsuspecting fighters to Namibia before his arrest by our forces in 1969-70. His visits led to the arrest and death of many fighters who, under police direction, he lured into traps. The police used to drop him in Zambia by helicopter. He would then proceed to 'report' to the SWAPO representative in Lusaka. He would feed him with a lot of disinformation about achievements on the battlefield and would ask for more guerrillas to be sent to Namibia to intensify the armed struggle.

The SWAPO leadership abroad swallowed his lies, unaware that he had been coached by the police. He would carry with him bogus maps which he claimed he himself had drawn up but in fact were drawn up by the police. Such maps would show false 'liberated areas', the route he had taken and those to be taken by the combatants. He would then give the maps, of which police kept copies, to the combatants with instructions to follow the routes as indicated. Thus the guerrillas would be under South African police surveillance throughout the journey. The police would strike when it suited them, sometimes with devastating effect.

He succeeded in bringing about the deaths of many combatants, including Tobias Hainyeko, the then Commander-in-Chief of SWAPO's armed forces. He lured him to his death by collecting him from Zambia in May 1967. He gave Hainyeko a map of the route he had to follow and put him on the Zambezi River Transport boat. The South African police then intercepted and boarded the boat before it docked at Sesheke on the Zambian side, a stone's throw from Katima Mulilo on the Namibian side. Before he died, Hainyeko shot dead a South African policeman and wounded another, who died later from his injuries. This took place on 18 May 1967, today commemorated as Namibia's Heroes' Day.

Our defence team was assisted by John Dugard, a professor of international law at the University of the Witwatersrand. He helped in drafting the argument that the court had no legality to try us, now that the League of Nations' mandate granted to South Africa over Namibia had been revoked by the United Nations. When we lost the legality battle, Dugard helped to draw parallels between our liberation struggle and that of the Boers against the British at the turn of the century. This argument was presented to the court because the Boers, who were now trying us, had felt justified in fighting what they called at the time British injustice and imperialism.

Carlson, being the instructing attorney, remained the main link between ourselves and our lawyers during the first days of the trial. But as time went on barriers between them and ourselves began collapsing and the ice melted. Mutual understanding developed between us and the junior advocates, especially with Ernest Wentzel. One day during a court recess he strode up to John Otto Nankudhu, the Omgulumbashe base commander. He wanted to ask him something about the attack on the base. But before he put his question to him, he jokingly asked how he should address him. Should he address him as 'Comrade' or 'Sir'? Before John could reply, Ernest was standing to attention and saluting. On another occasion during the court proceedings, there was a heavy thunderstorm. A loud and terrifying roar of thunder sent everybody in the courtroom going for cover. Wentzel's comment was: 'That was Omgulumbashe!' This sent us all roaring with laughter.

I was not on good terms with Philips, our defence team leader. One day he wanted me to give him some information on communism and also wanted to know whether I believed in it. His questions surprised me because I did not expect it to come from my lawyer but from the prosecution side. I politely asked him to explain to me what communism was.

'You were militarily trained in communist countries but you do not know what communism is?' he asked.

I told him that I had not been trained in any communist country. This exchange of words soured our relationship at a time when some of my co-accused thought he was a particularly good member of the team. In addition to our personal antipathy, I did not like the way he refused to put our questions to the witnesses in cross-examining them. He treated our requests as irrelevant.

It was alleged that Philips engaged in horse-trading with the judge as well as with the prosecutor. It was said that to remove the death penalty and possibly to secure some acquittals the judge demanded that some 'leaders' enter guilty pleas, a suggestion which Philips did not contest. Clearly there had been some kind of deal struck, because when the prosecution completed its presentation of evidence around November 1967, the defence (or rather Philips who was de facto in charge) produced no evidence to refute the basic charges.

At that time Matthew Joseph (Jo'burg) and Simeon Iitula were acquitted and discharged. At the same time Ya-Otto,

169

Mutumbulwa and Maxwilili changed their plea from not guilty to guilty under the second alternative charge of violating the Suppression of Communism Act in order to escape the main charge, the Terrorism Act. I was sure as was everybody else that they would not have changed their plea without Philips' advice. We had not been forewarned that they were going to change their plea. Philips had not even briefed his colleagues or Carlson let alone us as to what was happening.

After an adjournment, the trial resumed on 11 December. The prosecution submitted a 300-page typed document, asking for the conviction of all of us under the Terrorism Act – except the three who had changed their pleas to guilty. To our surprise, Philips declared that he would not contest the state's claim, and that we had all 'clearly contravened' the Terrorism Act. What a shock such a pronouncement gave us! Did we hear him correctly? was the question on everybody's face. He went on to argue that not all the defendants should be held responsible for what the others had done, but should be 'punished' according to the extent of individual participation.

I felt anger mounting within me and again asked myself the question: was this really our defence lawyer or was he on the other side of the divide? I thought he was worse than a pro deo. Carlson was not only shocked but was very angry and felt let down by the man he had entrusted with his confidence and our lives. And he, as an instructing attorney, thought that he should have been the first person to be consulted in advance of any new developments. He came close to giving Philips the sack but thought better of it.

Carlson worked tirelessly in highlighting our case to various international bodies, such as the United Nations and the International Commission of Jurists. During a recess he travelled to the United States, Britain and Switzerland to get support, speaking to government representatives and international organisations. The International Committee of the Red Cross, in Geneva, sent several delegations to come and investigate our treatment in prison. We received sympathetic letters of support and telegrams from all over the world. The UN General Assembly voted overwhelmingly in December to demand that our trial should be stopped forthwith and declared that it was illegal. A letter also came from the President of the UN Council for South West Africa protesting against the trial. We even received, to our surprise, a letter from the Association of the Bar of the City of New York, a normally conservative organisation, which issued a strongly-phrased resolution of protest and condemnation. The Association rarely took an active position on controversial 'legal' matters; it was indicative of the depth of indignation produced by our trial that support came from such a source.

Carlson also visited Namibia to drum up support and gather more information from our families. The police learned that he was returning on a certain flight and lay in wait for him at the airport to apprehend him and possibly confiscate any information he might have gathered. They missed him because he arrived earlier by a chartered plane. They were trying by all means to find something with which they could incriminate him. But he was always steps ahead of them.

17

The judgement

When the case resumed in January 1968, Judge Ludorf delivered the judgement of the court: it took him five hours to read his statement. He found thirty of us guilty as charged of violating the Terrorism Act and Ya-Otto, Matumbulwa and Maxwilili guilty under the Suppression of Communism Act. Simeon Iitula was acquitted. Ephraim Kaporo, accused No. 33, had died during the course of the trial in hospital. His death was, however, surrounded by some mystery. The police, who were the only source of information about his hospitalisation, led people to believe that he died from 'natural causes'. But according to Philemon Shitilifa, who received medical treatment at the same clinic, he believed that Kaporo's death was caused by negligence. Philemon said that Kaporo told him he was taken to the clinic to have one of his teeth, which was giving him some trouble, extracted. He was not given a proper anaesthetic before the extraction nor any treatment thereafter. An infection set in and his head swelled massively, leading to his death.

Judgement was deferred on Michael Nghifingilwa Moses, accused No. 16, who had also been taken seriously ill during the trial and was in prison hospital. He was unable to walk or stand on his own but was dragged out on the day of judgement despite protests from our lawyers that he was not fit to be brought to court. Everybody, the judge included, was horrified when he was carried into the court on a stretcher by the police medical staff. His eyes were sunk deep into his head. He was a mere skeleton with all his bone joints visible. His voice was gone and nobody expected him to live. Later, in April 1968, he too was convicted.

In summing up his judgement, Judge Ludorf referred to our national liberation struggle as a 'communist' plot and described us as 'conspirators' whose cowardly actions were feeble and without the slightest hope of success. He thought that we were inspired by 'powers' abroad, especially in the United Nations. He made a statement in open court outlining his concept of the crime. In his own words:

> In my view, it has been proved that the accused, because of the level of their civilisation, became the easily misguided

172

dupes of communist indoctrination. Had it not been for the active financial and practical assistance which the accused received from the Governments of Moscow, Peking and other countries, they would never have found themselves in their present predicament. I also think that had it not been for the loud mouthed support and incitement by representatives of foreign countries and the persons who published SWAPO newsletters, who have absolutely no respect for the truth, the accused would never have embarked on their futile and ill-conceived exploits.

SWAPO received all sorts of support from the Soviet Union, China and African and other countries but what the judge had failed to see was that SWAPO was founded not through this support but as a result of the South African oppression of Namibians. We as a suffering people could feel our pain without Moscow or Peking telling us that we were suffering. By the same token we could devise means to alleviate our own pain without becoming 'misguided dupes'. If there was anyone misguided it was Justice Ludorf himself, who was imbued with a racist and apartheid mentality. One minute, he was making an example of us to others, the next he was saying, as if he was sympathetic:

It also weighs with me that all the crimes whereof the accused were charged were committed before the Act was passed by Parliament, and that this is the first trial in which persons are charged with contravention of the Act because of the retrospective effect thereof.

For these reasons I have decided not to impose the death penalty in the case of any one of the accused. I will, however, take into account the common-law offences which the accused have been proved to have committed in the assessment of the appropriate sentence, although they were not so charged.

In fact Justice Ludorf had dropped the death penalty after horse-trading with Philips as described earlier. International pressure to stop the trial altogether was mounting and this too must have contributed: the UN Security Council had just passed a resolution calling on Pretoria to 'discontinue forthwith this illegal trial and to release and repatriate the South West Africans concerned'.

The judgement infuriated many of us. Most of us were determined to go into the witness box to refute all the judge's insults when the opportunity came for hearings in mitigation.

Our lawyers, however, felt that we would have made matters worse for ourselves, and decided against our testifying in mitigation, except for Ya Toivo. In his statement, Ya Toivo made up for all of us. He touched on the subjects we all wanted to. He told the court:

I speak of 'we' because I am trying to speak not only for myself but also for others as well, and especially for those of my fellow accused who have not had the benefit of any education.

He went on:

My Lord, we find ourselves here in a foreign country, convicted under laws made by people who we have always considered as foreigners. We find ourselves tried by a judge who is not our countryman and who has not shared our background.

We are Namibians and not South Africans. We do not and will not in the future, recognise your right to govern us, to make laws for us, in which we had no say; to treat our country as if it were your property and us as if you were our masters. We have always regarded South Africa as an intruder in our country. This is how we have always felt and this is how we feel now and it is on this basis that we have faced this trial.

. . . I am a loyal Namibian and I could not betray my people to their enemies. I admit that I decided to assist those who had taken up arms; I know that the struggle will be long and bitter. I also know that my people will wage that struggle whatever the cost.

. . . We believe that South Africa has a choice – either to live at peace with us or to subdue us by force. If you choose to crush us and impose your will on us, then you not only betray your trust but you will live in security for only so long as your power is greater than ours.

I particularly liked the part:

My Lord, you found it necessary to brand me as a coward. During the Second World War, when it became evident that both my country and your country were threatened by the dark clouds of Nazism, I risked my life to defend both of them, wearing a uniform with an orange band on it. But some of your countrymen, when called to battle to defend civilisation, resorted to sabotage against their own fatherland. I volunteered to face German bullets, and as a guard of military installations both in 'South West Africa' and the Republic was prepared to be the victim of their sabotage. Today they are our masters sitting in judgement and are considered the heroes, and I am called the coward. When I consider my country, I am proud that my countrymen have taken up arms for their people and I believe that anyone who calls himself a man would not despise them.

Justice Ludorf fumed with rage during and after Ya Toivo's speech. He was embarrassed because the court was full of diplomats who had come to hear the verdict, and some cheered Ya Toivo on when he read his speech. The judge did not like it, but there was little he could do. The prosecutor, Oosthuizen, was also visibly uneasy in his chair, as were many senior policemen in court who were opposed to the dropping of the death penalty. Packed together like sardines in our dock, we enjoyed their discomfort.

Afterwards, arguing against mitigation, the prosecutor emphasised the 'defiant' character of Ya Toivo's statement which he described as displaying no proper sense of 'remorse' and which maintained a spirit of opposition to the existing arrangements for governing South West Africa. And to counter Ya Toivo's statement that 'it was apartheid and South African colonialism that were being condemned by this trial', the prosecutor alleged that we were 'hypocritical' as we 'now denied the advocacy of violence or the encouragement of racial enmity'.

While it could perhaps be argued that we had advocated violence I could not see how the prosecutor could accuse us of having encouraged 'racial enmity'. To hear such an accusation from the mouth of an agent of a government espousing racial segregation policies, filled me with revulsion. I wanted to stand up and challenge him on that point. I wanted to point out that we, the accused, were the victims of and in no way responsible for any racial segregation. We did not pass the Separate Amenities Act, Group Areas Act, Immorality Act or any other racially biased laws. And here we had the culprit pointing an accusing finger at the innocents for the crimes of his government.

*　　*　　*

175

On the morning of 9 February 1968, Judge Ludorf handed down sentences to the thirty-three remaining defendants. The court was packed to capacity as it was on the first day of our appearance. First to be ordered to stand and hear their sentences were the three 'political' leaders: Nathanael Gottlieb Maxwilili, Jason Daniel Mutumbulwa and John Ya-Otto. They were all given five-year sentences under the Suppression of Communism Act, but they were to spend only one month in jail.

Next came Nathanael Lot Homateni and Jonas Nashivela who received the minimum sentence of five years each under the Terrorism Act for giving food and water to guerrillas. They received no suspended sentences, parole or remission. Having originally thought that many of us would face the death penalty, when I heard the sentences of the first two groups, I thought that maybe Philips' deals with the prosecutor and judge were not that bad after all. I started calculating that we who remained would get away with sentences varying between ten and fifteen years.

But Judge Ludorf was hurt by Ya Toivo's statement and because of his earlier undertaking not to impose death penalties, he was determined to give us the severest prison sentences possible. He repeated the conclusion he had reached earlier in the verdict that each of us was a willing party to the plan to 'wage war' against the South African administration in South West Africa. He refused to consider or take into account the age, health or family responsibilities of any defendant. He indicated that the South African courts would not, in the future, shrink from imposing death penalties. We were clearly to be made an example to deter others with intentions of opposing the South African occupation of Namibia.

Andimba Hermann Ya Toivo's name headed the list of the eight of us who received twenty-year sentences. The other six were Lazarus Zachariah Shakala, David Humunime, Eino Kamati Ekandyo, Festus Nehale, Nghidipohamba Jesaja Haufiku and Naftalie Amungulu (and myself).

There was an almost audible intake of breath in the court when Judge Ludorf pronounced the sentences. Not many people expected that we would be dealt with so severely. But more shocks were to come. The nineteen remaining defendants were all sentenced to life imprisonment. The silence that followed nearly brought down the roof. Eliaser Tuhadeleni, accused No. 1, headed the list of the lifers.

Though many people were shocked, Carlson was devastated. He could not control the tears streaming down his cheeks. He was too overcome by grief even to thank his defence team. Despite the harshness of the sentences, none of us showed any sign of emotion. We took the sentences calmly and as something natural bearing in mind that our accusers were none other than our colonial 'masters'. And as masters, they had to put their 'servants' in their place and show them who had the power.

The police on the other hand were disappointed and angry because none of the defendants received the death penalty. They felt the judge was too lenient in passing sentence. They felt that their 'hard' work in bringing the 'terrorists' to book was not rewarded.

Immediately after the sentencing, Philips entered notice of appeal on the jurisdictional phases of the judgement and the harshness of the sentences. The judge was quick to point out that the jurisdictional issues had already been dealt with. He did, however, grant leave to appeal.

In the cage behind the court room, our lawyers came to say goodbye and here emotions broke down. Carlson again cried unashamedly. But there was no time for the lawyers here. They were told by the police that their services ended with the end of the trial. We bade them goodbye and that was the last time we ever saw them.

Back at the prison, we found a van waiting and ready to take us to Robben Island. Prison garb was dumped in every cell for us to change into. Security men were all over the place and warders were shouting 'Haak, Haak!' We stripped and put on the prison garb – which did not include shoes – and within minutes we were on our way to Robben Island.

There was still a legal case outstanding. During the course of the trial I had been involved in proceedings to seek the courts' protection for one of the detainees, Gabriel Mbidi.

Mbidi was one of many Namibians arrested and taken to Pretoria for questioning before our trial. He was in his late 60s and came from Windhoek where he was a member of SWAPO's elders' council. He was detained in the same prison block as we were and during his last interrogation session, he was so badly beaten up by his interrogators that for a week he could not raise himself from his cell floor. He could neither speak nor hear properly for several days and pus oozed out of his ears. We tried to communicate with him by shouting to him but we did not receive any response.

We first thought that he had left but we were later told by common-law prisoners that he was still there, unable to move. We managed to send a written message to him. Because he was unable to write he asked one of the common-law prisoners to help him write his response to us. This was how we came to know of his plight and reported it to Carlson. But because Mbidi was not charged with us, he could not legally be represented by our lawyers. Carlson, however, wanted to take up Mbidi's case, to seek a court order protecting him from the police, and to link it with our trial to expose the torture we had been subjected to. He picked Sidney Kentridge to take up the case – he had a record of successes in defending political cases. Carlson had also wanted Kentridge to defend us in the main trial but he had been busy with two cases; one in Basutuland and the other in Southern Rhodesia.

Carlson needed someone from our own ranks to represent Mbidi and to act as the link between the two cases. After others had turned it down, I was approached. I agreed wholeheartedly as I knew Mbidi very well – he had been my next door neighbour in Windhoek's Old Location.

Carlson and I set to work. We drew up affidavits from those of us who had been assaulted, to support Mbidi's case. We could not meet Mbidi and talk to him face-to-face but since I was in the same wing as he was, I was able to communicate with him by 'broadcasting' after he had regained his voice and hearing. I would then pass on the information to Carlson. Thus, before our trial ended, an urgent application was made on behalf of Gabriel Mbidi to the Pretoria Supreme Court complaining of maltreatment and torture and seeking protection from further assaults. An interim order was granted on 19 December but the hearing was twice postponed on the grounds that it was not urgent. When the news appeared the police wasted no time in sneaking into the prison to interrogate John Ya-Otto and myself in relation to the case. This alarmed some of my colleagues who felt that we were already faced with the prospect of being sentenced to death and should not make things worse. But the death sentence did not frighten me. I told my friends that when you were dead you were dead and I could not make things any worse.

So by the time we left Pretoria for Robben Island on 9

February 1968, the case had still not yet been heard. I even left Pretoria without having met advocate Sidney Kentridge. He came to see me on Robben Island around March or April 1968 and informed me that Mbidi had been released and taken back home to Namibia just a few days before the case was due to be heard in Supreme Court on 20 February. As to the assaults on us, there was nothing they could do to reopen our case.

Our appeal was heard by a full bench of the Supreme Court later in 1968. They threw out our appeal on the right of the trial court to judge us, but reduced five of the life sentences to 20 years.

18

Robben Island

I heard about Robben Island in the early 1960s when a group of Poqo, Pan Africanist Congress (PAC) members, had become the first political prisoners in our time to be imprisoned there. I had no idea what sort of place it was. I had never dreamed that I would one day end up there. The picture I had in my mind of the island itself was just of a prison floating in the sea on oil-drums with no plants growing anywhere. Robben Island is in fact a fairly large island off the south-west coast of South Africa and about seven miles from Cape Town harbour.

When the van carrying us to Robben Island moved out of the Pretoria Local prison, I was thinking of how I would survive twenty years on a floating rock. There were many horrible stories told about the island. Stories of maltreatment and torture of the inmates, some of whom were shot dead while trying to escape, or of people drowned in the sea. Despite these horrific stories I was heartened by the feeling that many people had survived such horrors – if they could survive them, why couldn't I? During the trial the military/political training my colleagues and I had received had helped to sustain us in difficult times; it would help on Robben Island.

Our group of 30 Namibians, all of whom were SWAPO members, was now joined by Gerson Veii, who was then the SWANU President. He was convicted of sabotage and sentenced to five years' imprisonment. SWANU under Gerson Veii was a close sister organisation to SWAPO. His conviction came as a result of a speech he made in Windhoek in 1966 demanding the release of all SWAPO members detained in Pretoria. He had allegedly said that if they were not to be freed, then they would be obliged to meet force with force.

We left Pretoria at about noon on 9 February. The three-ton van carrying us was too small for a group of 31 people packed together like sardines and who had to travel a distance of over 900 miles. We were handcuffed in pairs and each had leg-irons on. There was hardly any space in which to move our limbs without discomforting others.

Going to the urinal, which was at the back of the truck, was a nightmare, especially when one had to drag one's unwilling companion along. To make matters worse, the prison garb had no buttons – the trousers had to be pulled up or down with force. The air in the van, despite wire-meshing, was stale from both the uncovered urinal and the suffocating stench of the bodies and breath of 31 individuals. Luckily we were all comrades who found ourselves in the same predicament and we were ready to accommodate each other and overcome our discomfort.

Our only meal of the day was 'breakfast' at 0730h in Pretoria Local before sentencing. No food was provided in the van and when we had a break to stretch our limbs at about 1700h in Kroonstad, Orange Free State, we were not offered anything to eat. We travelled for the whole night non-stop and arrived in Paarl, in the Cape province, at noon. There we were given a token lunch; only a few managed to nibble at the little which was offered. Eventually we arrived at Cape Town harbour.

A verbal tussle ensued between the police who had brought us from Pretoria and the warders who came to meet us from Robben Island. The cause of the problem was that every prison had its own issues of prison equipment. The prison clothes, handcuffs and leg irons we had on were therefore to be returned to Pretoria Local, but the Robben Island lot had not brought clothes into which we could change, only handcuffs and leg-irons. We refused to strip when we were ordered to take off the Pretoria Local garb, especially when we were expected to go naked into the boat. The problem was resolved, however, when Robben Island accepted the 'loan' of the equipment with the proviso that they had to pay a price for it.

We climbed into the Blouberg, the Robben Island prison boat, with the same 'Haak! Haak!' choruses which we thought we had left behind in the Transvaal. On the boat, we were forced to go down below into the smelly hold. It had just been vacated by someone who had been sick all over the place and no effort had been made to wash away the vomit. The stench was so strong that many of us began to feel sea-sick before the boat had even left the harbour.

The sea was rough and by the time we were half way the boat was rocking from side to side, sending everybody hurtling across the floor and struggling to find something to hold onto. As if this was not enough, we found ourselves subjected to powerful jets of water from the open hatch. Two men stood on deck on either side of the hatch; each one held a hosepipe and they appeared to be talking to each other, oblivious as to where they directed the jets. The water jets stopped, and an adjutant peeped in over the rim of the hatch. 'Hey!' he shouted down, 'Where are you hiding?'

Gerson Veii, who did not have a partner handcuffed to him, went into the open to complain about the treatment we had received, only to be caught in another blast of water. A shout of delight went up on deck. Many faces appeared, accompanied by a chorus of, 'Waar is julle? (Where are you?)' Nobody ventured in the open this time despite calls of 'Come out, Kaffirs!' Because we could not see outside, we were not aware that the boat had docked at Robben Island. A number of warders came down below to drive us out. 'Kom! Haak!' they howled. We climbed down from the sides of the hold where we had sought refuge earlier. Everything was under water and to find our belongings was a nightmare.

With our soggy belongings tucked under our free arms and pulling the heavy metal chains on our legs, we tried to ascend the ladder from the hold. This was impossible, and they had to remove the handcuffs to enable us to have one hand free. The same song, 'Kom! Kom! Haak! Haak!' met us on deck and accompanied us all the way to the gangway. Waiting for us on the landing were two lines of warders. They were part of the 'welcoming' party. Each warder was armed with a 'donkeypierie' (truncheon). Two other warders were standing at the head of the gangway, ready to grab a pair of us and push us between the two waiting lines.

The welcoming party's song was different to that of the rest of the warders. Here they sang according to the rhythm of their donkeypieries as they landed on our heads. 'Robbeneiland hier, Kaffirs! (This is Robben Island, Kaffirs!)' Bang! bang! went the truncheons on our heads. 'Welkom aan Robbeneiland! (Welcome to Robben Island.) Two! Two!' We were ordered to walk in twos. Bethuel Nuunyango, one of the pair in front of my partner and myself, lost his balance and nearly fell between the boat and the quay. He was saved only by his partner who held onto him. Nuunyango received a nasty cut on his right arm and tried to complain only to be met with a rain of truncheons and 'Kaffir! Move!' He and his partner were targets for every available truncheon.

They marched us in twos to the prison 200 yards away from the harbour. The prison had a brick section and a zinc section made out of corrugated zinc sheets on a wooden frame. We were taken to one of the zinc sub-sections where we found an army of about 50 warders waiting for us. The section had three communal cells measuring 50 feet by 24 feet to accommodate about 40-50 inmates each. The cells opened into a yard 100 yards long and nine yards wide.

We were all put in one cell: it was filthy and smelly and the bare cement floor was covered in specks of dried blood. There was a heap of prison clothes in the centre of the cell. We were ordered to strip and find something from the pile to put on. Each one of us had to take two pairs of shorts, two khaki shirts and two canvas jackets. There were no shoes and we were still barefoot. The clothes were not only unsuitable for the cold Cape climate but they were covered in all sorts of dirt. We protested and refused to take anything dirty from the pile. We wanted to keep the Pretoria Local clothes which were new and relatively clean but our protests fell on deaf ears.

They lined us up against the zinc cell walls while several warders went to the pile of clothes and started picking at random and throwing them at us to put on. In the meantime, warders came to stand next to each one of us to make sure we put on the Robben Island garb. They did not care whether the clothes fitted or not. We were also each given four blankets, one felt mat and two sisal mats. This provision proved to be totally inadequate for the cold.

We were later told to collect a few tin plates dumped outside our yard. They contained some cold boiled mealies (maize) with a few pork crisps here and there. This was our first real meal of the day. In a tin bucket were 31 stumps of spoons with their handles cut off – so they could not be used as weapons, we were told. How on earth they expected us to eat with those stumps was beyond our understanding, but we had to try because there was nothing else. The mealies were left-overs and not sufficient for all of us. Only a few managed to grab a few morsels but many went without food for over 48 hours.

We made our beds and tried to make ourselves as comfortable as we possibly could. This was our first night together in the same cell and we had a lot to talk about. The 'pleased to know you' session was in full swing when we were stopped by a loud noise on the corrugated zinc wall of our cell. A warder was scratching the wall from one end to the other with a piece of metal. It was the night curfew and we were expected to go to sleep. Everything fell silent and everybody was now alone with their own thoughts. The only sound we could hear was that of the foghorn booming in the distance.

The following morning, at about 6 am, we were rudely woken by the same terrible scratching noise on the corrugated zinc. We all jumped out of our blankets not knowing what was happening.

At about 7.30, a warder, Sergeant Richard David, whom we later baptised 'Kulundalali' (horrible one) and three other warders opened the cells. Kalundalali told us to get ready for inspection: officials would come around after breakfast. In the meantime, he said, some of us could come out to collect our breakfast while others continued to clean the cells. Breakfast consisted only of soft maize porridge and a mug of black coffee without sugar or milk.

After breakfast, which we had in the yard, we went back in the cell to clean it and to get ready for the inspection. 'Fall in!' Kalundalali shouted from the yard entrance. A no-nonsense captain was taking the inspection, we were warned. We fell in in threes in the cell. The captain came in followed by a stream of junior warders. Pens, wrist bands and anything 'private' were thrown out. They were not standard prison articles and we had no right to keep them, we were told. We wanted to complain but the captain did not take complaints, he said. If we were caught with anything 'contraband' again, it could cost us a day's rations – the usual practice in South African prisons. It was as simple as that.

Kalundalali and his team wanted to take us out to work but we told them that we could not go out without shoes. Kalundalali reported to his seniors and the man in charge of the prison, Major Rensberg, whom we baptised Nasser (because he resembled President Nasser of Egypt), arrived. He was sympathetic to our argument and promised that we would not be taken out to work without shoes. We had won our first battle the very first day on Robben Island. There were many more battles ahead to be fought.

During the day, a doctor arrived from Cape Town to examine us. He ordered us to strip – privacy was forgotten. 'Bend down, open your legs, raise your arms, run around the cell,' he barked. It reminded me of my experiences at Ondangwa years previously and the contract labour system. 'Get dressed!' he ordered and the 'medical' examination was over.

Bethuel Nuunyango, who was injured when he was getting off the boat the previous evening, requested the doctor to look at his injuries which he thought needed a few stitches.

'Where would you have got medical treatment if you were in the bush?' the doctor asked.

Nuunyango responded by saying that he was not then in the bush but in prison. If he were in the bush he would know where to get his treatment. 'I hope you will not politicise your medical ethics and take sides in your treatment of prisoners?' Nuunyango asked.

This must have had some effect on the doctor. He agreed to look at Nuunyango's injuries and ordered that he should be taken to the clinic to have some stitches in his cut. By the time he left, the doctor's attitude of hostility towards us had changed. We thought that too was a victory. Though small, it was still important to us.

Our yard did not get the sun until two o'clock in the afternoon and given the cold weather of the island, it was uninviting to spend our time outside the cell. Besides, we did not have shoes and the sharp-edged pebbles which covered the yard made it painful to walk. We therefore spent much of the day in the cell trying to keep warm. We wanted to stay curled up under our blankets but this was against the rules. We had no indoor games to keep ourselves busy or books to read and our boxes containing our private clothes and other things were locked up in the prison store room. We could not get anything out because we were not yet 'processed'.

Eventually a team of warders under Sergeant Bonzair arrived to process us and take down our personal background particulars. Beside Afrikaans, Bonzair spoke Zulu and Xhosa, two of the main black South African languages, in which he addressed us. Presumably he thought we were South Africans or maybe he had some notion that since all blacks 'look alike', they must also speak the same language!

Like many other South African whites, Bonzair was obsessed with tribalism. Eliaser Tuhadeleni, who was accused No.1, was the first to be called in to be confronted by Bonzair with: 'Umthloko wako ngubani na? (What is your tribe?)' Although he had worked in Cape Town for some time, and understood a few words in Zulu and Xhosa, Tuhadeleni could not express himself in either language. He called Gerson Veii to translate. But because Veii did not speak much Oshikwanyama nor Tuhadeleni Otjiherero, they could not communicate properly in some places. This was then my area because I was fluent in both languages.

The grading process took about two weeks and the questions

centred mainly around our family members and our relationship to them, 'tribes', previous convictions and criminal records. Bonzair and his team also took down our weight and height measurements as well as finger prints. Personal features such as birthmarks and scars were noted down. I could not at first understand why they found all these necessary and I protested that I found the whole process boring and unnecessary. I was told that it was for the prison records and was compulsory. I later learned that they needed our particulars in case we escaped – the information would help to track down the escapee.

The prison system requires that prisoners should be classified into several grades known as A – D Groups. At the end of the whole process, we were all classified as being in the D group, the lowest category which was afforded the fewest privileges. Promotion to a higher grade and more privileges had to be 'earned' by good behaviour and we would be re-assessed after three months. We were now confirmed Robben Island Prison community members.

After processing, they wanted to burn all our personal belongings. It was not in the prison's interests for the state to pay for our things to be sent to our relatives, they told us. We ourselves had therefore to pay for them if we didn't want them to be burned. If it was in the interest of the state to imprison us, it must also bear the responsibility to send our things, we insisted. They gave in and we had won another battle. We were the first ones whose possessions were not burned.

19

Prison life

Robben Island Prison covers about one square mile and is surrounded by a 19 foot high double corridor fence patrolled by guard dogs at night and overlooked by four watchtowers with armed guards. The administrative buildings are in the main section where commissioned officers from the rank of captain have their offices. Adjacent to the office block is the prison clinic, with 20 to 30 beds, staffed by three or four medical orderlies and a doctor from Cape Town who visited the clinic twice a week.

The solitary confinement section, known as Makulukutu, is also found in the same block of buildings. It has one yard 60 yards long and 30 yards wide, and harbours about 100 inmates in its single cells at a time. The cells have no toilets and the people had to empty their chamber pots in a shower/toilet block. Prisoners in the solitary confinement section spend 23 hours each day locked up. In addition to those permanently housed in the solitary confinement section, prisoners found out of step with the system are sent there from other sections for periods of one day to six months or more.

The majority of the prison population is housed in three main 'communal' sections. Each section is built in an H block style with brick and stone walls 3 feet thick, consisting of four cells, each with a capacity of around 50 inmates. They all have washing troughs and toilets – there are no doors on the toilets so privacy is non-existent. Each block has two small rooms opposite each other. One of the small rooms is used as an office for the warder in charge of the section, the other can be used as a temporary detention unit for anyone found guilty of petty offences before they are committed to the solitary confinement section.

A communal hall was built in later years to cater for authorised activities such as church services and film shows. Still later it was partitioned into three sections, a shop, a library and a main section for the events mentioned above. Adjacent to the hall was a kitchen. This was manned by the common-law prisoners before they were moved to another prison in the warders' township. When they left, political prisoners took over.

When we arrived on the island the common-law prisoners had their quarters in the zinc section which was built outside the main prison. It had three separate divisions – the common-law section, our section and one adjacent to ours which later was to be occupied by ANC members convicted, like ourselves, under the Terrorism Act. Though the common-law prisoners were allowed to mix with the other political prisoners, they were not allowed anywhere near us. We were considered to be the most dangerous people and our contamination of others was to be prevented at all costs.

Other installations on the island include the warders' township where the commanding officer and some of his junior officers have their offices. The township is south of the prison and well hidden from the cold Atlantic winds. It has a warders' club, a clinic, a shop, a power station, a shooting range and a school for their children under 16 – the over-16s go to schools in Cape Town.

The island harbour, which guards the entrance of Cape Town, was a military fortress for the South African forces during the Second World War. Gun turrets can be found everywhere. Other military installations such as underground bunkers, tunnels, pillar boxes and 220mm cannons are scattered around the island. South African navy and army personnel visited the island from time to time to check and maintain their military installations but no military personnel were permanently there.

Robben Island also has an all-weather airport which can land aircraft of all sizes – from small chartered aircraft to huge Hercules military transporters. The airport is to the west of the prison, to the east is Murray Harbour where the boats dock. The island is serviced by a network of good gravel roads built by political prisoners and a short tarmac road runs from the township to the prison.

A factory on the island processes a kind of seaweed known as bamboo which grows in abundance in the sea. The seaweed is thrown up by the tide and pulled out by the prisoners, loaded onto trucks and then taken to the factory to be cut. It is then dried, ground and put into bags for export to Japan where we understood it is made into 25 different by-products.

Before the 1970s, prisoners were mainly put to work in gathering seaweed, working in lime and granite quarries and on gravel roads. In the 1970s new workshops were built as a result of our demands for creative jobs, partly funded by the

International Committee of the Red Cross in Geneva. They provide training jobs like carpentry, brick-making and brick-laying as well as plastering, upholstering, tailoring and shoe-making.

*   *   *

When we arrived on Robben Island, we were informed by other prisoners that there were over 900 inmates on the island. These comprised mainly ANC and PAC members who had been convicted in the early 1960s. Prominent among them were Nelson 'Madiba' Mandela, Walter Sisulu, Wilton Mkwayi, Andrew Mlangeni, Ahmed Kathrada and Govan Mbeki of the ANC as well as Robert Sobukwe, John Nyati and Jafta (Jeff) Masemola of the PAC. There were also well known individuals like Dr Neville Alexander and Dr MC Naidoo. Robert Sobukwe was later removed from the main prison and given a 'bungalow' outside prison. Later, he was removed from Robben Island and taken to the mainland where he died in suspicious circumstances while still under house arrest.

In addition to the political prisoners there were also many common-law prisoners. By the end of 1968, the political prisoner population had grown to over a thousand. People were still arriving in their tens and hundreds and none were leaving the island. Michael Nghifingilwa Moses, who we had left behind in Pretoria because of illness, and who we expected not to survive, miraculously recovered and rejoined us, bringing our number to 32.

In the middle of 1969, six more Namibians joined us. Eight of the over 250 Namibians detainees held in Pretoria since 1966 were taken to Windhoek in 1969 to face another show terrorism trial. Two were acquitted. Those found guilty were Gaus Shikomba, Joseph Hipangerwa, Jonas Shimweefeleni, (all sentenced to 20 years), Massach Victory, Solomon Festus Heita and Justice Festus Heita, brothers, who both got life imprisonment. Their prison numbers ranged from 358/69 to 363/69 – an indication of the number of prisoners who arrived on Robben Island before the year was out. The Heita brothers were both kidnapped in 1967 from Angola to where they had fled the same year. Solomon had been arrested in Namibia before he fled to Angola. He escaped from Oshakati detention centre, met his brother and they crossed into Angola.

We had been following our comrades' trial but had not

heard of their conviction until they appeared one evening in the yard of our section. We had just 'retired' to bed when our signal man told us that the yard was full of warders and prison dogs. It was a raid! Quick! Hide the newspapers (the most highly valued commodity on the island – we were not entitled to read newspapers or any books other than the Bible)! We quickly managed to hide our bundles of papers which had been smuggled in despite intensive searches. Hiding places are difficult to find in prison, especially when you are surprised. One has to be really quick in order not to be caught. We quickly spread the papers near to the entrance and covered them with a sisal mat then went back to our beds as if nothing was happening. We settled down and appeared to be as cool and calm as we could (our hearts were drumming loudly). Then we noticed one black face, then another and another . . . six men stood in the yard surrounded by warders and barking dogs. We did not recognise our colleagues after years of separation. The cell door opened and the six were led in. Accompanying them was Brigadier Aucamp, the man in charge of prison security throughout South Africa and who, I believe, authorised many prison deaths, dubbed by officials as suicides.

Some of us remembered one face, then another and it was then that we realised that they were our comrades. We all got up and rushed to the door to meet them. We hugged and embraced while the warders, who were standing on the mat hiding the newspapers, watched. After a while Aucamp called us to order. He could not understand our stupidity, he said. How could we be pleased to see our comrades coming to prison? he asked. We were pleased to see them alive and to know that they had not fallen out of windows or committed suicide like many who had died in South African jails, we told him.

Other 'terrorism' trials were going on in many parts of South Africa. By the beginning of 1970, the section next to ours was occupied by about 16 ANC members. Though there were problems in contacting them, we managed to establish communications. The first problem was that we were not able to know what was happening in the other yard. The second problem was that there was almost always a warder present in one or the other yard. It was therefore difficult to know when the coast was clear on the other side.

For smooth communication, a signal was devised. The first

step was to throw three stones in one direction at intervals, after which they were to be reciprocated. If they were not reciprocated, that meant that the coast was not clear on the other side. If it was, then parcels of paper were thrown across. Communications with other sections were even more difficult than with our immediate neighbours. Because the system used was so obvious to the warders, many messages were caught before they reached their destinations. Another system was devised whereby we exchanged news via the kitchen.

All messages were coded; sections and names of prison officials were all in code. All prisoners had assumed names, also in code to protect their identities if messages fell into the wrong hands. Names and codes were changed immediately it was suspected that they had been intercepted. Those in the kitchen had a tough job to pass on the parcels to their respective destinations according to their code names. They had not only to put the well wrapped parcels inside the right food drums, but they also had to learn as quickly as possible the changed codes and when there was likely to be a raid. Meal times were always critical moments. Warders were often out searching food drums for messages before we got to them.

We on our part were always vigilant, looking for hidden messages on our plates, or in the food which might have escaped the caterer's attention. Contacts with other sections were handled by very experienced and sometimes daring people - they had to be prepared to destroy or even swallow the parcels when they found themselves under threat. Not to admit to anything was, however, every prisoner's trade mark.

Solomon Heita, who was one of the 'operators', one day failed to deliver a parcel destined for our ANC neighbours. He was to throw two newspaper packets across the yard. The warders in charge of the sections had their office overlooking the yard. One packet landed safely but the other landed in the middle of the yard. The warders rushed down to retrieve it and then began a search of our cells.

By now we had dug holes in our yard to bury our unauthorised materials under the very eyes of the warders. The warders searched the cells but found nothing. Many of us were thoroughly searched. Nothing was found despite the fact that we had many newspapers with us. Other sections were also searched, we learned later. Suspicion fell to our neighbours, the common-law prisoners, because they were the only ones allowed to read papers with official approval.

The following day, we heard the common-law prisoners screaming. They were being assaulted at the orders of Lieutenant Fourie, known to us as Shapota. We could see through holes in the wall of our enclosure that Shapota was in charge of the operation and took part in the beatings. Dogs were let loose in the cells to savage defenceless prisoners. The prisoners, who had their legs in leg irons, were manacled together with heavy chains and marched to the Commanding Officer's office where they were again assaulted in front of the Commanding Officer. The assaults went on for a couple of days after which the common-law prisoners were moved to another jail in the warders' township.

* * *

In April 1968 we were issued with shoes and, at our insistence, were taken out to work. We asked to be sent to work because we wanted to see outside the corrugated zinc walls of the yard and cells. We were tired of being locked up in the cells day in and day out and we wanted fresh air. We did not know what kind of work we would be given or what the working conditions would be: all we wanted was to get out. What followed was not what we had bargained for.

Sergeant Richard David (Kalundalali) told us that our request to go out to work had been met and he himself would be in charge of the span. He turned up next morning with a group of four warders. After breakfast, they ordered us to fall in. A huge seven-ton army truck covered with a heavy tarpaulin had backed into the entrance to our section and was waiting to take us to work. Two dog handlers stood guard in the gap between the truck and the section and two warders armed with FNL Belgian heavy calibre rifles stood a few yards from the truck. Kalundalali himself was armed with an army standard issue revolver.

In dog training blacks are often used as 'guinea-pigs'. The dogs thus develop colour consciousness and start barking immediately they see anyone with a black skin. The powerfully built, vicious-looking Alsatian dogs of the prison service began barking, dragging their handlers towards us as we were getting onto the truck. They howled and growled, determined to get at us. The warders with guns readied their arms. 'Kom, Kom! Klim op! (Come on! Climb up!)' Kalundalali shouted, shifting his revolver into position. We were pushed onto the truck. The tarpaulin was pulled down at the back and we were in darkness.

The truck pulled out of the yard followed by a van carrying dog handlers and armed warders. We undid the tarpaulin immediately the truck began moving to let in some light. The truck stopped at an 'asgat' or rubbish-dump one or two miles from the prison. We had nine warders in all looking after us. They took up their positions before we were let out of the truck. The place was littered with all sorts of rubbish – from old cars and barbed wire to rusting First and Second World War steel, covered with a carpet of ashes and all sorts of other rubbish from all over the island.

Kalundalali called Veii to give him instructions. We were expected to 'clean' up the rubbish dump. To clean up a rubbish dump? There were no tools: it seemed that we were expected to use our bare hands to pull barbed wire, rusting steel, cars and other rubbish from the dump and move it into what had been a granite quarry.

Before we started, the Commanding Officer's minibus pulled up. He told us that we were not expected to clear away rubbish as a permanent job. He assured us that he only wanted us to get out to get some fresh air. This was the only place he could think of at the moment.

We did not know what would have happened if we had refused to clear away the rubbish. But because we wanted to get fresh air and believed the Commanding Officer's word that it was only temporary, we did not make a fuss. We made some crude tools out of rusting iron and ropes. With these, we pulled all the old cars, wire and the like into the disused quarry. We spent about four weeks working there until all the rubbish was safely down in the pit.

Robben Island is a wooded place; its woods are unbelievably thick and provide enough firewood for the warders' hot water boilers. When we had finished clearing the ash pit, we were made to 'prune' the woods. They did not want to give us axes and we had to make do with our bare hands. With iron bars and ropes we managed to clean up large areas. The prison authorities were amazed at what we achieved without proper tools.

In the end they gave us axes, but they made sure that they were blunted by chopping them into metal or stones. It was difficult to chop wood with blunt axes but because many of us were experts with metals, we managed to sharpen them with stones. However, each morning we would find the axes blunted and chipped again.

Later, we were sent to work in the two lime quarries, chipping away at the rock-face with only picks, shovels and spades. It was very hard work, and a dazzling glare came off the white rocks when the sun shone – as we had no sunglasses, the eyesight of many of us was damaged.

* * *

While many countries are signatories to the UN's code of prison conduct, South Africa is not and the laws and regulations governing the prison services are based on apartheid principles. Blacks, who are at the bottom of the racial set-up in all fields, suffer some of the worst prison conditions in the world. Blacks are always at the receiving end of everything evil in South Africa. In prison, they are at the mercy of those who run them. In most cases, prison governors are a law unto themselves. Many deaths in the South African jails could have been prevented but due to the lack of controlling mechanisms, governors are free to manipulate the situation and get away with it.

John Shipponeni's case bore all the hallmarks of the worst features of the South African prison system. Shipponeni, prisoner No.19/68, had been injured in battle and one of his legs had been savaged by dogs at the time of his capture. He was involved in an accident which affected his injured leg in September 1969, while working in one of the quarries on Robben Island. Though there had already been bad relations between us and the warders, the way he was treated after the accident annoyed us and exacerbated the situation.

We had just finished our lunch and were getting back to work when Shipponeni slipped and fell about 20 feet down into the quarry. In the process, he twisted his right knee so badly that his foot was facing back-to-front. We carried him to the shade under a tree and asked the warders to give him first aid and to twist his knee back into place. To our surprise and annoyance none of the warders with us had any first aid training or experience. Fortunately, many of us had basic training and we managed to twist his knee back into place.

We requested that he be taken to hospital immediately for medical attention before gangrene set in but this was rejected.

194

We felt angry and frustrated: here was a man groaning with pain and left to lie in the shade under the tree with no medical treatment, because he was black.

Shipponeni was not given attention when we got back to prison nor was he admitted to the local clinic. Instead he was allowed to come with us to the section. We asked for a medical orderly to come and see him. No orderly was available, we were told. The man was in great pain. He groaned throughout the night and we all tried our best under the circumstances to alleviate his pain by wrapping his injured leg in cold cloths.

The following day, although his leg was so swollen that he could not move it, he was not allowed to stay behind to see the doctor who was due that day from the mainland. We were made to carry him onto the truck and offload him when we got to our working place. He lay down in the shade under the tree in the quarry to wait for the doctor to arrive. Why on earth did they have to bring him out? Was it really necessary? we asked in frustration. Under the prison regulations, no prisoner had any right to stay inside when the span went out, was the response.

The doctor came to see him immediately after lunch. We watched him from where we were working. He bent over him, poked his finger in the leg then straightened up. He turned then left without a word.

'What did the doctor say?' we asked Shipponeni later. He had not suggested any treatment nor did he bother to prescribe any pain killers. He gave no instructions for him to be taken to hospital and no instructions were left with the medical orderlies.

We later realised that many doctors were acting under the influence of the prison officials. Even when they wanted to give the best medical treatment to prisoners they were often over-ruled by medical orderlies. They were either told that the medicine was not available from the dispensary or it was too expensive.

While still working, we discussed what line of action we would take if they told Shipponeni to come out with us the next day. Since we had not been given a copy of prison regulations, we should demand that such copies be made available to us as the first step. We needed to know our rights. Secondly, we would refuse to carry him out of the cell. We would keep up the pressure for him to be given immediate medical attention and we would consider a hunger strike if all else failed.

We refused to carry Shipponeni out to the truck the following morning. The warders threatened us with punishment for having refused what they called a 'lawful' command. We stood our ground and in the end they carried him out to the truck themselves. We felt guilty about leaving our comrade's fate in their hands. We warned them not to mistreat him, or we would respond in kind. Fortunately for all of us, some warders were sympathetic and heeded our warning – taking great care in putting him on and off the truck. It was really sad to see this happening and it continued until early October when we threatened the prison authorities with a hunger strike unless he was given the necessary medical attention. Fortunately this was averted as shortly afterwards he was taken to Cape Town for treatment.

Shipponeni and I came from the same area. We grew up together and because he was a year older than myself, he was like an elder brother to me. After my military training and other personal experiences, I became a hardened individual and thought I could never be emotionally moved by anything. But when in November 1969, Shipponeni returned from hospital in Cape Town, I found that I was not as 'tough' as I first thought and that my eyes were not dry wells without a drop of tears.

We had just finished our dinner one afternoon when the door to our section opened. Walking on crutches and standing on one leg was Shipponeni. He had had his right leg amputated above the knee. I stared at him through misty eyes and in disbelief. My voice was gone and my body turned to lead. The mist changed to tears which poured down my cheeks. Not long ago my comrade had two healthy legs! Today he had just a stump! Nobody moved or uttered a word. In the end, my legs regained some life and I started moving towards Shipponeni, one step, two steps.

I stretched out my arms to embrace him and in the process I knocked down one of his crutches and through my tears I saw him fall. That brought me to life and I managed to catch him before he hit the ground. Others too rushed forward to catch him. He tried to regain his balance but dropped the other crutch and we were locked in a strong and emotional embrace. I was now sobbing and he too began crying. Warder Kalundalali, who had opened the door and was watching us, was also moved. He shed one or two tears, and went into his office nearby. Was he human after all? I do not know how long we stood in our embrace, but we were there until we were told to go into the cell.

He told us that he did not know what happened. He was made to understand that he was only to undergo an examination. For his leg to be thoroughly examined, the doctor told him that he had to be anaesthetised. When he came round, they showed him the lower part of a leg wrapped in a plastic bag and told him that it was his. The doctor told him that the leg had developed an advanced cancer. To have waited for Shipponeni to regain consciousness and to ask for his permission to amputate, would have risked the infection spreading to other areas where it would have been more difficult to stop. It sounded logical enough but it seemed incredible that the doctor had operated without the authorisation of the person concerned.

It was difficult to come to terms with Shipponeni's situation, though in the end he and everybody else came to accept it. The prison department was not prepared to give him an artificial leg. The system did not even recognise disability nor did it try to alleviate his discomfort. Beds were available at the hospital but instead of taking him there they made him sleep on the cell floor with the rest of us.

After Shipponeni's accident, which shook us rather badly, something even worse happened. The circumstances around it remained a mystery to us, even though we had some suspicions. Though it happened to one of us, it really affected us all and touched our hearts because he was one of our dearest comrades and a stalwart of our movement.

Comrades Festus Nehale, who was accused No. 9 and whose prison No. was 10/68, and Bethuel Nuunyango, accused No.15, prison No. 15/68, were found to have developed piles. For a permanent cure, the doctor suggested that they should undergo operations. These were carried out early in 1970, and were said to be 'successful'. Nuunyango recovered quickly but Nehale did not. A second operation was carried out on Nehale which was also said to be 'successful'. After the operation, he was allowed to remain in the Robben Island clinic to recuperate.

One day, however, when we had returned from work, we received a shock. Warder Jack told us that he had been instructed by the Commanding Officer to officially inform us that Nehale had passed away. Just like that. No regrets or condolences about our loss. His death was a result of 'natural' causes, we were told. We could not believe that Nehale was dead. After the second operation he was as healthy as anyone could be! How on earth did they think we would believe them? We thought they had a lot to explain and so we asked to see the Commanding Officer.

The Commanding Officer made himself available but said he had no information other than what we had been given already, and for security reasons he would say no more. He added that only his family were entitled to any further information and since we were not members of his family, he considered the matter closed.

True, we were not members of his family but we were his closest friends on Robben Island, who could reach his family quicker than the prison authorities. As a matter of principle, we felt that he should be given a decent burial and that his body should be taken back to Namibia where his family would be able to take care of his remains. But the Commanding Officer refused to consider our request, giving no reasons why. We did not press the matter any further but contacted his family through our own families.

As time went on, we found that there was something odd about the general health conditions in the zinc section and the unethical behaviour of the medical staff. Since our arrival, many people had begun to suffer from pains and colds, and we wondered what was wrong with us. Some of us who had never felt ill before began suffering from asthma, high blood pressure and tuberculosis. Some even suffered from arthritis, pneumonia and bronchitis. It was later confirmed to us that before we moved in, the section had been set aside for tuberculosis sufferers. We complained to the authorities and the visiting doctors that we should be moved from there to a healthier place and that the section be declared unfit for residence and completely shut down. The visiting doctors concurred with us and suggested to the authorities that we should be moved immediately. There was no 'safe' place to be taken to, was always the official excuse. But in the end we were taken away to the solitary confinement section, Makulukutu.

*   *   *

Tension had been building up between Sergeant Kalundalali

and ourselves before Shipponeni's accident and Nehale's death. Towards the end of 1969 the situation deteriorated. As a result, Kalundalali ordered two dark solitary confinement cells to be built inside one of the empty cells in our section. He wanted 'agitators' among us to be rooted out and confined there because we could not be taken for punishment to the solitary confinement section where Nelson Mandela and others were held. The authorities did not want us to meet with the rest of the political prisoners. We, as Namibians, were in total isolation.

We demanded that Kalundalali be removed from our section. He was too provocative and he used to pick on anyone he did not like. Our demands were not met and we gave the prison authorities an ultimatum that we would not take our meals the following day unless he was removed. When he came on duty the next morning we requested to see the Commanding Officer to complain. He was not available, we were told.

Without dishing out food, we sat down to consider the situation, especially the consequences which could follow a hunger strike. We looked into the advantages, if any, and the disadvantages in our future dealings with the prison authorities. We were aware of the dangers involved, especially when we knew that we were dealing with a system that did not give a damn whether we were dead or alive. They might rejoice at our deaths. But at the same time, we were also aware that they feared the world condemnation that would follow.

We discussed the matter fully. Would we all commit ourselves to the cause? Were we all willing to make sacrifices? Were we all fit to carry out our objective? At the end of the deliberations, we decided that the sick should be exempted because they had to carry on taking their medication, some of which could not be taken on empty stomachs. We understood full well that hunger strikes are difficult to undertake but they were the only effective measure left to us.

The breakfast was dished out but nobody went to take his tin plate. 'Kom! Kry jou kos!' Sergeant Kalundalali commanded, 'Come on! Get your food!' By now the number of warders had increased from the usual four to six. Two dogs were also brought into the section. This heightened the tension because the dogs never stopped barking.

When lunch arrived, nobody touched it except the sick. Kalundalali decided to lock us up despite our protests that we wanted to remain in the yard and also to see somebody in authority. An adjutant arrived in the afternoon. Instead of listening to our demands, he tried to persuade us to eat. They brought in dinner which we refused. Three warders instead of the usual one came on duty that night, one of them a dog handler.

The following day things remained tense. Kalundalali moved his office into the section and converted one of the cells so that he could keep an eye on us. Two lieutenants arrived to talk to us at midday. They brought a large contingent of warders with them. Tempers ran high because they were not ready to listen to our complaints about Kalundalali. They wanted to take Gerson Veii away and lock him up in one of the dark cells as punishment for 'incitement'. Veii was not only our interpreter, but he could argue well and put his point across clearly. Two warders grabbed him to take him away. We all surged to the front to stop them, and we demanded to be taken with him, so that they could not victimise him. The two lieutenants raised their truncheons to beat us but we grabbed them before they landed on anyone. The lieutenants panicked, thinking that their own truncheons were going to be used against them, and rushed out of the cell, but not before they managed to pull Veii through. In the middle of the scuffle, Kaleb Tjipahura, Simeon Hamulemo and I succeeded in joining Veii and all four of us were taken away to the dark isolation cells. Our comrades threw the warder's staffs after them and they were warned never to use them on us again. They never carried them again when they came for inspection.

In the evening they brought Michael Moses to join us in the isolation cells. Sergeant Kalundalali accused him of being the root cause of the whole problem. The day before the confrontation began, Kalundalali had exchanged sharp words with Michael over some pheasant's eggs which had disappeared. We were working near the rubbish pit where the two allegedly discovered the eggs. He accused Michael of stealing them because he was the only one who knew about them. Michael denied having anything to do with their disappearance.

The Commanding Officer arrived the following morning, the third day of the strike. He first went to talk to the comrades in the main cell before he came to us in the dark cells. We overheard him promising to deal mercilessly with the agitators. We challenged him not to judge us until he had heard our side of the story. He said that he would not listen to us until we called off our hunger strike. We on our part told him that we would not call off our hunger strike until he listened to us and removed Sergeant Kalundalali. The same message had been given to him by the comrades in the main cell.

At about 1400h, when the warders returned from lunch, we noticed that Kalundalali had not returned but we did not know whether he had been removed until the Commanding Officer arrived with an entourage of his junior officers. He ordered that we should be reunited with the other comrades. He said that he was ready to listen to our complaints and requests. Our main complaint was Sergeant Richard David (Kalundalali). We were not wanton 'agitators' as we had been incorrectly branded. All we were asking for was the removal of Kalundalali and things would be back to normal. The Commanding Officer wanted to stand firm but one of his junior officers remarked: 'If all they ask is for the removal of Sergeant David, I see no reason why we can't do that.'

'Where is Sergeant David?' the Commanding Officer asked. He was not back from lunch, Warder Lancaster (the only English speaker in the service), told him. Whereupon Lancaster was told that he would be in charge of this section from now on! Did that satisfy our demands? the Commanding Officer asked. We smelled victory but did not want to be too over confident or admit that we were satisfied. We would be happy not to see Kalundalali there again, we said. But we would also like to see the general victimisation of prisoners completely stopped. Not to miss the opportunity proffered by our victory, we also pressed for our repatriation to Namibian jails so that we could be near our people (our demand since we arrived on Robben Island). So far we had never been visited by anyone from Namibia. In the meantime, we went on, we would like all the privileges and rights, e.g. studies, library and sporting facilities, which were open to other prisoners. In addition, we demanded to be allowed to meet other political prisoners. The last bit brought loud guffaws and murmurs from the warders. Some were probably trying to tell their Commanding Officer, 'We told you so; if you give in one inch to the "terries", they will demand a mile!'

Warder Lancaster, whom we nicknamed Jack, had worked with us on several occasions. We found that he was reasonable and we were happy (though we did not show it) when he was placed in charge of our section. He and his colleague who we nicknamed Shikapute were always flexible. They sometimes let us through with our newspapers or, at times, did not search us at all.

* * *

After the UN General Assembly revoked South Africa's mandate over Namibia in 1966, and as a result of our trial, the Security Council had begun considering the Namibian issue. In the January 1968 resolution condemning our trial, the Security Council had described it as illegal, and in 1969 it confirmed the General Assembly revocation of the mandate and referred the issue back to the International Court of Justice. The South African Government was desperate and it needed to find out if it had succeeded in weakening our stand. In addition, the government was accused by the world community of the torture and victimisation of political prisoners, especially those on Robben Island. To counter this, it had to gain some support from outside sources to collaborate its argument.

It was while we were working chopping wood in the middle of 1968 that the government secured the co-operation of an American lawyer. He arrived early one morning accompanied by some high ranking officials. They found us chopping wood and asked whether we were enjoying the 'job'. The lawyer must have been told about Ya Toivo, because he called him aside to ask him a few questions. We overheard what was happening and when we realised that they were trying to corner Ya Toivo and persuade him to say that we were well treated we all flocked to where they were having their discussion. The warders tried to stop us from getting near. We told Ya Toivo to stop answering their questions. He was our spokesperson only if we had discussed a matter with him beforehand. He in turn told them that we were entitled to hear and participate in their discussions. That was not what the prison officials wanted and, realising the trouble which might follow by our intervention, they whisked their American 'guest' away.

Working close to the ashpit where all the rubbish was disposed, including newspapers, we were able to gather papers and at this stage we were the main source of the news throughout the prison. The following morning, we got hold of a paper containing a report of the American lawyer's visit to Robben Island. In his story, he spoke of having met the 'South

West African' prisoners on Robben Island. In his discussions with them, they told him that they were well treated and had never been assaulted, he said. We were infuriated but we could not complain to the authorities without exposing the fact that we received news items. However, it did make us even more wary of the government's intentions.

Not long after that, when we were working in one of the lime quarries, two prison vans pulled up. One carried officials from the prison department and the other carried lawyers and judges from Cape Town, among them judge De Villiers, one of the South African lawyers involved in the Namibian case at the International Court of Justice (ICJ) in The Hague in the 1960s and 1970s. With them was a lawyer from the Netherlands. He was recruited by the South African authorities to support the government's argument that we were well treated in prison and that the South African mandate over Namibia was still legal. If only they could get something from us to support their argument, they would have ammunition to back their claims over Namibia. This time, however, we were ready for them. We did not talk to them in the manner they wanted. If they wanted to speak to any of us, they had to talk to all of us.

They called us together amidst the menacing looks of the prison personnel. The message which the looks carried was always: Don't talk shit! Don't forget that we will always get back to you after they are gone! The menace did not, however, deter us from speaking out about prison conditions.

When pressed, De Villiers admitted that it was the first time a judge had visited Robben Island. We told them that while we could understand the reasons for a visit from the South African judges, who were responsible for sending people there, we failed to understand the interest of a lawyer from the Netherlands. It was at this juncture that the Dutch lawyer tried to explain his purpose in being there.

We asked him whether he had visited prisoners in his own country. If he had, would he describe the prison conditions there, the food and the treatment of political prisoners in general. If he had not, would he explain why he was more interested in conditions in South African prisons than in those in his own country. He admitted to not having visited prisoners in the Netherlands, adding that to his knowledge there were no known political prisoners there.

We asked him if he found it odd that everybody interned on the island was black. Do they have similar 'classifications' based on race and skin colour in the Netherlands? By now the lorry which brought our lunch had arrived and we asked him to look at the food. He was visibly disgusted at the sight of the food: two drums full of boiled maize and another half full with a drink called Puzamandla.

We now realised that we had created some confusion in the mind of the Dutch lawyer, and ignoring the South Africans, we addressed him on the subject of apartheid. We told him about the workings of the classification system, that blacks were at the bottom of the ladder and denied all rights, whether they were in prison or outside. They had not a single right they could claim as their own. They did not even have the right to eat decent food. The food we got in prison was the type many countries feed to their animals.

We demanded that he should tell us what his real mission was and what he wanted from us. Was he on the same mission as the American lawyer who told nothing but lies? The mention of this brought raised eyebrows from the warders (or so we thought). As Namibians and prisoners, we knew that money was more important to agents than the lives of Namibians, which they were prepared to sacrifice at the altar of the South African Rand, we said. We knew that his mission was not one of compassion and concern for our plight as prisoners but one of personal gain and profit, we told him. It was already bad to be black in South Africa. The situation became unbearable when one is black and in prison, especially for those who dare to oppose the apartheid regime.

Before they whisked him away, we fired our final shot: How much was he paid for coming to South Africa and how much was he promised on completion of his mission? This was not what his hosts had bargained for. They had heard enough and dragged him away and drove off.

When we got back to prison, we found that they had raided our cell while we were out. Everything was upside down and there was chaos everywhere. Even toothpaste tubes had been squeezed out. They were looking for the 'news'. And before we entered the section, we were searched as never before. They were convinced that we received news. Where did we get it from? Who supplied us with news? they wanted to know.

This experience made us wary of everybody visiting us in prison, even though some of these visitors wanted to help rather than elicit information from us for their South African paymasters. One example was when we received visits from representatives of the International Committee of the Red Cross (ICRC) from Geneva.

The first ICRC representative to visit us Namibians on Robben Island, and who was said to be the first to be allowed to set foot in the highest security prison in South Africa, was Dr Senna. We first met him in Pretoria immediately before we were committed for the Terrorism Trial in 1967. He was an old man with a frail body. In Pretoria, the discussions were in private. We were able to express ourselves freely though we knew that he would make his findings available to the South African authorities at a later date. There he insisted on private discussion and we were pleased with the arrangements, as well as with the outcome of the discussions. He managed to secure for us more exercise and better medical treatment for our sick. We were grateful for what he had done then and respected him for it.

When he arrived on Robben Island in 1968 he called us to see him in the office of the Commanding Officer. We were not happy with the arrangements as he wanted to talk to us in the presence of prison officials. Some of us, including myself, refused to talk to him.

Those who agreed to see him claimed to have given him a cool reception. They did not tell him much about prison conditions or our treatment for fear of harassment after he was gone. The only significant complaint they put to him was our general and commonly known one: to be transferred to jails in Namibia near our people. Before he left, however, he expressed disappointment at not having seen us all or heard significant complaints.

The second ICRC delegate was a young man in his 30s who arrived one day in 1969 while we were out working. He spoke to those he found in the section and told them that he wanted to see Ya Toivo. When he was told that Ya Toivo was out with the span, he left word that he would come back later. He did not tell them who he was or where he came from. When we came back, the only thing those he had spoken to could say was that there was a man looking for Ya Toivo. That had been a big mistake on his part: we immediately associated him with the South African agents.

When he returned, we could not even see his ICRC badge. All we could see was a man dressed in a dark blue blazer and carrying a black briefcase. He was allowed to come into the cell unaccompanied and this to us was a clear indication that he was an agent. We all stood watching him, seeing nothing but betrayal written all over him. We waited to hear what he had to say for himself. He introduced himself as Dr Zugger from the ICRC in Geneva. He asked for Ya Toivo whom he wanted to see alone and in private.

Due to past experience with the two agents, Ya Toivo had already made a decision not to talk to Dr Zugger. After some persuasion, however, he agreed to hear what Dr Zugger had to say. They went out in the yard but they were there less than a minute before Ya Toivo returned to the cell. He said that he had told Dr Zugger that he did not want to see him and that he should go away. Dr Zugger followed him inside to try once more to talk to him but it was in vain. We too refused to talk to him because we felt that we were not part of his programme and did not want to be considered as an afterthought. Pride? Maybe. But we later regretted our behaviour, and after constructive discussions among ourselves we agreed to see him when he paid us a second visit later.

20

Makulukutu

During the first half of the 1970s, Namibia was often in the news. To us in prison, it was interesting as well as disappointing to watch the unfolding situation although we often had difficulty in getting information. Many resolutions were passed one after another in the Security Council and the General Assembly of the UN and another advisory opinion was given by the International Court of Justice. In March 1969 the Security Council passed Resolution 264 endorsing the termination of the mandate by the General Assembly in 1966. The International Court of Justice delivered its Advisory Opinion on 21 June 1971, as requested by the Security Council. It held by 13 votes to 2 that South Africa's presence in Namibia was illegal. The Security Council by resolution 301 (1971) agreed with the ICJ's advisory opinion and called once again on South Africa to withdraw from Namibia. These developments raised the hopes of many Namibians but they were always dashed – thanks to the collusion of the Western Powers with South Africa's occupation, which they demonstrated unashamedly every time the Namibian question came up for debate in any of the international forums. They always expressed reservations on one point or another and used their veto powers in the Security Council to block any resolution they considered too drastic.

The UN initiated contacts with the South Africans to try and persuade them to allow Namibian independence. Secretary General Dr Kurt Waldheim visited South Africa and Namibia in March 1972 but came away disappointed by the vagueness of his hosts' pronouncements. Later that year, Dr Alfred Escher, a Special Representative of the Secretary General, visited Namibia and South Africa. He too came away empty handed but left with a wrong impression that South Africa was negotiating in 'good faith'. The UN was, however, being taken for a ride. They passed good resolutions, but to what end? Resolutions are only good if they are implemented: many of those passed on Namibia were castles in the air.

The Namibian people, however, were not waiting for the UN to free them. Our armed struggle was continuing and SWAPO had regrouped at the Tanga Consultative Conference in 1969. In December 1971 SWAPO co-ordinated a massive general strike in which virtually all contract workers participated. This in turn set off a resurgence of resistance and armed struggle, especially in the north.

We remained as Category D prisoners for some years because we did not wish to be re-assessed. We wanted increased privileges by right and not as a reward for so-called good behaviour. The system refused to compromise and our privileges were therefore limited to group D category. We could not study or write more than one letter a month. Our visits were limited to one monthly visit of 30 minutes. But we could not make much use of the visits because we were so far away from our homeland: the journey to Robben Island was too expensive and difficult for our relatives, most of whom did not speak any of the South African languages. After four years on Robben Island none of the Namibian prisoners had received a visit. On the whole, we did not care much about privileges. We felt, in a way, that we were better off without them because immediately they were given, they could be taken away as punishment for 'misbehaviour'. In the end the authorities compromised and classified us as group C without asking us, which gave us the rights to more letters and visits.

Our first priority was our demand for release from prison, since we did not recognise the right of South Africa to imprison us. After that we pressed for our transfer to jails in Namibia. We kept up the pressure for repatriation because we wanted to be near our people, where it would be easier for them to visit us.

On the afternoon of 10 May 1972 a group of warders came into our section and told us to pack our things. A Dakota plane had landed at the airport during the day and we could hear it warming up its engines. The warders urged us to hurry because our plane was about to take off for Namibia. We did not at first believe what they were saying and so we demanded to know where we were to be taken, though we knew that they would not tell us. They kept repeating that we were to be taken back to Namibia and, because we were so eager to be transferred to Namibia, we began to think that maybe we had succeeded in persuading them.

They marched us out of our section and through the main entrance of the zinc section. Outside we found ourselves mixing with our neighbours, the ANC members. Though meeting for the first time, we were not allowed to talk to one another and this added to our puzzlement and confusion. Puzzled because we were allowed to mix with the people we were not supposed to mix with before; confused because we were told that we were leaving for Namibia and ANC members were surely not going to Namibia too! Were we really being repatriated? If not, where were we going then? We marched out in silence. Because of the fence around the main section to our right, we marched as though we were heading for the harbour and thought that maybe we were going by boat and no longer by plane.

But when we were almost parallel with the office block, the warden ordered us to turn right and we found ourselves in front of the offices. They told us to stop while they cleared everybody else out of the way. We were not allowed to meet or be seen by anyone. When the way was cleared, they marched us through several gates in the passage. We were lined up facing the solitary confinement section – Makulukutu in its Zulu/Xhosa name or Makulungungu in its Namibian name. Then everything sank in. We were being taken to the solitary confinement section!

All the gates and doors in the block had recently been fitted with electric mechanisms imported from Britain and installed specifically for us, the 'terries', as we were known throughout the prison establishment. All the equipment used in the South African jails is British – locks and keys as well as handcuffs and leg irons.

The gate to Makulukutu opened and we were ushered through. We assembled in the centre of the yard. Some warders were left to guard us while others went into the 'wings' to make sure no prisoner was peeping through the windows. Having met for the first time and not having been allowed to speak to each other as we had marched together from the zinc section, we started talking to the ANC comrades in the yard. We were now a group of 51, 16 ANC comrades and 35 SWAPO members (three of our colleagues, Gerson Veii, Nathanael Homateni and Jonas Nashivela had gone to the general section). The warders tried to stop us talking but we ignored their shouts because we were too busy greeting each other.

'Haak! Haak!' started and we were ordered into the wings where all the solitary confinement cells were. There were over one hundred confinement cells, of which about half were occupied either by permanent residents or by people sent there to serve limited periods of 'punishment'. There were about six people serving 'limited' solitary terms and whose meals were halved. Among them were Steve Tshwete (ANC), Indres Naidoo (ANC), Thompson Mrambo (PAC) and Abel China Chiloane (PAC).

The cells had double doors with master locks and iron bars on the inner doors. The outer doors were left open and warders went from cell to cell sarcastically taunting us: 'Fasten your belts! The plane is about to take off!'

I was placed in cell No.66. Its back window overlooked the yard and I was able to see other prisoners in the cells across the yard. Unfortunately, I could not open the window because it was welded so that no prisoner could pass me things and vice versa. It was directly opposite the cells of Nelson Mandela, Nyati, and Ya Toivo.

The warders in Makulukutu were hostile towards us immediately we were brought into the section. When I tried to sing the Internationale, Sergeant 'Mbwingo' Van de Merwe came at my door and warned me that the solitary confinement section was a 'holy' place and no noises were allowed. I first thought that he was joking but he threatened me with 'three meals' if I did not stop– the term used for deprivation of a day's meals.

The following day, Sunday 11 May 1972, was a day that I and my compatriots will never forget. When the cells were opened, and after we had emptied our chamber pots, we were told to go and have our breakfast in the yard. The breakfast was on long wooden tables and people were lining up to go and take their plates from the tables. When we fell in into threes, I found myself standing next to a tall, heftily built man, about 6'8", who extended his hand to greet me. I put out mine to greet him and found my hand in a vice-like grip. The man introduced himself as 'Madiba Mandela'. To catch his name properly, because I could not believe what I heard, I begged his pardon. He repeated his name but still left out Nelson. Was he Nelson Mandela or was he his brother? I asked. He was Nelson but liked to use his African name, he replied. All this time our hands were locked in a grip of greeting but when I realised who he was, our grip became even stronger. We changed from hand shakes to embracing. At the tables, he introduced me to Walter Sisulu and some of his comrades.

We went to have our breakfast together at their side of the yard and I could not stop myself staring at them. I had shaken

Nelson Mandela's hand and embraced him! I am having breakfast with Nelson Mandela and Walter Sisulu! Though I was part of the Robben Island community, I did not dream that I would one day be sitting and having breakfast with the South African leaders. I was overcome with elation to have met some of the best known political figures in South Africa and whose examples many people would like to follow. I cannot remember what we talked about that day but I know that we had a lot to talk about.

I also met several other 'leaders', as everybody in Makulukutu was referred to, and met two old acquaintances, Michael Dingake and Bengu. I had met Dingake, an ANC member, in Pretoria in 1966. His trial was in progress when some of my friends and myself arrived in the Pretoria Local. He was arrested in what was then Southern Rhodesia and handed over to the South Africans. He helped carry our messages abroad to his defence counsel who also helped to pass them over to our colleagues abroad. The messages were sent to inform our colleagues that Castro (Leonard Philemon) was in South African pay. Bengu I had met in Leeuwkop prison when I and some of my colleagues were taken there to make room for the Omgulumbashe comrades. Bengu was in Leeukop on his way to Robben Island and he was the one who gave us the names of George Bizos and Ernest Wentzel, the two advocates who later became members of our defence team.

We had lunch as well as dinner together again that day. Sergeant Mbwingo, who was in charge of Makulukutu that weekend, did not try to restrict or separate us from one another. He had shown hostility towards us the first day we arrived in Makulukutu, but not today. So we had what one would call a field day to ourselves. Was this relaxed policy the official line or was it his own attitude towards us, I asked myself. The answer was not long in coming.

The following day, Monday, two of our colleagues, Simeon Shixungileni and Jonas Shimweefeleni, were locked up for no apparent reason before we went out to work. We did not worry much when our friends were not allowed to come out with us to the span. We expected to find them out when we got back. Our expectations were wrong. They had never been let out - they had not even had lunch or been given exercise, they said. They were told that they were given 'three meals' for 'refusing' to go out to work. In fact they were apparently too slow in coming out of their cells. The cells were locked during the day, and we had to be quick to leave them immediately the order was called.

We decided we would not take our food if our two comrades were not let out to have their meal. We were having porridge and eggs for dinner that evening. The caterers dished out the food when it came. We had not sent word to the Mandela group that we were hunger-striking and we did not expect them to join us. But word had somehow got round to them and when 'Fall in! Take your food!' was called, nobody fell in. Sergeant Mbwingo shouted: 'Hey! you, Mandela! Get your food!' It was difficult for Mandela and his comrades because they did not know what the cause of the strike was and could not answer when they were asked why they were not taking their food.

Mbwingo left Mandela's group and came to tell us to take our food. We politely asked him to let our two comrades out so that they could come and have dinner with us. He refused and warned us: 'You must either get your food or I will lock you all up!' We told him that we did not want any confrontation with him. If he was not prepared to do what we asked then we left it up to him to carry out his threat to lock us up.

He reported the matter to his superiors on his two-way radio and asked for their advice. Lieutenants Shapota (Fourie) and Kayoo (Van der Westerhuizen) came over and we could see that they were agitated and were spoiling for action. They had a few words with Mbwingo and went out of the section again. After that Mbwingo ordered us into the cells. He locked the doors and was gone.

We started singing freedom songs (which was forbidden) as soon as the doors were closed and continued singing until after the curfew bell. I do not know how long I had been asleep when I was woken up by barking dogs in the passage. I stood up to see what was happening and then my door was thrown open. Five warders, armed with truncheons, came storming into my cell and ordered me to strip and stand facing the wall with my legs far apart and my arms stretched out high up on the wall. I assumed they wanted to do a search raid. Before I knew what was happening, I felt a number of blows landing on my back accompanied by: 'Jou fokken Kaffir! Fokken kommie! Fokken terrie! Vanaand jy gaan kak! (You will shit tonight!)'

I could take the blows on my back no longer, so I turned and grabbed one of their truncheons as it was about to descend on me. I held it with both hands and pushed the warder away from me – he fell backward and went tumbling onto the floor. I used the truncheon to ward off the assaults from the rest of the group. I wielded the truncheon at them and because they could no longer get at me, they all fled from the cell. But they had already left several welts on my back. I was aching all over and was relieved that they had left me alone for the moment. I pushed the inner iron bar door closed after them. I expected them to come back, possibly in a larger number than before, but I was determined to fight back and not to allow anyone in, be it a warder or a dog. They did return, but only to lock the door. I threw out their truncheon before the door was locked.

I looked out of my windows to see what was happening around me. I could see that people in other cells were also being beaten up. Shapota was conducting the operation and was going from cell to cell pointing out who should be beaten and who should be spared. He was clearly enjoying every minute. It was good luck to them because we had handed them a golden opportunity to assault us *en masse*. People were screaming everywhere, accompanied by vicious barking of dogs and Shapota and his men were chanting in the passages: 'We are Boere Boys!'

The assaults went on for about one and a half hours before everything went quiet again. About three-quarters of the Makulukutu inmates had been assaulted. Brigadier Aucamp, the head of the whole South African Prison security services, was on the island on the night of the assaults. I believe that he authorised them.

The following morning we tried to see the doctor who was due on the island that day. We wanted to get medical treatment for our injuries and to complain to him about the assaults but we were prevented from seeing him. We waited the whole day and then we were told by the warders that the doctor did not want to see us. We knew that was not true but there was nothing we could do except to complain to the prison authorities about the assaults.

We queued up to go to the office to see a senior officer to complain. There was a stalemate because they wanted us to take our meals before they allowed us to see a high ranking officer. We on our part insisted that we would not eat until our complaints were heard and our demands met. Breakfast and lunch were ignored when they arrived. We stood in the queue almost the whole day waiting to put our complaints to the authorities, but nobody came.

They clearly prevented us from seeing the doctor because they did not want him to record our assault complaints on our medical records. And to suppress information about the assault incident, they made sure nothing would be entered in the complaints book. They had made themselves scarce except for Mbwingo and other warders on duty. In the meantime, other sections heard about our hunger strike and wanted to join in solidarity with us but we sent them word not to.

On 14 May, we decided to take our meals again after we had voted the previous evening to end the strike. It was a strategic move taken to fight the system 'on a full stomach' from a position of strength. Mbwingo was joined on duty by Sergeant Warder 'Watawata' Carstens, who had equal responsibility with Mbwingo in Makulukutu, but who had been away on the weekend. Watawata was one of the rigid law enforcers. Immediately he arrived in the section, he ordered that our group should not mix with the Mandela group again.

We tried in vain for the whole week to see the doctor or anybody high up in the prison hierarchy. We were allowed to see Dr Gosling when he arrived the following week on a Thursday, eleven days after the assaults took place. Dr Gosling was considered by many prisoners, myself included, as liberal. We were, however, disappointed by his response – he was either brainwashed or totally controlled by the system. Everybody who went to see him about assaults came out complaining that the doctor was even worse than the warders. He either did not want to concede that we had been assaulted or he pretended not to see the streaks which were still visible on our bodies.

When I myself went in, he asked what my complaint was. Before I finished telling him, he cut me off, saying he had had already heard about the 'conspiracy' cooked up by prisoners against prison officers.

'Where are the scars?' he demanded.

I had about ten or so streaks on my back and all he could tell me was that there were no 'open wounds or scars'.

'When were you assaulted?' he wanted to know.

'Last week, doctor,' I told him.

'Why didn't you see the doctor last week?' he demanded.

He dismissed me by telling me that I was lazy and warned me that if I did not want to work, I would face ugly consequences. I felt demoralised. So the general assaults of 12 May 1972 went unrecorded by any doctor who visited the island during those crucial two weeks.

Not long after that, we were again visited by Dr Zugger of the International Committee of the Red Cross. He was careful this time and had secured an undertaking from the prison authorities that the interviews had to be private – they could take place within the full view of the warders but not within their hearing. We were satisfied with the arrangements he made and received him well. He had come only to see the Namibians jailed on Robben Island and not any other prisoners, he told us. We apologised for our behaviour to him when he first came to see us in the zinc section. It had not been our intention to rebuff him but our situation had been very delicate. He accepted our apology.

We told him about our demands for transfer to jails in Namibia and about the assaults and the way they were handled without being recorded. We then told him that we wanted to see the solitary confinement section closed down because it was unhealthy and people locked up in there were prone to several illnesses, just as they were in the zinc section. We pointed out that prisoners in Makulukutu had to carry and empty their chamber pots every day. We complained about the general treatment of all prisoners on the island. We pointed out the discrimination in diet. Indians and 'Coloureds' were given what was called the 'D' diet while everybody else was given the 'F' diet. Our diet was unbalanced: maize porridge at breakfast and dinner and boiled mealies (maize) for lunch day in and day out. Indians and Coloureds were given vegetables, bread with margarine, coffee and milk. We demanded the abolition of the discriminatory diet. We also wanted fruit.

We also told Dr Zugger that we had no privileges or rights like other prisoners. We were not allowed to study. We had no right to read any books except the Bible and we could not visit the library. We could not write or receive more than one letter per month. We could not be visited more than once by one person per month. We wanted to meet other prisoners without any restrictions placed in our way. We also gave him the general picture of medical treatment on Robben Island.

Doctor Zugger listened with great interest and took down everything we told him. We could see that he was pleased with the way things were going. We were also pleased to get so many things off our chests. He made it clear, however, that he himself could do nothing about our complaints. He was going to present them to the authorities, who were the only people who could deal with them. The duty of the International Committee of the Red Cross was to try to ensure that we received better treatment while in prison.

Dr Zugger had hardly left the island when we were subjected to more harassment. 'Now your Red Cross is gone, the Boer Boys are in charge again,' was the kind of remark thrown at us by warders. The doctors, too, joined in, saying that we Namibians were a bunch of idiots. 'The Red Cross will not give you medical treatment. It is left to us to give you what treatment we can,' one doctor remarked.

The South African regime hates to admit that it only does things after it has been pressurised by outside intervention. While on one hand they harassed us after the ICRC visit, on the other they introduced a number of changes. Typical of the South Africans, one might say! The doctors were more assertive in prescribing treatment to prisoners. Shipponeni was given a bed in hospital on the doctor's orders. For the first time, we were allowed to study and were given application forms to fill in. We were also allowed to get books from the Makulukutu library. Later, we were allowed to play sports on a field alongside the prison. But the most important thing for me personally came as a big surprise one sunny Saturday afternoon, with a visit from my Aunt Beata.

Anyone wanting to visit relatives on Robben Island first had to apply for permission which was either granted or refused on the grounds of family relationship with the prisoner concerned. The only relatives who counted were parents, or children or brothers or sisters. Permission was often refused on the grounds that they were either not in these second categories or were young or too politically oriented, but my Aunt Beata was allowed to come because I put down her name as my only close relative.

We were sitting playing chess in the yard when a warder walked in with a piece of paper in his hand. Because we were not known by our names he asked who was 5/68. He told me my visitor was waiting at the harbour. I could not believe that the warder was serious. When I entered the glass cubicle separating prisoners from their visitors, I saw my aunt's face peeping through. She was trying to adjust to the dim light in the cubicle so that she could see me better. I do not know what she was expecting me to look like – perhaps like an inmate of an asylum.

With my aunt in the cubicle was a Special Branch man I knew from Windhoek. I was about to object when another Special Branch man entered my cubicle. What did they want? Was this a family visit or an identification parade? I wanted to know. The officer in charge told me this was the normal procedure. The Special Branch men had come to monitor our conversation as they spoke our language. They were joined by warders on either side. I wondered whether my aunt had been forewarned about this kind of intimidation. I stood up to confront the officer in charge and nearly walked out but, considering the effort and money my aunt had invested in the whole plan, I swallowed my pride and sat down.

Several other cubicles were occupied by other prisoners who were all shouting to their visitors in order to be heard. I was pleased and happy to see my aunt after a separation of ten years. I was proud of her because she was the first Namibian to come and visit us on Robben Island. Not only that, she had suffered a lot. After my arrest in 1966, she had been picked up several times for questioning under Section 6 of the Terrorism Act. She spent periods ranging from two weeks to three months in detention and each time was released only to be picked up again after a few weeks or months. Yet she was not frightened but was determined to find out where I was imprisoned. She is a small woman by stature with a big heart who must have made huge efforts and sacrifices to come there.

Sitting behind the pane, I was only able to see her head and shoulders. I began shouting greetings to her and she shouted back. Such was the noise from adjacent cubicles that we could hardly hear each other, let alone understand what the other was saying. We tried to mix shouting with sign language but sign language was prohibited and treated as passing on secret information. So we were left with shouting very loudly as the only alternative. The louder we shouted the louder the others had to shout. We were like lunatics trying to outbid each other.

It seemed like just one minute when my 30 minutes of visiting time were up. They pulled a board across the window pane and the warder and the policeman in my cubicle grabbed me to take me back to prison. I shook them off, protesting at the length of time I was given. I demanded to see the warder in charge. 'What's your problem?' he demanded. Considering that this was my first visit in the four years I had been on Robben Island, and considering the distance my aunt had travelled to come to the island, I asked him to be reasonable and to extend my visiting time for at least another 30 minutes.

It was not in his power to change the official policy, he told me. I asked to be allowed to use his radio to talk to his senior who might consider my case as a special one. He himself radioed and it was agreed that I should be given an extension of another half an hour. My aunt was brought back to our window – there were fewer shouts in the buildings because many visitors had left after their 30 minute quota. We were forbidden to discuss anything political but 'family' matters only. Before our time was up, I applied for my aunt to return the following day for an hour. Normally, applications had to be sent to Pretoria before they were approved, but after a few radio messages here and there, my application was finally approved. Everything has to be fought for in a South African jail and more so on Robben Island.

The atmosphere was calmer when she returned on Sunday and I was able to ask about a number of things. I enquired about the girl I had been engaged to and was told that she was now married to one of my friends and they had several children.

My aunt had opened the door to Robben Island and before long, some of my colleagues also had visits from their families.

Throughout our stay in Makulukutu, beside psychological and mental torture, we were subjected to daily harassment and physical beatings. Mbwingo (Sergeant Van de Merwe) claimed that his brother had been killed in the Caprivi Strip by our forces. He was very bitter towards us and when he told Temba Linus Dlamini (an ANC prisoner who worked as a cleaner) about it, Dlamini responded by asking what his brother was doing in the Caprivi. Mbwingo picked up a broom stick and hit him several times before Temba could grab the broomstick and take it away from him.

We Namibians were the main targets of hostility and random assaults. We were singled out because we were the 'terries' responsible for the 'communistic' attacks and killings of South African soldiers: we were allegedly the spearhead of the 'communist onslaught' against South Africa. Among those who were assaulted while we were in Makulukutu were Eliaser Tuhadeleni, Ya Toivo, Julius Shilongo, Mathews

Ngcobo (ANC) and many others from other sections. Ya Toivo and Shilongo were first put into straight jackets before they were assaulted.

All the assaults took place in the offices or in the passage to or from the offices while someone was being escorted there. Tuhadeleni, Ya Toivo and Ngcobo were taken away from us and were given summary sentences of 6 months each in solitary confinement, without being charged or being brought before the court. Court cases were going on all around the prison. Prisoners found guilty had their sentences increased by several months or years where the 'offence' was considered to be serious. There was nowhere one could appeal against these sentences or convictions although there was a token prison review board which never exonerated anyone found guilty.

Ya Toivo was accused of incitement but never given a chance to defend himself before the court against the allegations. Others returned to us after they served their six month periods but Ya Toivo's was extended for another six months. When we left Makulukutu in 1973, we left him there still serving his second six month solitary confinement sentence. When he finished his time in solitary confinement, he was not allowed to rejoin us, but remained in Makulukutu until the day he left Robben Island.

21

Operation survival

After nine months in Makulukutu, our group was taken to one of the cell blocks in the general/communal section. It had four cells but we occupied only two of them. As a general rule of the prison department, officers and men had to spend a limited period working on Robben Island. There was always a movement of staff coming and going. After the assault in May 1972, a new regime arrived on the island. They changed almost everything, accusing the regime before them of liberalism. Most of the disturbing changes they introduced were in the diet.

They complained that the prisoners were too wasteful and to curb this, they cut the diet almost by half. By then we Namibians were given mealie rice (crushed mealies) at lunch as a result of us refusing to eat boiled mealies, which we do not eat at home. The new regime believed that we were spoiled and would eat boiled mealies if there was nothing else. So they decided to drop mealie rice from the menu, cutting costs at the same time. They were starving us. There were food shortages throughout the prison. Several hunger strike protests were considered in a number of sections.

The new commanders were a breed of fanatics who believed might is right. They were headed by a brigadier who did not look anyone straight in the eye, would not listen to complaints and about-turned immediately he saw prisoners coming towards him. If he found it impossible to make an about-turn, he looked away instead. He always behaved as if he had something to hide – his identity maybe? He would do anything to hide his face from scrutiny. His behaviour gained him the nickname Martin Borman after the Nazi wanted for war crimes. (I suspect that if Nazi war criminals are to be found anywhere in the world in large numbers, they could be found in Namibia and South Africa and possibly in the prison services, where they would be safe from the public eye.)

Our leaving Makulukutu did not bring an end to assaults and harassment. If anything, we were subjected to more daily assaults and victimisation. Prisoners in South African jails are not given a chance to serve their sentences as charged and passed by the courts. They are victims of revenge attacks by the warders who see them as presents from the government for them to vent their anger on.

Immediately we arrived in our new quarters, our lives were made miserable by Sergeant 'King Kong' Marais who was in charge of our section from 1974 to 1976. He was a sadist who pounced on young, defenceless victims.

For a time we were no longer allowed to go and work outside, but had to stay inside the prison. Chopping-blocks and axes were brought into the yard behind our section and lorries brought in logs for us to chop. They would not let us use the loo in the section, so a toilet was set up near to where we were working. To relieve ourselves, we had to ask permission to use the makeshift toilet only feet away. This made us rebellious and we objected to using the toilet on the grounds that it was too close to where we were working and it posed a danger to our health.

We thus continued using toilets inside the section in defiance of the system. This resulted in numerous scuffles, with prisoners being beaten up and sent to Makulukutu for 'rehabilitation' for several days or weeks. I was one of those who spent my days in and out of solitary confinement.

In 1974 we were joined by more prisoners. About twenty members of APDUSA (African Peoples' Democratic Union of South Africa) and one ANC member arrived at the peak of tension with the warders. There were two practising lawyers in the group, Kadar Hassim and Vusani. Another, Sunny Venkatheradnam, was a law student (by correspondence) at the University of Natal. There were three school teachers and several other highly qualified people, as well as some peasants among them. They were all charged with contravening the Internal Security Act, while the ANC member was tried under the Terrorism Act. We were reinforced in our fight against the repressive prison system.

With lawyers in our midst, we realised that there were other means than hunger strikes to force the issues in prison. We had obtained copies of the prison regulations and our legal department went to work. They came up with the suggestion of a petition. Petitions were forbidden in prison but they had thought of a way out. Before we submitted the petition, legal representation would first be secured. The lawyers would consult their partners outside and a case would be built against the prison services – to use as a counter-measure if the prison department decided to institute charges against us for writing a petition. Our counter-case would (if the need arose) target the Commanding Officer of Robben Island Prison, the head of prison services Brigadier Aucamp, and the Minister of Prisons as respondents. But first we had to set out our complaints and submit them to the prison authorities.

The idea of the petition was born after the prison services had brought charges against some of us who had been working at the bamboo seaweed factory. There were three groups – one group working as machine operators, another cutting bamboos into six inch-long pieces to fit in the machine, and the other unloading the bamboos from the trucks and spreading them to dry. I was one of the machine operators.

We had been working at the bamboo factory for about a year. The machine operators had insufficient protective measures against the great amount of dust emitted from the machine when it was operating. But the people who suffered most were those chopping bamboos in the enclosure between the machine room and a storage room. Dust coming from the machine room windows poured into the enclosure. They complained about this to no avail. One day they had had enough and walked out of the enclosure to wait for the machine to finish working before they returned to continue the job.

The warders would not have it and tried to force the prisoners back into the enclosure. The prisoners reasoned that they would go back there as soon as it was safe enough. We inside the machine room did not know what was going on. I was wanted to help to interpret, and because the machine was so noisy, communication was impossible.

A warder tapped me on the shoulder and beckoned me to go outside. The machine stopped and those inside came out to listen to what was going on. Everybody heard the order 'Fall in!' and to disobey it meant punishment. We all fell in and I expected to be called upon to interpret. But the next order that followed was to march back to prison. What was going on?

We silently marched back to the section and it was only then that we heard what had happened. A warrant officer had been called to talk to the bamboo choppers. When they repeated their refusal to return to the enclosure while the machine was still working he wanted no further argument and instead he gave instructions that we should all be returned to prison.

Later we were called to the office to be given charge sheets. We worked in three groups but were all charged with 'refusing to work'. Our case was to be heard by a prison officer/ magistrate in a month's time we were told. We immediately asked for application forms to apply for legal advice. These were to be approved by Pretoria, they told us. This would give us ample time to prepare and compile our petition before the bamboo case was brought before the court.

The petition was signed by most of us and we handed it to the Commanding Officer when he came for inspection one day. We did not want to hand it over to his junior officers because we were afraid it might not reach him. Included in the petition was a protest at the pending bamboo case and conditions in the section, especially a prohibition placed on us preventing us from visiting other prisoners in other cells in our block. We were not allowed to be in any other cell without permission. We often ignored the regulations and on many occasions were found to be illegally in other cells.

Some days later Kayoo (Lieutenant van der Westerhuizen) came carrying a piece of paper. He called us into one of the cells to read us some instructions. He told us that the Commanding Officer and his advisory committee had decided, after reading our petition, to suspend for six months all privileges which by that stage we had become entitled to. The prison authorities would come to take away all study books, library books and any other reading material except the Bible. Tobacco and other smoking facilities and sports equipment would also be taken away, and sports suspended. Our sports field would be turned into a working place. Indoor games also had to go. Letters and visits would be cut or even suspended. They were always slow to act on something in our favour but quick to inflict punishment. And true to their word, the following day we were sent to break up stones on our sports field, and they cleaned books and other 'luxuries' out of all the cells .

They wanted to establish who had organised the petition. We maintained that the complaints contained in it concerned us all. But our case was weakened by some of our Namibian comrades who, when the petition came up for signatures, would not sign it. The prison authorities thought they had found a weakness and wanted to exploit the differences between us. They took out those who did not sign and asked them who organised the petition but failed to persuade them to co-operate. They also took aside the two lawyers and two of the school teachers amongst us. They accused them of incitement and wanted to charge them for that. What they were not aware of was the strategy we had arranged earlier – that if anything happened, we would begin legal action through our legal representatives outside.

Sunny Venkatradnam was smuggled into Makulukutu to take particulars from the four colleagues. He made drawings of their cells and took down information contained in notice cards on their doors. He ascertained why they had been taken in and for how long. This and other related information was then passed over to lawyers in Durban and Cape Town. The lawyers were the same ones we had applied to for our defence in our bamboo case. Some of them, such as Advocate Kawalsky of Cape Town, had been dealing with cases on Robben Island for quite some time.

The lawyers wrote to the prison department and complained about the suspension of our privileges and the solitary confinement of our four colleagues. After that they released information to the press on behalf of families who were worried about their relatives in solitary confinement – the families had not been given answers to their applications to visit them in prison. They challenged the prison service to provide satisfactory answers or they would be forced to seek legal advice. The authorities promised to investigate the matter while playing delaying tactics.

Before these matters were resolved, another tragedy struck our community and our SWAPO movement. Comrade Petrus Simon Niilenge (accused No. 36 in our trial), who was suffering from chest pains, died in hospital on Robben Island. He was found to be suffering from an unidentified illness when taken to the hospital in Cape Town. Because he could not express himself in either English or Afrikaans, I was taken there one evening in a speedboat to interpret for him (I accompanied many colleagues to hospital for interpretation purposes on the mainland).

The doctors wanted to extract a blood sample from his liver for tests. I explained the position to him and he agreed to the sample. After a week, I was taken there again, this time to accompany him back to Robben Island. He was still in pain but there was nothing more the doctors could do for him and he was to be taken to the island to await his fate. The doctors confided in me that Niilenge was suffering from liver cancer and asked me not to tell him or anyone else. He died four months later. We tried to secure the transfer of his body to his family but because his wife could not finance its transfer and the state was not prepared to help, he was buried in Cape Town like comrade Festus Nehale who died before him.

The situation was getting worse as a result of the petition and the subsequent suspension of privileges. Smokers in particular were badly affected. It was distressing to see them unashamedly rushing out of the section in search of cigarette stubs immediately the cell doors were opened. Many who were normally jovial fellows looked depressed throughout the suspension period. But while some remained gloomy throughout, some came out determined never to touch the stuff again. And true to their word, they never smoked again after privileges were restored.

Despite the suspension of all privileges we were, however, not without support. Many people in other sections risked not only their own privileges but their skins to support us. Prominent among these was Abel Chiloane or 'Shikololo' ('corner dweller' because his cell was in a corner) whose daring was known throughout the prison. He would always turn up in a place and at a time when the warders did not expect him. He would suddenly appear, deliver his goods and be gone before they knew what he was doing. They would try to apprehend him, but they could pin nothing on him. Because we were no longer allowed to go out, Shikololo was our main news supplier. At times when he knew that warders were watching him, he would come with back-ups. While the warders would keep an eye on him, his back-ups would deliver. He kept us going until the restoration of our privileges. Everybody in our section, despite party political allegiances, had a high regard for him.

Before the restoration of our privileges we had another visit from the International Committee of the Red Cross. They sent a powerful delegation of four men this time. They were not prepared to compromise with the prison authorities. They had come not only to see the Namibians but also the rest of the prison population and they wanted to listen to personal as well as joint complaints and requests. Discussions would be private and confidential, although some of it had to be known to the prison authorities in order to solve the problems facing us in prison. The delegation was headed by a Dr Meaullierlo and he proved himself capable. Everyone in the delegation had a specified task to perform. Their visit was crucial and brought a number of really good changes on Robben Island.

Before they left, Dr Meaullierlo promised us Namibians some financial support because we had no regular contacts with our families and no financial support. He also said he would leave some money for our sport. The prison authorities did not object and for the first time we were able to buy a few things for ourselves. After the ICRC left and we had served our six months of deprivation, things started improving. A number of restrictions were removed. Many people were allowed to study. The discriminatory diet was replaced with a non-discriminatory one. We were allowed to go out to work again and sport activities resumed.

Although we were now all given the same diet with more variation, the quantities were smaller. They wanted to prove that blacks would not be satisfied eating a 'white man's diet'. They wanted us to complain about the quantity so that they would have an excuse to reintroduce the discriminatory diet. Some prisoners did just that and played straight into the hands of the authorities. Some of the South African prisoners staged a hunger strike despite advice from many of us that it had not been thoroughly discussed. It was a futile effort from the start. The authorities hardly noticed it because many of us were still taking our meals: we argued that we preferred to fight the system from a position of strength with something in our stomachs. We did not want to go back to them on our knees asking to have our diet back. After a few days, some strikers resumed taking their meals and the strike ended in failure with us Namibians accused of being responsible for its collapse.

The charges against our four colleagues accused of incitement were dropped, partly as a result of the ICRC's visit but mainly due to the publicity in the press.

The bamboo case was, however, to proceed and by the end of November 1974, we were formally charged. Our lawyers, Messrs Kawalsky of Cape Town and Pillay of Durban, came to see us. They conducted an inspection-in-loco of the factory and its surroundings immediately after the case opened in the office of the Commanding Officer. The presiding judge was Captain Trout from Pollsmoor Prison on the mainland. Prosecuting was Warrant Officer Du Plussis. The defendants were eight machine operators (myself included), twenty bamboo cutters and eight spreaders and driers. We were all accused of refusing to work and disobeying a 'lawful command' to go back to work. We objected to being tried by a prison officer because we believed that we would not receive a fair trial and that he would rule in favour of his fellow officers. We demanded to be tried by a magistrate, but we were turned down. The case was postponed for the December holidays until January 1975.

The bamboo case took place against the background of the escalation of the war in Namibia. The Portuguese *coup d'état* of 25 April 1974 shook the imperialist world and the racist minority regimes of Rhodesia and South Africa felt vulnerable. The frontiers of minority rule were pushed back and the so-called Portuguese colonies were liberated.

The Peoples' Liberation Army of Namibia (PLAN), as SWAPO's military force was now known, had been hitting the enemy very hard. By 1974, PLAN had opened up several more fronts and it had penetrated deep into the Namibian hinterland.

The intensification of the fighting had some repercussions on us in prison. On Christmas Eve 1974, SWAPO combatants launched a number of well planned attacks along the Namibian border with Angola, with devastating effect.

The first we knew that something was up was when stones were brought onto our soccer field and we were ordered to bring hammers to break them up – sporting activities had been suspended for the day. We knew something had happened by the look in the warders' eyes which was enough to make us shiver with fright. We were not given a chance to change, so we went to work in our sports gear without asking questions.

In the afternoon, the news came that the South African forces had been thoroughly beaten on the border. In the Caprivi Strip, several colonels and captains were reported killed. There was mourning throughout South Africa and Namibia. Though it was mainly the people in the 'war zone' in Namibia who bore the full brunt of retribution from the South African soldiers, we in prison did not escape. Whenever South African troops suffered heavy losses, the warders turned their anger on us – defenceless prisoners.

World news figured prominently in our priorities. Because we were completely cut off from the rest of the world we would go to any length to obtain news and we gathered information from any conceivable source. Prison officials were not excluded from our list of news suppliers and were often the main source of information. They often carried newspapers around with them in their cars on their inspection rounds of working prisoners. Prisoners would surge around the officers' cars when they parked and before they knew what was happening, their vehicles would have undergone thorough checks and any newspapers removed.

In order to find news, we risked the danger of being caught or even being shot. During the deprivation period, we used to burrow through the fence and find our way to the ash pits or to the warders' township in search of the papers. Many of us were caught in the act and convicted. Nghidipo Jesaja Haufiku and Jacob Joseph Kashea were amongst those caught: they were sentenced to one month in solitary confinement with reduced diet. When our bamboo case resumed in January 1975, our lawyers too were targets of our news-gathering service. To save them from being accused of supplying us with newspapers we had to steal them – we never found out whether they knew.

The bamboo trial resulted in the acquittal of the eight spreaders and the conviction of the machine operators and bamboo cutters. Those with previous convictions were sentenced to 15 or 30 days in solitary confinement. The first offenders were given 5 days in solitary confinement – all with half rations.

We appealed against both convictions and sentences and it was agreed that we should not serve the sentences before the appeal was heard. But Warrant Officer Du Plessis who prosecuted, and who did not hide his hatred of us, decided to send us to Makulukutu and refused to answer our questions about our appeals. Some weeks later, after we had served out our sentences, we were informed that the appeals were successful. Our complaints and requests for 'compensation' for wrongful conviction and sentencing were brushed aside with: 'You were found not guilty on a technicality.'

Though we lost the case, it was the beginning of our successes. Whereas it was difficult for us to employ the services of lawyers in the past, the bamboo case set a precedent for future cases. We were now able to be represented by lawyers and the era of arbitrary punishment had ended. In one case comrade Immanuel Shifidi was charged with disobeying a 'lawful command'. It was a Sunday and the weather was cold. To protect himself, Shifidi wrapped a blanket around his shoulders. The warder on duty did not like it, so he told Shifidi to put it away, but Shifidi reasoned that he was feeling cold. The warder took this to mean 'disobedience' and decided to lay a charge.

Shifidi was able to consult a legal expert but like many of

my compatriots he was unable to express himself clearly in the two official languages, Afrikaans and English. When he was taken to Makulukutu for a period of two weeks to await his 'court' case, he asked me to interpret for him. As a result, I ended up spending several days in Makulukutu with him. They would not let me go back to the section for fear of gathering some 'information' with which to win the case. I ended up suffering from a minor asthma as the cells were cold and the walls peeling from condensation. Shifidi lost the case – it was one battle lost but the struggle for survival continued.

Lazarus Zacharia was accused of assaulting a warder. His lawyer defended him successfully – the warders contradicted each other and he walked away free. Several more cases were brought against some of our colleagues and were thrown out because of lack of evidence. Kaleb Tjipahura was accused of writing and delivering 'political' lectures. Kanyeule was accused of collecting and distributing newspapers. Both were acquitted. But some did not get away with it. Martin Kapewasha was caught while on his way to collect some newspapers and was given 30 days' solitary confinement. Ruben Iitengula and Ben Uulenga were charged with attempting to escape from prison (they were going to the warders' township to get papers) and each served 30 days in solitary confinement.

In 1975, the ICRC delegates visited us again and reported on the things they had discussed with the authorities. They had made no progress with our request to do some 'creative' jobs rather than breaking up rocks, collecting firewood or digging quarries and cleaning beaches. We wanted to do jobs which could enable us to fit ourselves back into society. The ICRC doctor had diagnosed a number of TB cases but some doctors from the mainland together with prison officials had contradicted him. Then came Dr Rom, also from the mainland, who confirmed the ICRC's findings. But most importantly Dr Rom was his own man. He resisted being bullied into obeying instructions from the prison service.

The first major contribution he made was when he examined Jonas Shimweefeleni, prisoner No. 363/69, and found that his kidneys were deteriorating. He recommended that Shimweefeleni be released from prison so that he could undergo a kidney transplant operation. He was of a rare blood type, and the only possible donor would be a close family member, or else he would die in prison: he had only a few years left to live.

Dr Rom's recommendations were overruled by Lieutenant Shapota and some other doctors who said that his diagnosis was wrong – later examinations proved that Shimweefeleni's kidneys were indeed deteriorating. Dr Rom lost his licence to visit the island and was later found dead in Cape Town – the post-mortem said of a 'heart attack'. He was popular with prisoners and he was a great loss to us.

It was clear from their report that the ICRC delegation presented the authorities with constructive suggestions and recommendations, but the authorities did not commit themselves to anything tangible – they just made vague promises to make it easy for them to wriggle out of any situation later. But we were glad to find someone who was on our side and their regular visits led to some results.

*   *   *

Three SWAPO Youth League members – Jeremia Ekandjo, chairman, Jacob Nghidinwa, his deputy, and Martin Mvula Kapewasha – arrived on Robben Island early in 1974 after being convicted under the Sabotage Act. Everybody arriving on Robben Island for the first time had to spend two or three months in Makulukutu to be 'rehabilitated' before they were brought to our section. Warder King Kong Marais found these young men easy targets and preyed on them. He subjected them to continual physical, mental and psychological torture and harassment. Jacob Nghidinwa bore the brunt of the physical attacks because he was stubborn. Two more SWAPO Youth League members – Jacob Joseph Kasheya and Esriel Gabriel Taapopi arrived on Robben Island later in 1974. These youngsters had some strange ideas about Robben Island. They understood that there was 'free' education and thought that there was a 'university' on the island which offered studies. It was difficult for us to explain to them that it was not the case and studies were by correspondence only. 'Robben Island University' was an ironical term for the prison itself and not an academic institution!

Kasheya and Taapopi were the youngest of us all and King Kong was offered new targets. He would often pick on them for no apparent reason, accusing them of trivialities. He would take them to the office for punishment and would set upon them. On a number of occasions, they came back to the section with bruises. But if the bruises were too severe, they would be taken to Makulukutu and would not be allowed to see the doctor until their injuries were healed.

By 1976 things were getting worse and worse. We discussed the situation in detail and came up with a decision to send a delegation (which was illegal) to present our general complaints, with particular emphasis on unprovoked attacks against our young comrades. Though the officials were first averse to the idea of representation, they later understood its logic. This opened the way for further delegations and helped to ease the tension.

We had been raided and searched several times before but the 1976 raid was unlike any other. They came in the morning after breakfast, over 80 of them – 40 in each cell. Several dogs were 'on guard' in the corridor. We were all ordered into the bathroom and told to strip. They thoroughly searched the clothes we had on and everything in the bathroom. The raid lasted about three hours.

In our struggle for survival, we had managed to convert many warders who, against all odds, went out of their way to provide us with newspapers and even small transistor radios. They also used to tip us off whenever we were likely to be raided. They had to be really careful not to be seen by other warders, but most importantly by the 'lackeys' among the prisoners themselves. We had therefore been tipped off that there was going to be a big raid. They seemed to know that we had a small radio buried in our section which they wanted to find and confiscate, to cut us off completely from the rest of the world. Soweto was in turmoil. Namibia was again in the news on the diplomatic front, and the war had spread throughout the country. They knew that we were getting papers and a radio was something they could not allow.

We were, however, not the idiots they thought we were. After we had acquired the radio, only two people were entrusted with it and very few knew anything about its existence. Instead of it being kept in the cell, it was always kept buried in the yard and we only listened to the news when we were in the yard.

After the raid, which took three hours, we went back into our cell and found it in a mess. Many of us were now given some 'privileges' and were able to buy a few 'luxuries', like sugar, sweets and biscuits. There was chaos everywhere and the luxury items were strewn all over and on top of everything else. All our study books had been taken and study privileges were suspended. But still they could not lay their hands on the one item they were so desperate to find: the radio. It was safe in its hiding place.

While searching for our things in the rubble, we detected a newcomer, a sergeant, standing between the doorways of the two cells. He stood there with folded arms and looked into each cell as if he was trying to catch us picking up something from the rubble. He was so quiet and stood still for so long that we suspected that he was possibly the man who had led the raid - he appeared really unfriendly.

He was Sergeant Olivier, the new warder in charge of our section. King Kong Marais had been taken away. When lunch came Olivier told us to get our meal and return later to clear up our things. After lunch, he did not lock us in as King Kong used to do and did not restrict us from visiting other cells. Olivier was a member of the new regime which had taken over from the King Kong regime. There was also a new officer, third in command, Captain Harding, an English-speaking man from Port Elizabeth. As we later found out, he was pragmatic and diplomatic in his dealings with prisoners as a whole but he could be ruthless with 'difficult' individuals or a group of prisoners.

Captain Harding and his men were members of the establishment but they dealt with the situation as they encountered it and didn't rely on the 'book' to administer the prison. Olivier helped to bring the situation back to normal in our section and improved warder-prisoner relationships. Captain Harding was always ready to listen and tried to solve prisoners' problems and to avoid confrontations. He was someone one could do 'business' with. He was soon promoted to second in command although many of his juniors branded him as a 'commie' and a 'Kaffir boetjie', because he was too 'soft' with the 'Kaffirs'. But Olivier's popularity was to be short-lived because towards the middle of the year, 1976, many sections were fenced off with 19 foot high wire meshes and walls. We Namibians were again separated from the rest of the prisoners and moved to another section. The South Africans, some of whom were with us for four years, were moved to the general sections to join the other South Africans.

Many trials were going on in Namibia and South Africa in 1976. The war in Namibia had moved from the 'border' to cover half the country. Some of those who were on trial in Namibia were captured in battles around Otavi/Tsumeb/

Grootfontein or in the Otjiwarongo area and in later years, around Keetmanshoop in the far south. In 1976 some SWAPO/PLAN combatants were put on trial, the first since ourselves in 1967.

The trial resulted in Ruben Iitengula, Ben Uulenga, Lazarus Guiteb, Michael Shikongo and Naboth Iimene, all SWAPO combatants, being brought to Robben Island, despite an undertaking by South Africa some years earlier not to move any more Namibians there. When they arrived, they went directly to Makulukutu to be 'rehabilitated'. We requested that they should be allowed to join us because we didn't think rehabilitation was really necessary. Maybe because by now we were on 'good' terms with Harding, they joined us after only a few days in Makulukutu.

In South Africa the nationwide uprising which began in Soweto in June 1976 resulted in many political trials in several towns around the country. And by early 1977, Section D, the section we vacated, was filled with hundreds of young men, mostly from Soweto. They were arriving in their hundreds every day. Few of them had ever been in prison before and their attitude, like ours when we first arrived on Robben Island, was never to compromise with the system. But now we were wiser and could teach the new arrivals one or two things about how to survive in prison.

Most of the new arrivals were members of the Black Consciousness Movement (BCM). They were uncompromising and wanted to do their own thing without 'white liberals' trying to tell them how to run their own affairs. Immediately they arrived, they set up their 'Administration' consisting of all governmental departments. They had Ministers of Foreign Affairs, Labour, Defence, and Police, with a 'State President' as the head of the 'Government'. They would not take orders from the prison officials but only from their own 'Ministers'. Any warder or officials wanting to talk to them had to do so through the Minister of Foreign Affairs, otherwise nobody would listen to them. This led to heightened tensions and Captain Harding had one day to run for his life when he wanted to assert his authority. He wanted to talk to them without going through the Foreign Affairs Minister. He was hit with a brick on the head and he ordered the removal of all 'dangerous weapons'. Warders went in armed with FNL heavy-calibre rifles and dogs to remove all tools. Armed warders and dogs patrolled the section day and night. The prisoners remained locked up for 24 hours a day – they were allowed out only to get their meals. The noise of barking dogs nearly drove us mad – we were their immediate neighbours.

Instead of ordering in his warders with guns blazing, Harding employed divide and rule tactics. He found out who the 'ring-leaders' were and called them to his office one by one, where he would intimidate or beat them. The other tactic was to take one of them out, put him on a tip lorry and drive him to one of the quarries. Harding would give the prisoner a spade and order him to fill up the truck with gravel, not letting him pause to straighten his aching limbs until the truck was full. He would then order him to shovel back the gravel. Harding's tactics proved effective because many of those who received that treatment did not want to have anything to do with their comrades' advice. They would tell their 'Ministers' they had been alone at the office or at the quarry and nobody had gone to rescue them from Harding. He succeeded in dividing them and turning them against one another. In later years, and as things 'improved' in prison, they threw scorn on themselves, admitting that they had been naive.

We found the constant barking of dogs most unpleasant. They were not solving the problem but heightened the tension and nearly drove everybody in that section to insanity. We decided to send a delegation to talk to the authorities. It was well received and the following day the dogs were removed and the situation improved. Two days later the armed patrols were also removed, bringing the situation back to normal.

Amongst those brought to Robben Island after the Soweto uprising were many minors. For some reason, many of them concealed their real ages and the authorities never found out how young they were.

In 1978 a group of children from Port Elizabeth arrived and were brought to our section. I could hardly believe my eyes when, after a hard day's work, we returned to prison to find frightened small children in our section. All cells in other sections were overcrowded to bursting point but there was still room in our block. I shook their tiny hands and felt anger surging within my heart. The oldest of them was 15 years old and the youngest was 13.

What system could imprison its children without a feeling of guilt? How on earth could the so-called civilised world stand by and allow this to happen – it was beyond one's understanding. International laws provide that people under

18 should be taken into their parents' or guardians' custody or to special institutions and not be sent to prison. Yet South Africa could seemingly get away with the violation of these international provisions made to protect juveniles.

I felt bitter, not because I myself was in prison but because of what I saw as a racist attitude by many Western countries who were often quick to point the finger at countries they considered undemocratic, especially if the victims were white, but were always slow to show their disgust at the things happening in South Africa. Their silence seemed deafening when it came to injustices committed by the Pretoria regime, because the victims happened to be black. What right did the South African regime have to detain, try and imprison these juveniles, who were all sentenced to five years each, I asked myself.

Later I found the children in their cell sharpening their spoons. I watched them for a moment then asked what they were doing. They were sharpening their 'knives', was the response.

'What for?' I asked.

'To protect ourselves.'

'From what?'

They explained that in the prisons where they were detained before and during their trial they were subjected to sexual harassment by both warders and criminal prisoners alike. They expected it would be the same here and were taking no chances. We as Namibians were foreigners to them and they would not trust us.

Having been a permanent member of the delegation representing our section in dealing with the prison authorities, I asked them to stop sharpening their 'knives' so that we could talk. They took my suggestion as an effort to mislead them but reluctantly they agreed. I told them that there was not going to be any kind of harassment from us and that all we wanted was for them to feel at ease, to ask for anything they wanted and to complain if they saw or felt that something was wrong. Though we were not their fellow South Africans, we were comrades in arms fighting a common enemy, the South African Government.

They were ill-at-ease for several weeks but, as time went on, they accepted us as their comrades and together we fought for the right to meet others in other sections. Because they were so young, their bodies needed more exercise than ours, we reasoned with the authorities, and we pressed for their right to play sport with people of the same age group. It was interesting watching them growing up. When they left prison, the youngest was still under 18.

22

Attempts at co-option

In the second half of the 1970s the pressure mounted on South Africa to end its occupation of Namibia. Mass popular mobilisation, worker strikes and armed struggle in Namibia were coupled with growing diplomatic pressure. The OAU and the Non-Aligned countries were pushing for sanctions against South Africa to force it to give up Namibia. In 1976 and again in 1978, Britain, the USA and France cast a triple veto against sanctions resolutions. However, the UN did for the first time set out a concrete procedure for the transfer of power to an independent Namibia, in Resolution 385 of 1976. To help South Africa avoid sanctions, and to reduce the pressure from African and Non-Aligned countries, the Western powers set in train a seemingly endless series of negotiations. In 1975 Dr Henry Kissinger was involved in fruitless 'shuttle diplomacy'. Then in 1977 the so-called contact group – of which Canada, France, West Germany, the United Kingdom and the United States were members – came into being.

The contact group eventually came up with the plan known today as the UN plan, Resolution 435 (1978). This was a watered-down version of Resolution 385, which left much of the say during the independence process to South Africa. Pretoria, against its own principles, was advised to 'test the political waters' with the Namibian prisoners on Robben Island. Many voices, including that of Helen Suzman, an opposition member in the white South African parliament, were urging the South African regime to talk to the Namibian 'leaders' in prison.

They particularly wanted the regime to talk to Ya Toivo, who was still held on his own in Makulukutu. By so doing, some envisaged, the regime would be able to drive a wedge between SWAPO members in jail and those outside prison. They wanted to see a struggle for power develop which in the end would result in SWAPO breaking up into splinter groups, thus weakening its position at the polls and giving South African puppets in Namibia a chance of beating it in elections. Ya Toivo, SWAPO's founder member, would be the right candidate, they believed.

But the regime had a lot of difficulties in communicating

with us in prison. Ya Toivo, in particular, was uncompromising. A number of prison and government officials arranged meetings to talk to him but he always walked away from them, refusing to say a single word. To overcome this problem, the government sent agents.

Eight of my compatriots from our section as well as Ya Toivo from Makulukutu were one day called to meet someone at the visiting offices at the island harbour. Among them were Eliaser Tuhadeleni, Messach Victory and Eino Ekandjo. Waiting to see them individually was 'Professor' Jack Kemp, who claimed to be a researcher at UNISA (University of South Africa). He was writing a book on Namibia and wanted to add a section of opinions and views of the Namibians in prison on current affairs and on a future SWAPO government, he said.

I was not on 'Professor' Kemp's list but Eino Ekandjo, one of the eight, needed an interpreter because he felt that he could not talk to Kemp alone. He put down my name. They waited for me and we went into the visitor's room. The warder who brought me from the section closed the door and Eino and myself found ourselves with 'Professor' Kemp. I understood why Eino had refused to see him alone. The visit was unusual. There was no warder in sight to watch what was going on inside, as was the normal procedure for visits.

'Professor' Kemp introduced himself to me and asked Eino to brief me on his mission. Eino also told me the reason why he wanted me to be present. Two heads were better than one, he said. I told Eino that I was there as an interpreter only and not as a participant in the discussion. With the experience of meeting the ICRC delegates who always presented us with their cards whenever they visited the island, I asked for the 'Professor's' professional visiting card.

He was visibly shocked. 'What card?' he asked.

I repeated my request. He had never had one nor had he heard of anything like that before. Next I asked to see his passport. He did what I wanted him to do. He opened his jacket and removed his passport from the inside pocket. A quick glance revealed what I thought was the insignia of a captain in the South African Security Police over the inside pocket. We looked at his passport and gave it back. It revealed that his profession was a 'chef' and the passport was issued in February 1978. That was enough for me!

He wanted to know Eino's views on current affairs in Namibia. What form of government did Eino envisage in

Namibia after independence? What about the economic system? Would a SWAPO government nationalise all big private industries? Would SWAPO follow a multi-party system or introduce a one-party system when it came to power?

Before he responded to any of the questions put to him, Eino wanted to know where he had got his name from. To this 'Professor' Kemp replied agressively: 'From the UN, but I could get your names anywhere, if I wanted to!'

The policeman in him was now surfacing.

In response Eino said that he could not answer 'Professor' Kemp's questions as he was not a free man. Secondly, even if he was free he did not think he would like to be interrogated for a second time or, to put it bluntly, he did not want to talk to a policeman disguised as a 'Professor'. This made Kemp very angry and he called in a warder. He told the warder that I had asked him about a card and would the warder find out later what card I had wanted. We were unco-operative, he said, and he wanted us taken back.

Back in prison, the warder did as he was told. He called me into a small room. He searched me and wanted me to tell him what sort of card I was asking 'Professor' Kemp for. When I explained, instead of being sent back to the section, I found myself locked up for the day in Makulukutu. The same happened with everybody who saw 'Professor' Kemp – they all ended up in Makulukutu. We were only allowed to go back to the section after he had finished seeing those he wanted to see.

The next in the line of agents was 'Doctor' Fourie, a clinical psychologist and a lieutenant-colonel in the 'Social Services' section of the Prison Service. Colonel Fourie or 'Psychology' as we later nicknamed him, was specifically assigned to attend to the problems affecting the Namibian prisoners on Robben Island. This rang a warning bell in our ears. His task, as a clinical psychologist, was to listen to our complaints and problems and refer them to his department.

One day he moved his office into our section. Having heard that I was the interpreter to my comrades, he gave me a list of our names in the order we were to see him. He wanted me to help him interpret. He was annoyed by the first person to go in, who would not talk to a 'policeman'. Everybody else said the same, we all refused to talk to him. We did not like the manner in which he went about asking his questions which were reminiscent of 'Professor' Kemp's. But if everybody else made him angry, Jerry Ekandjo made him furious. Jerry was one of my colleagues who did not need an interpreter and he spent less time with Psychology than anyone else. There was a shouting match between them and Jerry burst out followed by a hail of shredded papers. Psychology called me in after Jerry. He wanted to know why everybody called him a policeman.

'Aren't you?' I asked.

'Do you also think that I'm a policeman?'

'Yes I do,' I said, rubbing salt into the wound. His face became redder than a tomato. Sitting down myself, I told him to tell me what had happened between him and Jerry.

He could not remember the questions he put to Jerry but remembered throwing papers after him. I deliberately burst out laughing. I wanted to infuriate him more before I made the point I wanted to emphasise. He was a 'doctor' in clinical psychology, I said, how did he think it helped him to lose his temper. I suggested that he was a victim of his own academic prejudice. He had failed to use his theoretical skills against the natural wisdom of less privileged people. He must feel disappointed in himself for letting his temper overtake his academic skills.

He said that he thought people did not want to talk to him because he was white. I disagreed and told him that the colour of his skin was not important to us. We could see underneath the skin, be it black or white. As I left I told him to behave more like a 'doctor' with psychological training than a policeman.

Subsequently we had a visit from Dr Mburumba Kerina who was the chairperson of SWAPO in the early 1960s. He left SWAPO and joined NUDO in 1964 but ditched it later and ran off to live in the US. Around September-October, 1978, he and many other exiles rushed back to Namibia to 'take part' in the elections envisaged in Resolution 435 of 1978, and were drawn into Pretoria's web.

Kerina came to Cape Town and stayed in Heerengracht Hotel - one of the few five-star hotels in Cape Town where blacks were allowed to stay. He wrote a 12 page letter to Ya Toivo. With it he sent several newspaper cuttings dealing with the Namibian question. He also enclosed a copy of the *Namibian Review*, a bulletin of the Namibia Independence Party. It carried a number of allegations against SWAPO, including the mistreatment of people in its camps. The bulletin carried photographs of 'starving' children who were 'taken away' from their mothers. SWAPO was running 'child battery farms', ran the accusations.

Ya Toivo was called to collect the letter personally from the office of the Commanding Officer, in the warders' township. When he got there, the Commanding Officer stood up and proffered him a handshake and a chair (which they didn't normally do). Ya Toivo declined both and demanded to be taken back to the prison, even before he was shown the letter. The Commanding Officer, in order to save the situation, had to act quickly. He handed the letter to Ya Toivo, who refused to accept it. He instead asked the Commanding Officer to tell him what was in the letter, otherwise he would return to prison.

The Commanding Officer managed to read the opening paragraph only before Ya Toivo turned to go. The Commanding Officer gave in and let him return to prison, sending the letter after him. He wanted Ya Toivo to give him his reply in a day's time. Ya Toivo wrote us a note telling us what had happened at the Commanding Officer's office and asking our opinions on the matter. We wrote back telling him to ask permission to come to our section to discuss it with us, because we did not know the contents. They would not let him come to our section but allowed him to give them names of those he would like to discuss the letter with.

He first gave them twelve names but they reduced them to eight. We would, however, be allowed to meet him only if we would confine our discussions to English, and there would be a warder stationed within hearing distance.

The meeting took place in one of the offices in prison. Present were Ya Toivo, John Otto, Eliaser Tuhadeleni, Kaleb Tjipahura, Immanuel Shifidi, Lazarus Guiteb, Joseph Hipangerwa, Lazarus Shakala and myself. Ya Toivo passed the letter and clippings to us. Kerina wanted to come and visit Ya Toivo. In his letter he said: 'Brother Kuhangwa and I as well as many others have returned to Namibia. As you can see from the documents enclosed, SWAPO is no longer the organisation we want it to be.' He held out the promise of our release from prison. After we had finished looking at the items, we found that we could not make a decision on behalf of everybody else. We wanted the decision to be unanimous and we proposed to take the documents with us to our section for thorough discussions with all other comrades.

Kerina had deserted us once before and we felt that he was

not now on our side and that his coming to Robben Island to visit Ya Toivo was not his own initiative. We were not allowed to read newspapers yet Kerina was allowed to send uncensored cuttings to Ya Toivo. Letters from our families were heavily censored but Kerina's were not. Our family members and relatives were vetted before they visited us but Kerina, who was not Ya Toivo's relative, was about to be granted that rare right to come and visit him. If ever there was anything fishy it was Kerina's intended visit!

After exhaustive deliberations over the issue, a unanimous decision was reached. We did not want Kerina anywhere near the island let alone near Ya Toivo. Our delegation therefore returned to deliver the majority verdict to Ya Toivo. He on his part had also reached his own decision. He did not want to see Kerina and he would have gone against us even if we had voted 'yes'.

Then General Roux arrived. General Roux was then in overall charge of all the prisons and was a personal advisor to P.W. Botha, the South African Prime Minister. He visited our section and was clearly frustrated by our decision not to allow Kerina to see Ya Toivo. Briefly, we pointed out the ironies which had made us suspicious.

They must have by then convinced themselves that none of their tactics would work with us. Here was Kerina preaching 'freedom' and 'independence' yet we did not jump at the opportunity he offered for our release from prison. What kind of people were we, they must have wondered. Not that Kerina had a chance of securing our release from prison – he was just gambling. He thought he might pull a rabbit out of his political hat and claim credit for our release. We knew we were merely pawns in a chess game.

Ya Toivo was uncompromising. In many instances, he refused to talk to the authorities and they found him too elusive to deal with. When they allowed us to talk to him, they did so hoping that we would persuade him to accept Kerina's visit as a 'foothold' to deal with him. The authorities again expected to find us tired of being in prison and thought we would grab at any chance of getting out. Given prison conditions, they thought that we would be easy targets. They were wrong, and what they did not know was that we were in secret daily contact with Ya Toivo and were united in whatever we were doing, despite the fact that Ya Toivo was separated from us. General Roux was finally convinced that there was nothing that would persuade us to give our views about the future SWAPO government.

Our trump card had always been that if they wanted to know SWAPO's views, there were many SWAPO members outside prison who were ready to discuss anything at any time with anybody. Their views were our views, and as long as we remained in prison, our 'personal' views would remain imprisoned with us. If they were really desperate, then they must let us out and we would enter into discussions as free men.

Towards the middle of 1979 we were given some beds for the first time. We also partially won the battle for news: we were allowed to listen to taped and censored news from the radio. Hot water, which was a privilege available only to a few with a doctor's prescription, was now available to everybody. By now the prison authorities had made a number of concessions. We were even allowed to mix and play sport with people from other sections, except people from Makulukutu.

But the main victory came in September 1979 when we were told that we could then buy and read uncensored newspapers. World news at last! There were, however, conditions attached. Only people in group A were entitled to buy and read them. Anybody allowing his paper to be read by somebody with no 'rights' would forfeit privileges and be relegated to another group. We were nonetheless pleased with our achievement and would try to be careful not to be caught smuggling them to our comrades who were not entitled to them. We had won the battle for newspapers but we were still fighting for the rights for our own radios. We failed on radios and they were still not made available to prisoners by the time I left prison in 1984.

We had been playing sport with other sections for about two months when there was another hunger strike. Three ANC combatants who had been on the death row for several months were about to be hanged. To show their solidarity with their comrades, the ANC members on Robben Island organised a hunger strike. Unfortunately, they started fasting before they let everybody else know.

They wrote us a letter requesting us to join and show our solidarity with them. The letter arrived on day one of their fast. After some discussion, we found ourselves in an awkward position. We sympathised and wanted to show our solidarity with them but felt that we could not take part due to the fact that they had already started fasting and we had not had time to prepare. Secondly, since the fasting was political and had nothing to do with prison conditions, we felt that a petition to the Pretoria regime would have been more appropriate. Thirdly, they did not state how long the fasting would last.

We indicated that we were engaged in political and armed struggles in which people were dying every day. The war in Namibia had escalated and we could not embark upon hunger strikes every time one of our compatriots was killed in battle. We understood that the struggle would be long and bitter and many would lose their lives on the road to freedom. We believed that hanging was part of the war of liberation and what we needed was to draw inspiration from fallen comrades and the determination to carry on the fight. The ANC prisoners responded that they understood and welcomed our advice and they immediately called off the strike. From then on, nothing was unilaterally undertaken by any organisation before proper consultations were made.

The condition of Comrade Jonas Shimweefeleni, who was suffering from kidney problems, deteriorated towards the end of 1978. Further examinations proved that Dr Rom's diagnosis had been correct and he underwent a kidney operation and was given a dialysis machine. But he could not have a kidney transplant done in prison and no donor could be found, and he died on 1 August 1980. Lt-Colonel Harding (now in charge of the prison) sent a message to us to send representatives to his office.

He was alone when we entered and he asked us to sit down. He then told us about comrade Shimweefeleni's death and he expressed his sympathy to us. We were touched by his behaviour and thanked him for his compassion. Before we left, we requested that Shimweefeleni's body be taken to Namibia for a proper burial, adding that we were prepared to pay for its transportation, if the state refused to help.

Unlike the previous cases where we had failed to secure permission for the bodies of our deceased comrades to be taken for burial to Namibia, Colonel Harding was sympathetic and helpful in the matter. He asked us to draw up all the arrangements and he would pass them over to the authorities. The body of comrade Shimweefeleni was thus taken home to his relatives for decent burial. However his death and the subsequent transfer of his body affected my relatives. He was my distant cousin and when we were trying to trace his close relatives, I asked my Aunt Beata Ishinda whether, in the event of his relatives not being found, she might accept some responsibilities for his burial. Bad news always travels fast and when this request reached my home people misunderstood it to mean that I was dead and my body was about to be sent to my aunt. Family members and relatives gathered for mourning and waited for my body to arrive.

Rumours were circulating in South Africa that Robben Island Prison would be closed down in 1983. All prisoners would be transferred to prisons near their families. The island was to be turned into a tourist attraction and prison buildings, especially the cells where Mandela had lived, would be preserved as museums - or so the rumours went.

In 1982 the first of a number of South Africans were transferred to prisons on the mainland. Some were even out on parole and others were given remission. The rumours multiplied. Then towards the end of 1982, Nelson Mandela, Walter Sisulu, Ahmed Kathrada, Andrew Mlangeni and two others were transferred from Robben Island to Pollsmoor Prison, outside Paarl near Cape Town. By the end of 1982 there were about 600-700 prisoners left on the island and we believed then that it was going to close after all. But Robben Island was still far from being shut down.

In 1983 the prison population decreased to about 400-500 but only one Namibian was released. By then we were doing the jobs vacated by those who had been transferred – jobs which had been denied us since we had arrived on the island. We were now doing tailoring, carpentry, shoe-making, brick laying and plastering. Towards the middle of 1983, we were again, however, involved in another court case similar to the bamboo case.

Colonel Harding had long left and a new regime had taken over. Changes in methods of tailoring, in which about twelve of my countrymen and I worked as 'apprentices', were proposed. We objected to the system because it required us to produce a quota of finished products as if we were working for wages. One person was responsible for bringing cut material into the tailoring room but the proposed procedure required everybody to collect and register his own material. This would have enabled the authorities to victimise those who they thought did not work hard enough to deserve 'gratuity'.

They went ahead and introduced the new system but we

refused to collect our own materials: we sat by our sewing machines waiting for the cut material to be brought in. This went on for about a month, after which they decided to take action against us. Lieutenant Jacobus Koetze arrived one morning after we took up our posts and ordered us to go and collect the material. We told him that we did not accept his new scheme and were ready to carry on with the old system. At this he ordered us to fall in and go back to prison.

A week later we were issued with charge sheets. We were to appear in a Robben Island magistrate's court for refusing to work. We were then given permission to write to our lawyers. After another week, the lawyers arrived, bringing with them their responses to our letters. After a further week the case started.

Mr Omar, as senior advocate, stood up to plead not guilty on our behalf. He then played our trump card: not all the accused spoke English. They had entered a request that they be given an interpreter, he said. We knew the authorities would find no one on the Island to interpret for them. They would import one from Namibia, they said, and were thus forced to call for a postponement for a month.

When the case resumed a month later, we were happy to find that the state had not found an interpreter and they applied for another postponement. It was now November 1983. But before the case resumed in December 1983, the chief witness, Warder Bruce, died from a heart attack. He had reported for work that day, took a team to the workshop and an hour later he was dead. This resulted in another postponement.

Eventually, we were all called to the office and told that the state had withdrawn the case against us. We were about to jump in jubilation when they dropped their bombshell. Since there was no longer any dispute between us they concluded that we should now go back to work under the new system!

We told them there and then that the new system was still out of the question on our part. Charge sheets were issued to us again and we were given permission to write to our lawyers. The new case started in March 1984 and it was still in progress when I left Robben Island on 7 May.

On 29 February 1984, Andimba Toivo Ya Toivo, Lazarus Guiteb, Sakaria Iihuhwa, Willem Biswa and Marius Amagulu were told to pack their things. The news reached us in our section about the drama which preceded their departure. The warders wanted to put them in leg irons and handcuffs but Ya Toivo refused to be put in either. When they told him that they were taking him to Namibia, he demanded that we all went together, otherwise he would not leave Robben Island. He only left when they told him that the helicopter taking him and his party from the island could only take a few people at a time and promised that we would follow him later. We were not allowed to go and bid them goodbye but we had a glimpse of them when the pickup taking them to the airport passed near where we were playing sport.

We later learned that Ya Toivo and Iihuhwa were released on 1 March 1984, but his three companions remained in jail. The puppets in the so-called 'transitional government' installed by South Africa in Namibia wanted to claim credit for Ya Toivo's release and were lining up to go and see him before he was freed. First to go was Sakaria Andreas Shipanga. When Ya Toivo saw him, he just turned and went back to his cell. The prison authorities tried to persuade him to talk to Shipanga but he told them that he did not want to see him. Moses Katjiuongua, who was next in line, cancelled his visit when he heard of Shipanga's failure.

The second drama was when Ya Toivo was told that he was then free to leave the prison and go home. He refused to go out until he had finished his sentence – he still had four years to go, he told them. They told him that he was given remission. He did not ask for that, he said, and requested to be taken back to his cell. Ya Toivo feared that he was being manipulated and that the South African regime and their puppets would exploit his release for their own purposes. He was also concerned that they would impose restrictions on him.

Not knowing what to do with him, the prison officials called for help from the Administrator-General's office. Sean Cleary, the secretary to the Administrator-General, was sent to tell Ya Toivo that his release was unconditional and he was given an undertaking that he would not be victimised after his release. But Ya Toivo would still not budge. It was only when he was threatened with dogs and removal from prison by force, that he decided to leave.

23

Freedom

We had just settled in on the evening of 6 May and were preparing for our studies when the door of the cell opposite ours was opened. We thought it was a raid and ran to hide our unauthorised paraphernalia. However, when our cell door was opened, the warders did not rush in as they normally did. Instead they stood outside and one of them carrying a piece of paper entered the cell. He called several numbers representing our names and said that we should collect our things and leave the cell within five minutes.

We grabbed the few things we could carry under our arms and were not given time to ask where we were going or to say goodbye to the colleagues we were leaving behind. Fifteen of us in all were herded towards the office block. Seven were taken to Makulukutu where they spent the night while eight of us spent the night in the clinic section. At about six thirty the next morning they took us to the office where we were told that we were to be transferred to Namibia.

They gave back some of our confiscated items, some of which we did not even know existed. I found three letters and photos from relatives and friends which had been confiscated without my knowledge and five letters and twelve photos which, I was informed, were kept with my 'private' property. We were not given a chance to look at them or complain. They gave back our other things such as watches and the books we were not allowed to read while in prison. They did not, however, give back my French and German Teach Yourself books which I had been allowed to purchase but not to use, because no 'foreign' languages were allowed to be studied in prison.

In the passage, they put us in leg irons and handcuffs and put us on a truck and drove us to the island's airport, where we were put aboard an army helicopter which flew us to the Ysterplaat air base near Cape Town. Dakota was waiting to take us to Windhoek. Four warders got in with us and it took off at about 9 o'clock in the morning. On the Dakota I practised a trick somebody had taught me – how to open handcuffs. I was amazed to find that, using a safety pin, one could easily unlock handcuffs. With warders looking the other way, I undid my leg irons as well.

After a couple of hours we flew over the Orange River and entered Namibian airspace. It was the first time I had flown over the southern part of Namibia. Many parts of the country, from the Orange River into the interior, are dry and barren. From the air it all looked like a desert until we reached the Rehoboth and Windhoek areas. It was a windy afternoon and the plane was buffeted by strong winds over the hills around Windhoek. However, we landed safely at Eros airport in the late afternoon. The Dakota came to rest at the far end of the airport. I was struck by the change around the place. Whereas in the past one saw only civilian aircraft there, now military aircraft outnumbered the civilian ones. All entrances to the airport were controlled by the military police – everyone leaving or entering the airport perimeter was thoroughly checked.

Two vans and a team of warders from Windhoek Central Prison came to meet us. In charge was Colonel Prins, seconded from South Africa. He had been posted on Robben Island and because he worked with us while there, he was an 'expert' on Namibians. He was now the Commanding Officer in charge of Windhoek Central Prison. He came over to greet us and wanted to shake our hands, but we declined because he did not try to shake our hands while he was on Robben Island. I had a personal grudge against him because he was responsible for the confiscation of my lecture books!

Windhoek was a changed place. Our drive through its wide streets made me feel as if I was passing through a foreign country. Many of its formerly narrow streets had been broadened into two lane roads. The prison itself, which had been in the centre of the city, had been moved to the outskirts. It was now a few miles from Katutura black township and the sprawling city itself was about to engulf it. Next to the prison was the Katutura State Hospital, where blacks are treated. This whole area which was a wilderness in the sixties was now a bustling suburb.

Security was tight at the prison when the two vans carrying us drove through the gates. In prison, they took down our particulars as if we were arriving for the first time. They then took us to the coloured section. Two young army doctors came to examine us under the supervision of a nurse from the Katutura State Hospital. We put our problems to them and for the first time we got a hint that we were about to be set free.

After examinations, the doctors told us where we could find the Katutura Hospital. 'You just turn left and the big building you see is the Katutura Hospital,' they said. When we reminded them that we were prisoners, they said they had heard that we were to be set free the next day. They left and we settled in for the night and waited to be freed the following morning.

No black warders were allowed to come near us and the night duty warder, who arrived at about six pm, must have been warned that we were 'dangerous' people and he must not talk to us. We tried to attract his attention and be chatty with him but he chose to stay away from us. But having been long in prison, we soon had him eating out of our hand. We first asked him for a lighter to light a cigarette. He hesitated for a moment, looked at the door to the section and then produced a cigarette lighter. He was offered a cigarette which he accepted and we asked whether he knew who we were. He said he knew that we were terrorists from Robben Island.

'Have you ever seen a terrorist before?' we asked.

He said he had not. Another glance at the door, then, 'They told us that you were animals and not human beings,' he said.

'What do you think now that you have seen us? Do you believe that we are animals?' we asked.

We did not ask any further questions because the door to the section opened, and the night duty commander came in to find out whether everything was alright.

The following morning, 8 May 1984, we waited to be freed, but we ended up waiting the whole day. Towards late afternoon, I asked if I could use a telephone to ring my family in Windhoek. They told me to ask the permission of the Commanding Officer. When I asked to see him, I was told that he had gone to see the Administrator-General, the South African 'governor'. Later, when we could no longer restrain ourselves and we asked what was happening, we were told that the Administrator-General had gone on holiday!

Our SWAPO comrades in Windhoek did not know that we had arrived the night before and thought that we were still on Robben Island. The following day I tried again to ring my people. Neither the Commanding Officer nor the Administrator-General were in Windhoek, I was told. So we waited for another day.

While still on Robben Island, we had received information that the security situation in the north of Namibia was very bad because of attacks by the police and army. And while we were now waiting to be released, we decided that we would all ask to be released in Windhoek in the care of SWAPO and to travel up north only when the security situation warranted it. But when the warders arrived on the morning of 10 May they had only six names of those to be freed into Windhoek. The rest were to be escorted to the north.

Eino Ekandjo, David Hamunime and Philemon Shitilifa were the first to be called to the reception. They never came back and towards three o'clock in the afternoon, Lazarus Zacharia Shakala, Nghidipo Jesaja Haufiku and myself were called. Before we left our nine colleagues, we agreed that we would make every effort to get them out before four o'clock, lock-up time, that day and that we would ask the movement to intervene to prevent them being taken to the north.

At the reception, my two friends were told that since they could not give an address to where they could be taken in Windhoek, they could not therefore be released. I stepped in and undertook to take them with me – I had given them the address of one of my cousins, Monica Kalomo, in Katutura. I then filled in a discharge form and we were given civilian clothes, our paraphernalia from Robben Island and our money.

Finally we were given certificates of release from prison and told that we were now free men. We looked at the 'certificates' and found that there was no mention of any conditions under which we were to be released. There was nothing except: 'This is to certify Helao Joseph Shityuwete was released from prison on 10 May 1984, Windhoek.' Nothing else. We demanded to know the reason why we were being released since we still had four years to go before we finished serving our sentences. We did not want to be released today and be detained again tomorrow, we said.

Since they could not answer our questions satisfactorily or give any guarantees, we refused to leave prison. Colonel Prins, the Commanding Officer, was then called. He told us that we were given four years' remission with 'no strings attached'. He also gave us his 'word of honour' that we would not be rearrested nor be victimized at any time after we were released from prison. After this we agreed to leave the prison.

They put us into two cars and drove us to Katutura. They stopped in front of the house whose number I had given them but the face of the woman who answered the door when the warders knocked was not familiar to me. She did not know anybody called Monica Kalomo, she said, when I asked her about my cousin, but she said she would ask somebody nearby who might help. The warders offered her a lift but she turned it down. Taking a short cut herself, she told the warders to get there by a circuitous route. This was a ploy to give her time to alert the people that the police (warders) had got some people in their cars. Our people often did not know the difference between police, army and prison personnel. To them, they were all the same.

By the time we arrived at the house where the woman was standing and waiting for us, there were already over a hundred people waiting with her and many more were arriving. She had spread the word like wildfire: they had all come to see who was arrested or released. The house belonged to Frans Kambangula – one of the SWAPO leaders in the country and Secretary for Transport. He himself had been in and out of detention many times. He was not at home but a car had stopped there just before us.

A handsome young man got out of the car. He closed the door and waited for the warders, who asked him who he was. He introduced himself as Daniel Tjongarero. They told him that they had some people from prison in their cars. Could he help them to find their families? When we heard that the young man was Tjongarero, a SWAPO official, we got out of the cars to meet him. He was the man we wanted to see! In prison, we gave his name to the authorities as the man we wanted to be put in touch with, but the warders would not hear of it. They did not want us to see any SWAPO members and we did not try to press the issue but they could no longer stop us now that we were free men.

We introduced ourselves to Danny as comrades from Robben Island. We had never met but he immediately knew who we were. He ignored the warders' questions and we hugged and shook hands. The crowd joined in welcoming us – women ululated with joy and began dancing in the dusty streets.

That area of Katutura, Donkerhoek, was known as a no-go area for the police and when the warders realised that they had no more role to play there, they jumped into their cars and drove off. Danny left us in the hands of the masses to make a phone call to London, to inform the SWAPO office there of our release.

In the group which gathered to welcome us were some old faces I remembered as our next door neighbours at the Old Location. There were also three cousins of mine who I did not recognise because when I left the country they were all small girls. Now they were mature women with a number of children between them. One of our former neighbours introduced me to them: it was a moving occasion for all of us, relatives and non-relatives alike.

I did not allow myself to be carried away by emotion and began organising people to volunteer to put up our colleagues we had left behind in prison. We were racing against time to get them out before 4 o'clock. When Danny came out I told him that we must get our comrades out that very same day. It was a matter of urgency, I said, adding that we were tipped off by one of the warders that they were planning to escort them to the north first thing in the morning.

Danny told me to go to the phone inside the house – Jacob Hannai, SWAPO's Deputy Chief Representative for Western Europe was on the other end of the line in the London office. He welcomed us and told me that Shapua Kaukungua, the Chief Representative, was not in the office at the time. I told him all about those of us who had been released and the comrades we had left behind on Robben Island. When I returned many more people had arrived and volunteered to put up our colleagues for two or three days until places were found for them. Sadly, we failed to secure their release that day and they were taken to the north the following morning.

Abbreviations

ANC	African National Congress
APDUSA	African People's Democratic Union of South Africa
BCM	Black Consciousness Movement
BCP	Basutuland Congress Party
CANU	Caprivi African National Union
CDM	Consolidated Diamond Mines
FNLA	Frente Nacional de Liberetacao de Angola
ICJ	International Court of Justice
ICRC	International Committee of the Red Cross
NUDO	National Unity Democratic Organisation
OAU	Organisation of African Unity
OPO	Ovamboland People's Organisation
PAC	Pan Africanist Congress
PLAN	People's Liberation Army of Namibia
SAP	South African Police
SARP	South African Railways Police
SWANLA	South West Africa Native Labour Association
SWANU	South West Africa National Union
SWAPO	South West African People's Organisation
UDI	Unilateral Declaration of Independence
UN	United Nations
UNIP	United National Independence Party (Zambia)
UPA	Uniao Popular de Angola
ZRT	Zambezi River Transport